Articulating Europe

Local Perspectives

Edited by

Jonas Frykman
&
Peter Niedermüller

MUSEUM TUSCULANUM PRESS
UNIVERSITY OF COPENHAGEN
2003

Articulating Europe. Local Perspectives
© 2003 by Ethnologia Europaea & Museum Tusculanum Press
Printed in Sweden by BTJ Tryck AB, Lund
ISBN 87 7289 848 8

Cover motif: Allegoric representation of Europe by the Danish artist Nicolai Abildgaard (1743-1809)
The Museum of National History at Frederiksborg Castle (Denmark)

This book is published with support from
The Sigfrid Svensson Foundation
Nordea Danmark Fonden

Reprint of Ethnologia Europaea. Journal of European Ethnology
vol. 32:2 (2002), Museum Tusculanum Press.

Museum Tusculanum Press
University of Copenhagen
Njalsgade 92
DK-2300 Copenhagen S
www.mtp.dk

Articulating Europe

Local Perspectives

INTRODUCTION

In only a short space of time, the number of works dealing with European issues, in ethnology, has multiplied dramatically. Although a well-known topic for the discipline, a European perspective has, for a long time, implied the study of traits within different traditional cultures. It is ironic that when Sigurd Erixon, in 1971, launched the term *European ethnology*, he transported many of the "Erixonian" historical, systematic and comparative elements that were starting to fade out on the national scene over to the European one. In their different ways of looking at "Abschied vom Volkskunde" stories from groups other than peasants, handling scenes other than the rural, studying periods other than the pre-modern, ethnologists have kept the material artefacts, traditions and folklore of rural society at the core of European studies. When the political scene in Europe slowly changed into a loose federal, multicultural and immigrant one, the study of traditional milieus prevailed. Having Europe as the framework of understanding meant that there were still so many challenges to meet. What had once been successful on the national level could not be transferred to the wider scene without encountering considerable difficulties.

As every reader of Ethnologia Europaea is aware, present day research strives for comparisons on a different level by asking pertinent questions. For example, how are national, regional or ethnic identities formed? How are borders and boundaries maintained, penetrated and made into zones of contact and conflict? Nowadays, no one wants to map the numerous "cultures" that make up the European space or explore their marginal areas and centres. Instead, ethnologists look towards border-zones as evidence of vital areas for the hybridisation of cultures as well as studying the power relations that constitute them. There is no longer any interest in describing what they *are*, but how they are *made* and what influence they exert. The Erixonian notion of making comparisons between different "cultures" brings to life the idea that each culture sits squarely in its own territory, although it might conceal the presence of innumerable immigrant groups, as well as the power structure and hierarchies of today's European politics.

A European culture is now more obviously produced in political life, in science, in entertainment and in tourism. European space becomes *re*-territorialized in ways that deeply affect people's everyday lives. What is considered as European increasingly takes on the illusion of an Imagined Community, and as such constantly seeks to be anchored to a place of safety. European territoriality becomes re-inscribed at the very point where it threatens to be erased. That is why place has become such a critical issue in today's discussion of what European identities could be about. That is precisely why places have to be seen in the making. Places are re-inscribed not only with a European presence, but also with heritage, history and a *folk*-authenticity that corresponds to the claims of present day democratic society.

What role has ethnology played in articulating what today has been lifted up as distinctive traits of both places and peoples? The definitions that were taken for granted have been questioned and deconstructed, not only by intellectual changes in the discipline, but also by political developments in Europe. There is a certain excitement in Academia about the fact that Europe is entering a phase where space has been created for new identifications – be they post-national, post-regional or post-ethnic. Compared to other sciences, the special position of ethnology is such that, as a discipline, it is so profoundly drawn into the question of cultural identity. The question, "Who are we, the people?" is constantly being asked both from above and below. Seemingly secure borders around home and country are taking on other forms – or are being lifted away. Our discipline is being asked to answer questions about roots, authenticity and purity. In all the European countries, museums and galleries are being compelled to make people feel more at home in "their own" culture. Exposing local, national and ethnic traits has become an issue about belonging and roots, while the obligation to safeguard or document the past takes second place.

How then do ethnologists answer the people, the politicians and the authorities? When notions and findings from earlier ethnological research are used in claims about the exclusive possession of country and culture, the ethnological answer becomes increasingly political. Concepts like *folklore, tradition, authenticity and identity* almost seem to be part of a collective process of loss and mourning. There is a notion that cultural achievements are being levelled out and trivialised. People who have "deep roots" are being looked upon as survivors, as the ones who still resist the contamination of modern society. They are made into victims as opposed to being the producers of culture. A whole world of distinction is being irretrievably lost. Places are seen as being connected to memory and nostalgia and, of course, ethnology and the whole antiquarian sector are being called upon to lessen the pain.

In this context, the contribution of ethnology seems to be twofold. In the first instance, researchers analysing the discourses of place, region and nation have shown the arbitrariness in the construction of cultural identities. The comforting message is that what has been constructed can also be *de*constructed and is therefore arbitrary. Never before has there been such profusion in the study of the history of ethnology as there is now. Never before have scholars shown such initiative in demonstrating how folklore and tradition have been created in discourse, in museum exhibitions and in pictures. So, what to some seem to be a navel-gazing activity, a dwelling upon the intellectual history of the discipline, could also be looked upon as a preparation for a *re*orientation. A lot of valuable and necessary research has now been produced within this field of deconstruction. But it still does not answer the question: "Who are we, the people?"

Secondly, ethnology continues to do what it has always excelled at – it shows how concepts like history, nation, region, ethnicity or Europe are constantly reworked and renegotiated in order to create something viable in everyday life. What kind of "Europeanisation from below" is going on? What will be learned through ethnographies of local cultural processes that are framed by a new European awareness? Will they unlock different interpretations of xenophobia or micro-nationalism? In order to avoid the countless pitfalls that become evident when discussing cultural identity from the point of view of nationalism or ethnicity as if they were examples of false consciousness, this issue tries to describe *places* where identity can unfold. Since places are sites for everyday activities, they must be somewhat vague, open and in the process of reformulation. Mourning the past, as described in different national Volkskunde-classics, is just one of many creative means of rendering new dimensions to the very place. The question about "us – the people" can be successfully met by stimulating a curiosity about the everyday life-world. Cultural heritage, tradition and folklore are just some of the resources that people can draw upon in order to negotiate a sense of self and identity.

Unlike the nation, Europe does not really have a centre or a sharply demarcated territory, as discussed by Reinhard Johler. This lack of place turns Europe into a diffuse entity or phantasmagoria, but at the same time maintains the concept of it as something in the making – a process. Europe seems to be perpetually connected to easily identifiable processes from above – a *construction européenne* – while the everyday "facts of life" still have to be studied.

For example, in his study of festivals in Budapest in Hungary and Scania and Jämtland in Sweden, Kjell Hansen asks if places can really be understood without taking into consideration what is happening on a European level. Eva Reme also discusses that when the city of Bergen, celebrated its year as a European Capital of Culture, it displayed strong elements of this new protective regionalism. The event also articulated many of its multicultural traditions and released the place to a multitude of impressions. It therefore became a "gateway to other places and other times". Today, when the Croatian region of Istria is emerging as a Euroregion, as discussed by Jonas Frykman, it is at the same time creating a space for the indigenous culture – and for the multicultural and multilingual as opposed to the national. Seeing it as a cultural imaginary, a region of mystery and magic means avoiding clear-cut definitions, and instead opening it up for agency and a multitude of practices.

Maja Povrzanović Frykman's article indicates that when the Adriatic city of Dubrovnik, was being shelled during the war of 1991–1995, its inhabitants relied on a very flimsy presence of European culture and civilization, while at the same time trying to save the city as a place for the many and the multitude, calling to life a past under the banner of *Libertas*. As is usual with violence, the bombardment created clear-cut definitions. Nevertheless alternative stories and experiences emerged where a unity between man, nature and animals created a truer truth and the horizon stretched in alternative directions.

The *Carnival of Cultures* in Berlin, as described by Peter Niedermüller and Michi Knecht, makes global trends meet the European in an urban setting. They remind us of the fact that the true continuity in the European culture of multiculturalism is closely linked to cities. Being places for commerce and encounters, they have always functioned as training grounds for everyday multicultural competence and sensitivity. By focussing upon the place, it becomes evident that what on the surface looks like a display of hidden patterns – sexual, ethnical, regional or national – is also part of a process of reformulating the local as well as the patterns themselves. It seems to be inevitable that the analysis of different levels of discourse will be combined with an increased attention to performance, action and agency.

In one and the same operation, places where Europe becomes real must be seen as having been constructed by power and discourse and as an arena where something authentic becomes palpably real. This is clearly illustrated in Kirsti Mathiesen Hjemdahl's article on the "themeparkisation" of cultural heritage. An understanding of why historical theme parks have become so successful can be grasped by tracking the children who visit them. The method used is "thinking with one's feet". This implies being captivated by the informant's fascination and trying to understand how he or she uses it in the factual life-world. It then becomes apparent that the past – as presented in the place – is an open area for action and for imagining and not just another instantiation of the "past".

Throughout Europe, ethnology has prided itself on its unique mastery of domestic culture and being in a position to do in-depth investigations into historical backgrounds, thereby taking the insiders view. In the future, European ethnology will have to make do with a rather superficial acquaintance of the sites in question. Being absorbed, trying to use one's body and sensitivity in order to understand what is taking place, points towards fieldwork where the researcher also reflects upon his or her own praxis. In writing about festivals, Kjell Hansen discusses the importance of trying to catch the gist of what is happening by "thinking with your feet". To be able to understand the presence of Europe in the local means being able to read the signs and symbols displayed, as well as grasping the sense of what they mean to the locals. In this issue, many scholars point to the importance of multisited ethnography in contemporary European ethnology. How is this going to change the character of ethnological fieldwork when the researcher is not doing "ethnology at home"? Here new fields wait to be investigated, located somewhere between the classic anthropological "case-studies" and the ethnological competence of reflecting the insider's point of view.

In the concluding contributions, Karin Salomonsson shows how place seems to be an absolute precondition for marketing European food products, while Anna Burstedt similarly shows how local food has become a restaurant sales feature. It seems as if food is the privileged site for enacting all the values that would be debated if they were openly displayed. Here you can freely boast about moral and cultural superiority, talk about the importance of keeping borders, sticking to the old traditions and promoting the notion that an authentic life is only possible in the countryside. These issues are usually associated with the populist appeal, but here the middle class and the elite embrace them. At the same time, however, distinctiveness of taste and the localisation of the product becomes a precondition for seeing the other, for imagining other regions and other cuisines. Sampling local cuisine is part and parcel of a process of an imaginary that does not really come with opposites or structured into dichotomies. Eating Italian does not imply criticism of French or Scanian cuisine.

The main aim of this volume is to publish a collection of articles that, in different ways, address the challenges that European ethnology is facing. Representing a variety of localities, they give new insights and perspectives to the importance of doing empirical fieldwork and of seeing the emergence of new patterns as well as the remaking of old ones.

This publication is the outcome of an ethnological work-shop within the European network "Articulating Europe" that was held in March 2001 at Humboldt Universität, Berlin. The network includes scholars from Austria, Croatia, Germany, Norway, Poland and Sweden. Research has been faciliated through grants from the Norwegian Research Council in the project "Annerledeslandet" and Centre for European Studies, Lund University. The articles by Anna Burstedt, Jonas Frykman, Kjell Hansen, Maja Povrzanović Frykman and Karin Salomonsson are revised versions from contributions to the book by Hansen, Kjell & Karin Salomonsson (eds) 2001: *Fönster mot Europa. Platser och identiteter*. Studentlitteratur, Lund. Copyright authors and Studentlitteratur.

Jonas Frykman

Peter Niedermüller

Local Europe

The Production of Cultural Heritage and the Europeanisation of Places

Reinhard Johler

> Johler, Reinhard 2002: Local Europe. The Production of Cultural Heritage and the Europeanisation of Places. – Ethnologia Europaea 32: 7–18.
>
> The "new Europe" is making a noticeable contribution to the reorganisation of "peoplehood and territory". By doing so, EU-Europe is really constructing with "Euroland" and "Schengenland" a "European space". But in a powerful process it is simultaneously creating "European places" and "European localities", whereby the "European" is becoming increasingly "local" and the "local" clearly "europeanised" at the same time. Using Brussels, Euralille and Vienna as examples, this essay will look into this process of the localisation of Europe and the Europeanisation of the local. In doing so, my ethnographical perspective is directed at cities, setting its sights on the various forms but also on the respective protagonists of Europeanisation, because the Europeanisation of the local and the localisation of the European are often contested and linked with the construction of a specific "cultural heritage".
>
> *Professor Reinhard Johler, Dr., Ludwig-Uhland-Institut für Empirische Kulturwissenschaft, Universität Tübingen, Schloss, D-72070 Tübingen. E-mail: Reinhard.Johler@uni-tuebingen.de*

The "European Pavilion" at the World's Fair

At the World's Fair in Hannover, Germany, in 2000, the European Union had intended to present itself by means of an "exciting and lively style". Accordingly, visitors were invited to participate in a "journey through time" at the "European pavilion", which had been erected for just this purpose, displaying in seven show rooms the "unique history," the "unprecedented diversity", and the future destiny of a United Europe. Through select images of urban street life and various cultural icons, the first exhibit on "The 1950s" attempted to document the "beginning of a new era" after World War II, simultaneously narrating the "origin of the European Community." In the second exhibit, the gradual formation of the European Union was reimagined via memory icons like the "Time Shuttle", in which the high point of the millennium – the introduction of the common European currency, the EURO – was staged on a so called "Euro Disc". The subsequent installations, titled "The Blue Planet", "The Bridge" and "The Tunnel of Reflection", were concerned with the "European" engagement with the themes of the World's Fair: "Humanity, Nature, Technology." In the last exhibit called "Here and Now", by repeatedly addressing the recent past through sounds and images, European diversity was praised as a perspective for the future of the European Union. In its self-representation, European Union (EU)-Europe declared itself, promising to oversee the step-by-step creation of a multi-cultural society that would be on guard "against racism and xenophobia".

When leaving the "European pavilion" after the estimated 30-minute visit, visitors stepped out onto the "Robert Schuman Square" and the "European Boulevard" from where they could see the various pavilions of other European countries extending beyond. For Viviane Reding, the EU Commissioner in charge of Education and Culture, this ensemble was most appropriate due to the symbolic arrangement in which the "European Pavilion" took center stage, indeed having been built at the "intersection of all cultures of Europe" – including both the member-states as well as those applying for membership. Of course, many of the visitors as well as most of the journalists whom I inter-viewed did not partake in this message. For in comparison to the larger national pavilions, the EU contribution seemed rather modest and, in addition, according to one newspaper commentary, it merely accentuated the "dilemma of Europe's career professionals" (*Berufseuropäer*) and their difficulty in properly presenting their own supra-national creations. The seemingly less than imaginative European "view" was "obviously" lacking "any kind of vision" (Schümer 2000b), just like the rest of the European Union.

This dissatisfaction with the content and design of the "European Pavilion" can be linked to the current lack of support for European institutions and the overall invocation of European unity. Such a critique, however, is primarily directed against the scarcely successful "cultural politics of European integration," which have been attempting to convince citizens about the legitimacy of "building Europe" since the 80s (Shore 2000). Indeed, the propagated historical understanding of the EU, the commonly deployed European symbols, and the readily implored European identity have – so it appears at first glance – encountered little acceptance, whether in the "European Pavilion" at the World's Fair in Hannover or in the daily lives of the citizens of Europe.

The Production of a European Cultural Heritage

Nevertheless, it is worthwhile to take a closer look at this phenomenon – specifically in the context of the World's Fair. At some distance from the "European pavilion", located among the various projects centered on the "Future of Work" in the "Global House", there was an interesting exhibit on the regional development policies of a small valley in Western Austria (Bregenzerwald). There, for quite some time, and through numerous initiatives, it is cultural heritage that is being discovered, cared for, and in many ways economically marketed. For example, a well-known local cheese had been chosen as the "leading product" (*Leitprodukt*) of the region. Here, the maintenance of the "cultural landscape" and the fostering of small local structures have been pushed on stage by regionally practiced identity politics. Local specialties are offered for sale on a European organized and interconnected "rural market place." It is this regionalization (or perhaps rather this localization) that is of special interest in a global context: as previously mentioned, it was also staged in the "Global House"-exhibit at the World's Fair – a process that may be described with the commonly used phrase "glocalization." At this point I need to add that such a "mobilization of cultural heritage" has first been made possible by ample EU assistance. And this is not a unique case scenario in Europe. One of the objectives of the European subsidy programs for local farming areas is – directly or indirectly – concerned with the main-tenance and further development of regional culture. In the context of the European Assistance Policy, whether it concerns foodstuffs, landscapes, product designs or culture – and the thereby invented cultural heritage – all is understood in a double sense as having potential value: Culturally produced differences are viewed as an opportunity for the economic development of disadvantaged areas. And, in addition, with the invention of key phrases like "unity in diversity" (McDonald 1996) and "Europe of regions" (Kockel 2002), the concept of culture itself has been discovered as an important resource for European identity politics (Johler 2002).

In this respect, the EU has become, at least for people living in the countryside of certain regions in Europe, an important "fact of life" involved in the current "production of identity." Inasmuch it is worthwhile not only to pursue the question of how cultural heritage is articulating Europe, it is above and beyond also important to focus on how the EU itself defines this European cultural heritage in its programs, how it utilizes it in its policies – and along with all that allows "Euro-Culture" (Wilson 1998) to become a reality in Europe on the local level. Or, in other words, at present, the diverse and observable mobilization of cultural heritage is strongest in the interaction between Europeanization and localization. For this interaction not only allocates new political leeway to both local and European protagonists. It has also set into motion a powerful process. The "European" is becoming increasingly "localized", and simultaneously, the "local" is clearly being "Europeanized". Thus to pursue these closely interwoven practices of (European) localization and (local) Europeanization ethnographically means not only to investigate – as in agricultural policy (Johler 2001b) – where EU-Europe is present, but above all where it is perceptible and visible by means of designation, symbols, and rituals.

But if the EU-Europe is in this sense already a reality, then it is also worthwhile to turn this "local Europe" into an ethnological topic. My main ethnographic example is Vienna and with it – at least in the European context – a large city. In this article, I try to show how an old and a new infrastructure of the European, including European projects and European festivals in Vienna, are stimulated by the concurrent processes of localization and Europeanization. And in addition, I would also like to demonstrate how the cultural heritage of Vienna is thus precisely defined, strategically utilized, and to some extent reformulated as European. Cities, however, as M. Estellie Smith declared, have barely been noticed by EU policymakers and even ethnological research has rather neglected the "urban entities in the European Community" up until now (Smith 1993; Chesire 1990). And yet it is the cities that are the agents of Europeanization and of cultural differentiation – and thereby also act as a pronounced and exerted mobilizer of cultural heritage.

The question included here thus aims at a special perspective. EU-Europe is, necessitated by the numerous sponsoring programs, present and perceptible, especially in the economically underdeveloped areas of Southern and Western Europe as well as in the rural agricultural regions of the continent. Thus it is not by chance that the majority of anthropological EU studies also concentrate on these zones (cf., e.g., Dracklé 1996; Ekman 1999; Giordano 1987; Gray 2000; Jurjus 1993; Martin 1993; Nadel-Klein 2002, Shutes 1993). In contrast, however, the "super regions" of Northern and Central Europe, and along with these the cities have been studied to a much lesser degree. But "European practice" can be experienced here, and, according to Donald Judt, it is here that the "great success stories" of Europe are being written (1996: 130).

A EU-European Space

A comparative study of European cities from this vantage point would be productive and could further verify the reality of a "local Europe" based on the ethnographic material thereby ascertained. Such an examination would also have to take into consideration those positions formulated, e.g., by the French philosopher Jean Baudrillard. In a recent interview Baudrillard suggested that Europe had been turned into a "virtual reality", into an "archetype of simulation." This "simulated Europe", according to Baudrillard's conclusion, will indeed "exist", but no one "will be a part of it" (Der französische Soziologe Jean Baudrillard 1997).

On the level of public discourse, this assumption seems to be confirmed: The EU is often termed a travelling "citadel of tents" („Zeltburg") or a "modern road show", lacking a recognizable center with "soul" and its buildings appear to many as "faceless" and anonymous. The EURObank, e.g., notes also consciously display only stylized "typical" constructions which do not exist within the reality of Europe, and the "Eurocrats" at once violently contested the fact that the "Pont du Gard" bridge in the south of France had served as a model for the 5-EURO note.

In some sense, EU-Europe is indeed "placeless," even when, as for instance in the EU-advertisement campaign "At Home in Europe", it attempts to emphasize belonging and concreteness, but with the settings quickly changing in pictures and words – in the course of the few pages of this advertisement brochure, the citizen becomes a car buyer in Spain, an apartment seeker in Italy or a corporation interested in women's issues in Denmark.

The message of such images is clear and often described: The European Union is an "unfinished construction site", always in a "continuous process", signaling "growth", "modernity", and "future". For the citizens, it does not

Der Zirkus ist in der Stadt! KURIER-Karikatur: M. Pammesberger

Images of Europe: the EU as a "citadel of tents".

convey a sense of "belonging", but rather means a constant "moving." And the term "Europe" or rather European symbols have been systematically deployed. The European stars against the blue background are mainly found on international travel buses and transportation companies active throughout Europe. In addition, Europe has not merely lent its name to the "Eurostar" – the train between London and Paris – and to the "Eurofighter", but also to the "Euro Airport Basel-Mulhouse-Freiburg", the "Eurogate" in Zurich, and the seemingly futuristic city district "Euralille" in France.

Such an understanding of the EU-Europe, as suggested by the described usage of the symbols of Europe, may confirm French anthropologist Marc Abélès' diagnosis of the EU: Europe has no center, it corresponds more to a method than a territory, and it has triggered above all identity-building processes of "deter-ritorialization" and "dehistorization" (Abélès 1996).

However, skepticism seems to me to be appropriate in relation to this diagnosis. "Schengenland" and "Euroland" have allowed national frontiers to largely disappear, however in the words of the Thomas M. Wilson (1998) "boundaries remain" in Europe – and these are directed toward the outside as well as the inside. And at present, the observable tendency towards localization or regionalization is according to this perspective to be regarded as an important result of the current reorganization of European space.

For although Europe has not been defined geographically and regards itself as being principally "open-minded" with regard to expansion, "Europeanization" has clearly contributed to a reordering of "territoriality and peoplehood" (Borneman & Fowler 1997: 487). EU-Europe, along with "Euroland" and "Schengenland" makes up a "European space", but in doing so it also simultaneously creates beyond this, at least according to the hypothesis contained in this essay, "European places" and "European localities". Thus, however, "virtual Europe" (Abélès 2000), a Europe that is more an "idea" than a "place" (Judt 1996: 19), mutates into a "real Europe", at least in the initial stages.

Thus the EU is in a catch-22 situation because there is a simple reason for its caution with regard to a representation of tangible places. Every presentation necessarily makes a selection and thus cannot do justice to European diversity. Simultaneously, however, the EU has long since become a tangible reality. Propagating "the house of Europe" or the "fortress of Europe" (Mandel 1996) is just a part of this strategy, as is the annual award of "the European cultural capitals". And finally it should be remembered that all European treaties – and it is on these that the European Union is based – are linked with definite places – Rome, Amsterdam, Cork or Maastricht. The "Treaty of Nice", e.g., containing in an appendix a "Declaration on the Future of the Union", was indeed negotiated in this city in the south of France by government leaders in December 2000, but in order to affix the signatures to this treaty in a ceremonial act at the "Sardian Palace" in February 2001, these leaders had to travel to Nice for a second time.

It is unnecessary to overrate this "symbolic reference to a specific place" (*symbolische Ortsbezogenheit*) of the EU. Its content has, however, already become a matter of popular discourse. For example, the journalist Dirk Schümer has recently discovered "The face of Europe" in European cities, in Rome, Aachen, Ausschwitz, Bukarest, Frankfurt, Den Haag, but also in Strasbourg and Brussels, "the merry swamp in which the bureaucrats wallow" (Schümer 2000). Where, then, does Europe "happen"?

Transit-Europe

As is the case with EURO notes, the European Union likes to employ bridges as signs of the European, since these do indeed symbolize identical goals. They unite what was hitherto separate, thus encouraging the process of growing closer together and increasing the mobility of both goods and people. Thus, since the 60s, there are many bridges (e.g. the "Europe Bridges" in Tyrol or near Strasbourg) which have "Europe" as part of their name, and it is also not by chance that the bridge that openeed a few years ago linking Sweden and Denmark led to the birth of the European "Öresund Region", and thus to a new kind of "transnational metropolization" (Berg, Linde-Laursen & Löfgren 2000).

Orvar Löfgren has described this tangible bridge as a "moving metaphor", but many such "moving metaphors" can be found in present day "transit Europe": names of airports ("Euro Airport", "Eurogate"), the "Euro Squares" in front of railway stations, the "hotels de l'Europe" in cities, the names of large liners ("Europe") and international trains ("Eurostar" and "Euronight"), or the international haulage contractors that not only incorporate Europe into their name (e.g. "Eurotransport") but also print on their lorries icons in the form of a European blue color logo complete with a European star, which serve as unambiguous signs of a mobile Europe on European transit routes.

As "moving metaphors", they propagate the "new Europe", simultaneously exploiting the metaphoric meaning attributed to this Europe. They are "movable European places", just like the "places" that organize European mobility such as urban squares and hotels. It is through these – as the German historian Karl Schlögel has aptly noted – "the new Europe grows": "It grows on the routes used by the haulage contractors reconnecting Europe. New areas are being formed: areas of traffic and communication, networks of science and knowledge, an infrastructure of modern communication, commuter movements of labor migration, and branches and offices of international firms. People are on the move everywhere, gathering new experiences. They are the explorers of the new Europe, the pragmatists of European unity." As Schlögel goes on to say, the fast, everyday "histories of the new Europe" could be told through these places alongside those, because it is here that "thousands of Europrofessionals are determining the very sphere of European institutions and structures, the sphere of European traffic and communication and the sphere of working migration." They are also in motion, but their "place" is more stable and their "history" correspondingly slower (Schlögel 2002).

The Center of Europe: Brussels, Strasbourg or Suchowola?

Irrespective of specific geographical definitions, Europe has many "hearts": a small place in southern Belgium, the largely unknown small city of Cölbe in the German provincial state of Hessen, a farm in Lithuania or the Polish community of Suchowola. In the latter place, its few visitors are directed by means of many signs toward an acclaimed central locale. From an ethnographic point of view it would be worthwhile pursuing these extremely diverse symbolic markers of European geography in detail, but here it will suffice to point out one thing: the many "hearts" reveal the divergent and politically controversial designs of modern Europe. But apart from this quest for a geographical center, the cities and communities mentioned here lack what the political centers of the EU have in common: they hardly have any share in the "Transit-Europe". Both Strasbourg and

Brussels are centers of surplus-European immigration. But it is these migrants, just as much as the officials and politicians of the EU, who are creating "the new Europe" by the way they carry out their everyday lives. And they also have something else in common. As "new Europeans", they are living in Brussels and Strasbourg in secluded colonies just like the present-day designers of the EU.

Whoever wants to comprehend the institutional centers of the EU as "places" must observe immigrants and "Eurocrats" simultaneously and regard their varied places of work and residence as a common urban iconography of European politics. It is also necessary to perceive the connection of these new "European places" to the historic city centers of Brussels and Strasbourg in order to grasp the language of symbols and forms of the "new Europe". Astonishingly, here critics of architecture, journalists, tourists and field researchers agree in one respect: the structure of the European edifice is, as in the case of the political structure of the EU itself, to a large extent without face or vision.

It is exactly those "tours of inspection" by journalists in Brussels that reveal the same picture (Hénard 1999). Dirk Schümer, e.g., maintains that "the EU has left its mark here like in no other city on the continent, and no other city has suffered more from its mania for destruction" (Schümer 2000c). The high-rise buildings made of asbestos originating from founding times and the post-modern glass buildings erected in the meantime have left a "nowhere" surrounding the Round Pont Schuman, thus making Brussels into the ideal "capital of Europe" because it has become so average and hardly recognizable any more. "A clean sweep has been made here, in a shocking way. Europe is being built not on the foundations of its heritage but by destruction. Just look down. The smart Place Luxembourg has become the miserable remains of a once charming quarter which had to give way to Euro buildings" (Fritz-Vannahme 2000).

But what went wrong in the center of Brussels seems to have succeeded in Strasbourg. With the newly erected European Parliament in the "nowhere" at the edge of the city, a European "icon" has been constructed. According to the opinions of architects, Europe has thus finally received an architectonic "face" – and perhaps also a genuine "center" (Rautenberg 1999).

Euralille

Euralille, the newly constructed part of the northern French city of Lille, really does have European architecture – and also history. This began in 1984, when the French Prime Minister, at that time Pierre Mauroy, was able to push through the idea of building the Channel Tunnel at the summit conference of Fontainbleau. As advertising leaflets proudly proclaimed, by virtue of this construction the city was once again situated "at the intersection of European high-speed tracks between London, Paris, Brussels and Köln", thus having "100 million European consumers within a 300 km radius." Mauroy, who was, incidentally, a convinced European, seized this chance to have Euralille built as a modern center of the service industry alongside Lille, the old, economically run-down workers' city. With its 70 hectares of building land, Euralille is directly linked with the newly erected TGV railway station "Lille Europe" and, alongside schools, hotels and banks, consists primarily of the technology park "Eura-Technology" as well as a center of genetic re-search ("Eura-Santé"). These terms alone reveal the political aim of Euralille. The metamor-phosis of the city is seen in direct connection with the process of European unification. Here, the "European destiny of Lille", a much conjured up phrase, is also expressed by the fact that by 2004 Lille will be "the cultural capital of Europe" and thus – as has already been announced by the tourist advertising agency – "the Gateway to Europe".

Joined to the "Communauté Urbaine de Lille" and having been a member of the EU networks "Eurocities" since 1993, the city and region ("Euroflanders") in the "Europe of the Regions" have perceptibly gained political importance and therefore also influence on the organization of the EU. Praised as "one of the most striking urban landscapes in Europe", Euralille, nevertheless, is described as a simple survival strategy in the "new Europe":

"More recently, a new spate of urban projects has emerged, sparked by the approaching deadline for the construction of Europe, in particular the opening of the single market. The logic and strategies of urban planning must now be adapted to fit in with a European context. As the notion of territory expands – whether in a political, geographic or economic sense – the traditional national hierarchies (state/region/cities) have exploded only to be replaced by a reconstruction of space. Borders have become mobile, giving rise to new relationships, new complementaries, and new rivalries. Euro-regions are being mapped out; Euro-cities are being drawn up. The newly defined face of Europe has impli-citly generated new distributions, new flows, and new networks where large cities, motors of deve-lopment, have become poles of magnetic attraction around which smaller or less-wealthy local areas tend to gravitate. At the heart of Europe, which is currently under construction, possessing the know-how required to join the ranks of the 'big cities' (or even the 'metropolis'), means concentrating on welcome facilities, accessibility, amenities, and environ-mental issues (the criteria of excellence); this has become a genuine 'object of desire' for a number of medium-sized cities in France and elsewhere. It has also become, for some, simply a matter of survival" (Kolhaas et al. 1996:13).

But it is just as interesting that the "European dimension" of this project, which is intended to promote Lille to the rank of one of the "European hub cities", is also reflected in the very architecture of Euralille itself. This regards itself – as does the EU – as not being completed but as directed with open-mindedness towards the future. Euralille is meant to embody "European modernity" and as a result, the architects did not establish any connection to the old city of Lille. The architect Rem Kolhaas countered the violent criticism that was expressed because of this with two arguments: Other attempts to introduce "modernity" into Europe (e.g. "Euro-Disney" in the vicinity of Paris) had been described as "cultural and contextual massacres". And he wanted to express his objection to exactly this criticism of "European modernity" in one

Using European Symbols: "Wien im Zeichen der EU".

sentence: "No ground against a non-place" (Kolhaas et al. 1996: 189–190).

"Local Europe" in Vienna

The possible discovery of a new type of European urbanism in non-place Euralille can be read as a consequence of "hyper modernity" (Augé 1988) and understood as a part of the powerful process of "deterritoralization" to which the "new Europe" contributes significantly. The architec-ture, history and intention of Euralille then correspond exactly to the "future orientated narratives" of the EU (Borneman & Fowler 1997: 492). And doubtlessly European identities could also result from this, oriented towards the future and bearing little relation to the past (Macdonald 1993).

But this interpretation needs to be supplemented: Orvar Löfgren has demanded, not only to see the processes of the "de-", but rather also those of the "re-" – and he is correct in this assessment with regard to Europe (Löfgren 1996). "Local Europe" can be interpreted as a "reterritorialization" and, in this context, the uses of cultural heritage can be seen as a "re-historicization" – precisely as it is attempted by the creation of a "Europe museum" in Brussels. And even if it is still uncertain what should be exhibited under "European", the research director has nevertheless – perhaps naively it appears – perspectives for the near future: "In the next few years Euroland will experience the beginnings of a common history anyway which will then in turn employ more and more identity and togetherness as for example through the common peace policies in Kosovo or the unified reaction against Haider-Austria."

It is still unclear whether or not the sanctions against "Haider-Austria" have contributed to a European identity or will even produce a "European Value Community". In any case, in Vienna the sanctions have indeed shown effects. Because even if the city never tires of upholding its own politics and demonstrating a critical distance to the new conservative-nationalistic government, its stance – and thereby its own narrative of an open, international, even European city – has nevertheless been put to question. "Whoever boycotts Vienna," so has been the complaint, "hits the heart of Europe".

This geographic or rather cultural self-positioning is not new. Here, however, the often-claimed "Middle of Europe" has achieved a new meaning with Austria's membership in the EU in 1995. And since then the European substance of Vienna has been re-worked in content matter in several ways. One wants to be "The bridge to the East" and "the door into the West" and the flag of Europe, which hangs on the Vienna City Hall, should not merely – as perhaps in other places – show the belonging to the EU, but it should also symbolize a particular openness in relation to the neighboring Eastern countries.

In the middle of the 90s, the re-working addressed therein was accompanied by a strong mobilization of the national "cultural heritage". That Vienna was befitted with a particular role as dominating capital city was also demonstrated in a "Festival for Europe", e.g., which was held on July 1, 1998 on the Viennese "Heroes Square" on the occasion of Austria's taking the chair of the EU (Schallenberg, Thun-Hohenstein 1999). There Vienna wanted – this is only cited here – to emphasize its new "function" as a European "Culture Capital" with an extensive cultural program. More important at this point is, however, that the President of Austria used this "Festival for Europe" to give a new interpretation of Austrian history. With its membership into the EU, Austria, "after several detours rife with victims, found its way back to its European calling". And the "Heroes' Square" – the infamous place where, i.a., Adolf Hitler announced Austria's annexation to an enthusiastic crowd in 1938 – thereby gained a new, a European meaning. In the future, it will show that Austria has learned from its history.

That Beethoven was not only played at this "Festival for Europe" but also at the April 2000 opening of the "European Monitoring Centre on Racism and Xenophobia" in Vienna – the only such EU-institution of its kind – corresponded to this European self-image. Nevertheless, what both events had in common was that the European positioning of Vienna was also founded on the cultural resources of the city's history. The director of the "European Monitoring Centre", Beate Winkler, e.g., saw herself in Vienna as being in the "right place":

"Vienna is a very good place for the location – also due to the momentary political situation. We can only do this job well if we are as close as possible to the problems of the people. There are a lot of positive things in Vienna. Vienna has quite a large potential – also in regards to history. One can't forget that Vienna is the city of cultural dialogue. Vienna is the city of Sigmund Freud – the man who introduced a whole different perspective in coming to terms with xenophobia."

This argument – which by the way was also advocated by the city of Vienna – still has another interesting angle: current EU-activities in Vienna were always legitimatized by EU representatives as well as Viennese politicians by invocation of a European destination derived from history – and this was the case even at such trivial events like the opening of a "Europe Garden" in Schönbrunn Palace or the planting of a ring of trees in the "Sigmund Freud Park", which was to symbolize Europe several years ago. Something else, however, can be observed in Vienna: A well-known Austrian author recent-

European places: The "Café de l'Europe" in Vienna.

ly compared the damage done by the new government to the European style of the country with the renovation of the "Café de l'Europe" located in the center of Vienna. Without getting into more detail here on the underlying metaphor, a brief explanation would be in order: the "Café de l'Europe", which opened its doors at the end of the 19th century, also represented mobility in Vienna's city history. And at the end of World War II, it was the first sought location particularly by Jews fleeing from Hungary. Its name "Europe" – as an old coffee house visitor recently stated – therefore offered its guests a "program, vision and perspectives." And the re-opening of the "Café de l'Europe" in May 2000 was perceived – despite the unchanged political situation in Austria – as the confirmation for the notion that "Europe even now still begins, as always, in the middle of Vienna."

"Europe is located in Vienna" has, however – and this has already been implied – still another meaning. The "Café de l'Europe" belongs, along with the "Hotel Europe", the "Europe House" or the "Europe Square" to those wax-works of the European, which can be found in many cities and at the same time connects sediments of past European constructions. These histories of Europe were reconciled with the present EU – and thereby likewise "re-worked" in substance: The "Europe Square" in Vienna, e.g., was given its name in 1958. It is located – like many of the like-named squares throughout Europe – directly in front of a large train station and as an important traffic intersection point it did not undergo any significant design changes for quite some time. When Austria joined the EU, it was initially distinguished by a monument designed by school children entitled "The Path to Europe". In the meantime, "Europe Square" has also become a architectural topic of the city. And in the future, it should – according to a prominent architectural duo contracted with its new design – "no longer smell of the Eastern Bloc" but instead show a modern, a "European ambiance".

A "European ambiance?" – the EU has directly supported several projects in Vienna for city renewal. The most important – and seemingly most prominent – targets the rehabilitation of a quarter marked by abandoned apartments and houses, burdened by heavy traffic and struck by strong ethnic ghettoism – the "Gürtel". The EU considers this largely successful revitalization as one of its "success stories" and has thereby – according to its own proud depiction – "created a noticeable sign post in Vienna" (Veigl 1999). On the other hand, the so-called "Gürtel night-walk" takes place every year in this quarter. In 2000, alongside numerous cultural events, the film *Thank you Europe?* could also be viewed. It is this decidedly Europe critical film, which largely disputes the EU in its justification of existence.

Contested "European places"

As Tony Judt has maintained, Europe exists from an ontological point of view (Judt 1996: 130). And in fact the many places of "local

Europe" bear witness to the presence of the EU. But these "European places" must at first be provided on site with symbolic meaning and charged with European content by means of ritual. As we have already seen, this is, however, a matter of continual political controversy among the public. A further example may serve to underline this. On the 40th anniversary of the "Treaties of Rome", a strange scenario of European diplomacy took place in Vienna, about which Viennese residents were not informed until the following days by the media. In the Sigmund Freud Park in the heart of Vienna, diplomats of the EU member states planted a circle of trees typical of the various countries with a yew (as a typical EU-tree) in its center. Such planting of trees has been part of the EU's stock of rituals for years and was understood as it was intended in Vienna: The respective trees typical of each country were interpreted as signs of the propagated European "unity in diversity". The act itself was understood as a "symbol of growth of the EU". But the tree rondeau did not survive a year. In January 1998, an until then unknown group named "the underground" cut the trees down. In this way these people wanted to protest against existing manifestations of power which they particularly saw manifested in the introduction of the EURO and generally in militarism, and at the same time they wanted to draw attention to local problems with the Viennese tramway. In the meantime, the anniversary-trees have been replanted, although in the absence of any ambassadors. And a small board explains this "European place", which is hardly noticed any more (Johler 2000).

Agencies of Europeanization

The tree-rondeau in the Sigmund Freud Park together with the "European Garden" in Schönbrunn Palace belongs to the "European places" sponsored by the EU, which are part of a EU infrastructure. As in all other European capitals, the Information office of the European Parliament as well as the Delegation of the European Commission have been set up in a grand shopping mall in the center of Vienna. Not far off, there is the office of the only EU

European places: The "Europa Cafe" in Nicosia.

institution in Austria: the "European Monitoring Centre on Racism and Xenophobia". The EU-Office of the City of Vienna is in the City Hall. At a significant distance from these, the EU has its "Objective 2" sponsoring offices in the problem areas in the city. All these institutions propagate the EU and are easily recognized in public by means of the EU flags and symbols.

But in Vienna, as in many other European cities, the use of the term "Europe", but also of European symbols, is not restricted to the EU. Thus in Vienna there is a bar called "Europe", a "Europe Hotel" and also a "Café de l'Europe". And in the direct vicinity of "Europe Square" typical European meals and drinks can be consumed in the recently opened "Europe Brewery" or electronic goods can be bought in the "Europafunk" shop. These few examples can be listed alongside with shopping centers named "Eurospar" or numerous other businesses that have Europe as part of their name ("Eurojobs", "Eurolingua", "Eurokredit", "Euromed"). In this terminology, "Europe" means the internationality and diversity of the goods offered, and the modernity of the goods and services rendered. In Austria, however, it also refers to the rather low prices. It would be worthwhile carrying out a comparative study of these "European places" of business life. But it is certain that these, as for example in the case of "Euro-Disney" (Korff 1994) or the "Europarks", contribute to the formulation of what is currently understood by "Europe" in Europe, possibly corresponding to EU propaganda but also differing from it.

Conclusion

The "new Europe" has made a noticeable contribution to the process of deterritorialization. But what Akhil Gupta and James Ferguson have formulated as the anthropological task is also valid here: "instead of stopping with the notion of deterritorialization […] we need to theorize how space is being reterritorialized in the contemporary world" (Gupta-Ferguson 1992). At present, this reterritoriali-zation can be observed in the creation of "European places". In doing so, however, – and this is an observation originating from Jonas Frykman – we note that EU-Europe not only defines "European places", but these in turn determine what Europe is or what is should be in the future. The ways in which this "belonging to Europe" (Frykman 2001) is constructed, the manner in which it is put into practice varies across the whole of Europe in the same way, as the concept of Europe is variable. Recently a Viennese EU-politician made the proposition that there hardly existed a city, which could be as European as Vienna. I am not sure exactly what he meant by this but the idea in itself, in every superficiality of thought, is interesting and worthy of further comparative ethnological investigation.

This research has been supported by a grant of the City of Vienna (Being in Europe: Eine Ethnographie Europas in Wien).

References

Abélès, Marc 1996: La Communauté européenne: une perspective anthropologique. In: *Social Anthropology* 4: 33–45.
Abélès, Marc 2000: Virtual Europe. In: Iréne Bellier & Thomas M. Wilson (eds.): *An Anthropology of The European Union. Building, Imagining and Experiencing the New Europe*. Oxford: 31–52.
Appadurai, Arjun 1995: The production of locality. In: Richard Fardon (ed.): *Counterworks. Managing the Diversity of Knowledge*. London-New York: 204–225.
Augé, Marc 1988: *Orte und Nicht-Orte. Vorüberlegungen zu einer Ethnologie der Einsamkeit*. Frankfurt/M.
Berg, Per Olof, Anders Linde-Laursen & Orvar Löfgren (eds.) 2000: *Invoking a Transnational Metropolis. The Making of the Oresund Region*. Lund.
Bhaba, Homi K. 2000: *Die Verortung der Kultur*. Tübingen.
Borneman, John & Nick Fowler 1997: Europeanization. In: *Annual Review of Anthropology* 2: 487–514.
Cheshire, Paul 1990: Explaining the recent performance of the European Community's major urban regions. In: *Urban Studies* 27: 311–333.
Dracklé, Dorlé 1996: Europäische Bürokraten und Fisch. Feldforschung in Südportugal. In: Waltraud Kokot & Dorle Draklé (Hg.): *Ethnologie Europas*. Berlin: 109–127.
Der französische Soziologe Jean Baudrillard über die Wahlen in Frankreich, die europäische Illusion und die Sexualisierung der Gesellschaft. In: *Die Zeit*, 23. 5. 1997: 39–40.
Ekman, Ann-Kristin 1999: The Revival of Cultural Celebrations in Regional Sweden. Aspects of Tradition and Transition. In: *Sociologia Ruralis* 39: 280–293.
Fritz-Vannahme, Joachim 2000: Die Erfindung des Surrealen. Brüssel zwischen Wahnsinn und Gemütlichkeit. In: *Die Zeit*, 14. 9. 2000.
Frykman, Jonas 2001: Belonging to Europe. Modern Identities in Minds and Places. In: Peter Niedermüller & Bjarne Stoklund (eds.): *Europe. Cultural Construction and Reality*. Copenhagen: 13–24.
Giordano, Christian 1987: The 'Wine War' between France and Italy: Ethno-Anthropological Aspects of the European Community. In: *Sociologia Ruralis* 27: 56–66.
Gray, John 2000: Rural Space in Scotland. From Rural Fundamentalism to Rural Development. In: *Anthropological Journal on European Cultures* 9: 53–79.
Gupta, Akhil & James Ferguson 1992: Beyond "culture": Space, identity, and the politics of difference. In: *Cultural Anthropology* 7/6: 6–44.
Hénard, Jacqueline 1999: Die Farbe Farblos. Europa und die Kultur – eine Ortsbesichtigung in Brüssel. In: *Frankfurter Allgemeine Zeitung*, 11. 3. 1999.
Johler, Reinhard 2000: Ethnological Aspects of "Rooting" Europe in a „De-Ritualised" European Union. In: Regina Bendix & Herman Roodenburg (eds.): *Managing Ethnicity. Perspectives from folklore studies, history and anthropology*. Amsterdam: 171–184.
Johler, Reinhard 2001a: Telling a National Story with Europe. Europe and the European Ethnology. In: Peter Niedermüller & Bjarne Stoklund (eds.): *Europe. Cultural Construction and Reality*. Copenhagen: 67–74.

Johler, Reinhard 2001b: "Wir müssen Landschaft produzieren". Die Europäische Union und ihre 'Politics of Landscape and Nature'. In: Rolf Wilhelm Brednich et al. (eds.): *Natur – Kultur. Volkskundliche Perspektiven auf Mensch und Umwelt*. Münster: 77–90.

Johler, Reinhard 2002: The EU as Manufacturer of Tradition and Cultural Heritage. In: Ullrich Kockel (ed.): *Culture and Economy*. Aldershot: 223–232.

Judt, Tony 1996: *Große Illusion Europa. Herausforderungen und Gefahren einer Idee*. München-Wien.

Jurjus, André 1993: Farming Styles and Intermediate Structures in the Wake of 1992. In: Thomas M. Wilson & M. Estellie Smith (eds.): *Cultural Change in the New Europe. Perspectives on the European Community*. Boulder-San Francisco-Oxford: 99–12.

Kockel, Ullrich 2002: *Regional Culture and Economic Development. Explorations in European ethnology*. Aldershot.

Koolhaas, Nouvel, Portzamparc, Vasconi, Duthilleul 1996: *Euralille. The Making of a New City Center*. Basel.

Korff, Gottfried 1994: Euro Disney und Disney-Diskurse. Bemerkungen zum Problem transkultureller Kontakt- und Kontrasterfahrungen. In: *Schweizerisches Archiv für Volkskunde* 90: 207–232.

Löfgren, Orvar 1996: Linking the Local, the National and the Global. Past and Present Trends in European Ethnology. In: *Ethnologia Europaea* 26: 157–168.

Macdonald, Sharon 1993: Identity Complexes in Western Europe: Social Anthropological Perspectives. In: Sharon Macdonald (ed.): *Inside European Identities. Ethnography in Western Europe*. Providence-Oxford: 1–26.

McDonald, Maryon 1996: 'Unity in diversity'. Some tensions in the construction of Europe. In: *Social Anthropology* 4: 47–60.

Mandel, Ruth 1996: "Fortress Europe" and the Foreigners Within: Germany's Turks. In: Victoria A. Goddard et al. (eds.): *The Anthropology of Europe*. Oxford-Washington: 113–124.

Martin, S. 1993: The Europeanization of Local authorities – challenges for rural areas. In: *Journal of Rural Studies* 9: 153–165.

Nadel-Klein, Jane 2002: *Fishing for Heritage. Modernity and Loss along the Scotish Coast*. Oxford.

Olwig, Karen Fog & Kirsten Hastrup (eds.) 1997: *Siting Culture. The shifting anthropological object*. London-New York.

Rautenberg, Hanno 1999: Ikone im Nirgendwo. Das Europäische Parlament in Straßburg bekommt ein neues Haus – und Europa erstmals ein Gesicht. In: *Frankfurter Allgemeine Zeitung*, 15. 7. 1999.

Ray, Christopher 1997: Towards a Theory of the Dialectic of Local Rural Development within the European Union. In: *Sociologia Ruralis* 37: 345–362.

Schallenberg, Alexander & Christoph Thun-Hohenstein 1999: *Die EU-Präsidentschaft Österreichs*. Wien.

Schlögel, Karl 2002: *Die Mitte liegt ostwärts. Europa im Übergang*. München-Wien.

Schmale, Wolfgang 2000: *Geschichte Europas*. Wien-Köln-Weimar.

Schümer, Dirk 2000a: *Das Gesicht Europas. Ein Kontinent wächst zusammen*. Hamburg.

Schümer, Dirk 2000b: Fünfzehnerratssitzung. Wer nicht mitschunkelt, fliegt raus: Europa auf der Expo. In: *Frankfurter Allgemeine Zeitung*, 16. 8. 2000.

Schümer, Dirk 2000c: Eine schrecklich tolle Stadt. Moloch als Promenadenmischung: Brüssel, Europas Haupt. In: *Frankfurter Allgemeine Zeitung*, 5. 6. 2000.

Shore, Cris 2000: *Building Europe: The Cultural Politics of European Integration*. London-New York.

Shutes, Mark T. 1993: Rural Communities without Family Farms? Family Dairy Farming in the Post-1993 EC. In: Thomas M. Wilson & M. Estellie Smith (eds.): *Cultural Change in the New Europe. Perspectives on the European Community*. Boulder-San Francisco-Oxford: 123–142.

Smith, M. Estellie 1993: The Incidental City: Urban Identities in the EC of the 1990s. In: Thomas M. Wilson & M. Estellie Smith (eds.): *Cultural Change and the New Europe: Perspectives on the European Community*. Boulder-San Francisco-Oxford: 48–60.

Veigl, Christa (ed.) 1999: *Stadtraum Gürtel. Wien. Natur-Kultur-Politik*. Wien.

Wilson, Thomas W. 1998: An Anthropology of the European Union, from Above and Below. In: Susan Parman (ed.): *Europe in the Anthropological Imagination*. Upper Saddle River 1998: 148–156.

Festivals, Spatiality and the New Europe

Kjell Hansen

> Hansen, Kjell 2002: Festivals, Spatiality and the New Europe. – Ethnologia Europaea 32: 2: 19–36.
>
> The principal purpose of this article is to pay attention to events that emphasize and give profile to local, everyday life. It also focuses on "the multiplicity of Europe" and the politics of distinction through local markets, national commemoration days and open-air museums. Cultural heritage is presented as an ongoing process of production and re-production of meaning in these events. The article raises questions about how we can conduct fieldwork on matters as elusive as "the presence of Europe", and the sensory experiences of taking part in ceremonial activities.
>
> *Kjell Hansen, Ph.D. Department of European Ethnology, Lund University, Finngatan 8, SE-223 62 Lund. E-mail: Kjell.Hansen@etn.lu.se*

European Multiplicity?

During the last ten years "Europe" has grown from being an element in a speech of honour to become a designation full of different and changing contents. These include almost all the spheres of life, from claims for the quality of simple everyday goods to ideas on a political federation and a common currency. In this way the concept of Europe stands out as a special case of "globalisation". It is at the same time transnational and an expression of a specific cultural heritage directed towards "Americanisation".[1] The concept of "Europe" is to a high degree created out of a feeling of a shared culture – a distinctive feature pointing both towards the past and towards the future. At the same time the rhetoric about Europe is imprinted, for example, in appearances in official documents from the EU, by a strong underlining of Europe as a varied continent. When one talks of "Europe" reference is made to all the different cultures that go into the continent, from the Greek archipelago to the Arctic area of the Scandinavian countries to the Kola Peninsular, and "Europe" becomes in itself the creation of precisely this mixture. Here I appeal to the ideas of specific – often implicitly national – cultural heritages with deep historical roots.[2] Multiplicity becomes thus a prerequisite for the existence of specific cultural heritages. Images of "the multiplicity of Europe" appear accordingly in reality as being opposite to the notions of the USA as a melting pot where multiplicity has a completely different meaning.

One problem is of course that no one actually knows where this "Europe" really is or more precisely how it is composed. The concept has been used and misused in so many different ways that its meaning threatens to be completely dissolved (cf. Goddard *et al.* 1994:26). In recent years there has, nevertheless, been a distinct shift in how "Europe" has come to be understood. Every now and then the continent's name seems synonymous to all the activities that are undertaken by the agencies of the EU. In that way "Europe" has had a tangible presence in everyday life. But at the same time that the EU has become increasingly present processes that signify a striving for cultural differentiation have also appeared. There can be a number of different reasons for this, but without a doubt the EU's supranational challenges towards the national States and the establishment of a type of matrix for broader comparisons between regions in the whole of Europe has played an important role. Not least is this distinct in regions that are defined as peripheries. There a large part of regional politics de facto has been taken over by the EU. This has created a situation where a region has to compare itself not only with other national areas, but just as much with other marginalized regions within the boundaries of other nation states. Regional policy has become a field where the *Jämtland* countryside, the Scottish Highlands and the Greek Islands immediately and directly are compared with each other. Obviously these types of real and possible comparisons in competition for limited resources become a driving force for a policy that depicts distinctions.

The principal purpose of this article is to pay attention to events that emphasise and give profile to local, everyday life. Thus it deals with actions that are experienced as profiling those that carry them out and that are often used to indicate individual character. It can, for example, be about berry picking in the thinly populated areas and elk hunting (cf. Ekman 1983). In this way I will try to make "the multiplicity of Europe" and the politics of distinction clearer. In order to look for the constantly escaping "Europe", I have therefore not tried to contact the Brussels bureaucracy (cf. Shore 2000), but rather to attend to the phenomena that can be considered as its contradiction, namely local fairs, national commemoration days and open-air museums. With this I have also stated the article's second purpose, to concern myself outside the really commonplace so as to throw light on ceremonial acts and events.

My methodical starting point has been an aim to capture the experiences of being a visitor and participator in these events. Consequently, my intention is not to present any detailed ethnography on the phenomena. Rather I have aimed to use them as pointers in the discussion of more general questions about how affiliation can be articulated in a world that increasingly is characterised by transnational influences and activities. Festivals[3] and museums are phenomena in which local life stands out as a clear performance. They separate themselves from the everyday run-of-the-mill but at the same time form part of this framework of routine existence. One has sometimes described these phenomena as "symbolic statements on local social order". But they can just as well be seen as an occasion when this order is examined. Regarded in that way they become parts of an extra-parliamentary political field, phenomena such as those the British social anthropologist, Abner Cohen, named politics disguised in everyday life (Cohen 1993), even if national holidays and fairs must be said to belong to the Sundays of everyday life. They appear as political expressions without some "case" to put forward. In an article on the distinction of cultural policy the human geographer, Susan J. Smith, has summarised the political function of the fair; "festive forms are spectacular, yet routinized events whose political content expresses and shapes the character of the society in which the political is articulated through the cultural to inform the sameness and differences that make up local life" (Smith 1999: 135).

Fairs are consequently, in their celebration of some form of community, also political expressions for a desire to be different. This obviously doesn't mean that they are necessarily carried out in a striving for change; then they would of course have conveyed a "case" to fight for and turned into something other than quite simply fairs. Rather it is reasonable to interpret them as expressions of a striving to keep an imagined status quo or to re-establish a stability that is experienced as threatened. Naturally, we shall not let ourselves be deceived by formulations like these either. Neither is the preservation any "case" for the fair. Most of those that visit a fair do that either to sell something, or to buy something or quite simply to have a nice time.

Europe's constant presence, in both the obvious and the not so obvious, signifies among other things that every local phenomenon and occurrence potentially can be compared with "the European". In contrast every local occurrence may then also become a possible comment to the supranational context. Naturally this doesn't mean that local occurrences, such as fairs or national holidays, should *aim* to make comments on the world situation.

However, here is an essential difference between local fairs and the celebration of national commemoration days. The latter are ceremonial expressions for the nation state's "imagined community" (Anderson 1983), and as such exponents for a policy of separation. On the contrary, the local fairs have a completely different articulated purpose – or rather they are characterised by a lack of expressed purpose. Even so they can be seen as expressions of political commentaries, by virtue of being examples of policy distinction that isn't characterised by some "case", except that which emerges in the celebration of localised community and by that an indication of a localised distinctive character.

In such connections it can be said that the presence of something outside the locality, within Europe, also makes the local context more actual, transforming it from something obvious to a project (cf. Bringslid n.d.). The fair can accordingly be seen both as an identity producing discursive field (cf. Bauman 1993), and as a lifeworld (cf. Schutz 1970). Festivals and museums stand on one hand in relation to an existing agenda for discussion about what a European social structure can express and imply. On the other hand they are also parts of the total experiences a person has when one meets things, people and events in their pragmatic striving to survive (cf. Wagner 1970). To visit a fair or share in a national celebration day for the purpose of research is accordingly the same as trying to capture their meaning as areas of action in real life. Thus the fieldwork doesn't deal so much with making ethnographical observations as with experiences, and with empathy as the tool tries to capture the ceremony's policy that speaks more to the senses than to reason. As occurrences that stand out from the daily routines, festivals can be seen as a type of drama. In that sense they present a possible narrative structure (cf. Ricoeur 1991:99), which we can take in, not through reading, but through participation and action. It is through participation rather than through the expressed message – the words – that one understands "the story" in the event.

Hungarian Seriousness

Festivals seldom function as unambiguous statements. Rather they are events that can be seen as occasions when the consequences of affiliation become manifest in all their ambiguity. But as much as festivals stand out from the routinely everyday life, they are strongly limited in idiom. Every festival utilises a limited repertoire of possible collective forms (cf. Tilly 1995). This makes it naturally possible to physically understand what takes place, even if one cannot understand everything with the intellect. That was my experience on a beautiful spring day in 1998, in Budapest, when I was present – participated is too strong a word – at the celebration of one of Hungary's national days in March. In the morning of the beautiful, sunny early summer's day, the streets crawled with people in their best Sunday clothes. To my eyes they seemed to walk around without any clear direction and didn't seem to be waiting for anything special. My prior information was vague. My knowledge of the Hungarian language was non-existent. However, I had, being Norwegian, a clear idea of a national day's celebrations from the schoolchildren's parade in Oslo, a strong icon as to how a celebration "ought to" be. In one part of my brain I accordingly walked around the streets of Budapest and tried to construct the celebration of the Hungarian national day with the 17th of May as a model. In my striving to find an intelligible meaning in the celebration, recollections of parts of my past became emphasised and focused. At the same time my bodily presence in the crowd was a source of mental difficulty. Being a participant in another nation's celebration of itself made me feel like a phoney – a kind of 'peeping Tom' – close to being an impostor. The feeling that at any time I might be unmasked and thrown out of the celebration pressed on me. A feeling of inability to be able to read the surroundings, both linguistically and with regard to its general cultural meaning grew strong. It didn't diminish when I too bought a green, white and red cockade and attached it to my lapel, even if it was an attempt to disguise the 'foreign' body – or at least to indicate it as friendly.

After a while people began to gather in the park, at the foot of the National museum's magnificent steps. The flags fluttered. Some men high up on the steps played the kettledrums. Women in some kind of national dress, that directed the thoughts to one of Wagner's operas, stepped forward and began to sing something serious. Speakers in suits succeeded them.

Because I wasn't in command of the language other impressions became much more important and forced me to navigate the atmosphere with a kind of sensitivity. At the foot of the National museum's steps the atmosphere was rather listless. The speeches were many and long. The applause more dutiful than enthusiastic. Actually, nothing much happened.

Why the National museum? The place itself is really what the name indicates: A kind of essence of the nation where Hungary distinctly stands out as the final outcome of a historic development. In the museum's exhibitions the nation begins with the arrival of the Magyars to the high tableland and concludes with the fall of Communism. Throughout difficulties and distress the nation has been brought forward to the light. The place itself, the vague yet determined meaning that has materialised in the buildings with columnar facades, the wide, long and imposing steps and the little park between the building and the busy main street is in no way an accidentally chosen arena. Without the monumental illusions in front of one's eyes, the story wouldn't be other than a mere abstraction, remarks the French social anthropologist, Marc Augé (1995:60), and he could have made that remark specifically about the event I was attending.

I later came to know that the celebration at the National museum was the government's official arrangement. In that lies also a political charge that didn't reach out to me during the event, but which I started to suspect when, at the end of the speeches, I accompanied the stream of people through the streets. In what for an outsider stands out clearly as a commercial centre, we encountered a demonstration. Neither here could I really understand what was actually going on; whom it was that demonstrated, against what and how it was related to the national day's celebration. In contrast to the activity by the steps of the National museum the atmosphere around the demonstration was loaded. The demonstrators expressed their anger and their dissatisfaction in choruses, placards and banners, and it spread out to the body language of the marchers and the bystanders. I imagined that someone had tried to (politically) " steal" the nation. Whether this someone came from the left or the right I couldn't judge. In contrast to the government's celebration – and,

as we will see, that of the mayor – the demonstration wasn't tied to a specific place. It moved through the centre in order to, precisely through the movement, ritually seize the town. But at the same time it became much more transient. As soon as the demonstration had passed, it was as though it had never taken place. Only the sound still echoed when the marchers had disappeared out of sight.

The third scene was a small place, half way under one of the new traffic system's bridges but centred round a statue of some hero. Also this place emitted a marked historicity. It carried a story, materialised in the monument. Again, it got the outsider to tax his power of association. People began to gather and I took my place amongst them. The preliminaries went on for a long time. Here were the military and dignitaries as well as soldiers, a TV team on the fringes of the event interviewed those who were prominent, and security guards ran around and spoke keenly into their wristwatches. Perhaps my preconceived ideas played a part, but the total gave me a definite "Eastern European feeling". I expected to be questioned by a KGB agent at any time. But on the roads round about, the traffic raced forward as if nothing was going on. And not much happened either. After a couple of hours there was a speech. Cameras hummed and clicked. People applauded politely. Then it was over. The mayor had spoken.

Peeled of the significant elements – the content of the speech and the slogans on the banners – the celebration of the national day stood out precisely as a ceremonial community celebration.

The spring day in Budapest was something other than an emotional show. This concerned the items on the programme as well as those of us who were participants on the streets. What was shown up was, in general terms, a connection to the place. This way to turn the research to approach the expression of affiliation towards focusing on the experience means that we move ourselves from a concentration on identity that is shaping expressions towards an interest in experience, participation and feelings. But what happens then when the visitor's experience of participation isn't realised?

Scanian Triviality

It is a quite warm, sunny day in April. Far away in the Scanian countryside, amongst verdant fields and bursting leaves lies Lövestad, a former railway village. The railway station building has been turned into a pizzeria, the centre is composed of a supermarket, a parking area, a bus stop and a green open space as big as a football field situated behind the Farmers' Co-operative. There, in this area is a fair. There are carousels and tombolas and three small "streets" lined with market stalls. People move to and fro at a leisurely pace, look, talk, buy, halt, say hello, chat. Everyone seems to already know each other, at least by sight. Unexpected meetings scarcely happen here. The selection of goods is what we have come to recognise as a typical market assortment: kitchen gadgets, clothes, ornaments, cassette tapes of dance band music, flowers, toffees and sweets. In reality nothing much happens. But many are here and seemingly enjoy sauntering around. Here, there are only small features of that specific cultural heritage that we later will meet in Östersund. One stall sells pyramid cakes (made of eggs and baked on a spit), another smoked eels, a third homemade jam. The field worker's problem is above all that everything is so well known. There is nothing to challenge the imagination.

This experience, which at first seemed to me to be empty, can in itself be used to illustrate the boundaries between what it is to be inside and to find oneself outside the adherence that the event creates. To adhere can be said to be about being recognised. In Lövestad greetings were absolutely showered on people. Here there was an immediate confirmation of belonging. We, who no one said hello to, found ourselves on the outside. That's why the fair also clearly stood out as being rooted in all the daily trivialities. The routine and ceremonial *celebrating* of the everyday presupposed the presence of the actual everyday to be able to form the basis for the creation of a feeling of participation. It was through the daily meetings and the awareness that one found oneself in the same place that lifted the fair to a place of ritual recognition.

Festivals of this kind are striking but yet ordinary events. They attract us because they offer a break from everyday routines, yet of course we know very well what goes on at a fair: They have their own routines whereby they create affiliation and a sense of being rooted. As a celebration of community it is perhaps not their exoticism that creates interest, but rather the ritual emphasis of the commonplace?

However, one can ask why I experienced a greater presence during the celebration of Hungary's national day than I did at Lövestad's fair. As a Scandinavian it should be likely that I feel myself more at home in a Scanian village than in a big Central European city. The answer to the question lies above all in the scale of the events and thus in how participation is defined. In a town with more than a million inhabitants no one can expect to say hello to everyone. Not to be greeted is not stigmatising. A cockade

The small fair in Lövestad takes place in the open space behind the Farmers' Co-operative. It is marked by rural tranquillity and slowness.

attached to a lapel can serve as camouflage, and in a nation's imagined community, everyone can indulge in fancies that they belong.

There are few metaphors in our times that are charged with meaning like "roots" (cf. Malkki 1997). Roots become a useful metaphor for affiliation precisely because they are invisible. Roots lie below the surface, hidden from our eyes and are acknowledged only through our actions. This way, roots become flexible. If the challenges don't become too great – e.g. if one avoids being addressed – the cockade on the lapel can make it possible to feign common roots with all the others that move about in the crowd. Only the imagination puts boundaries as to what we can picture ourselves to be in such situations. At the same time I was of course very conscious that I was only posing. The feigned roots, as distinct from those that I experience as more genuine and true, gave no secure affiliation either in time or place. They didn't bind me to the place.

My presence on the streets of Budapest was, in itself, an expression of the globalised world, above all of the increased mobility that is one of its distinctive features. On the other hand, though, I was definitely there – it was the question why, that was problematic. The general, historical process that globalisation expresses, appeared as problematic in relation to my specific, genealogical history: Mobility and the cockade made it possible to fake an affiliation that, after all, in an insistent way stood out as being false for me.

The desire to establish a genealogical order – roots – is closely associated with the feeling for the local, that is to say, the capacity to be able to create and re-create locality under changing conditions (cf. Appadurai 1997). At the basic level the feeling for the local can be said to deal with creating localised affiliation in the globalised world around us, even if this world around us – as in Lövestad – can seem to be at safe distance. But this production of affiliation doesn't happen as a compensating and ordering intellectual activity, but rather as a practical dealing in everyday business. At the same time the genealogical story – the establishment of roots – gains special authenticity by emphasising the unique and by having its origins in feelings that are perceived to be expressions for what is personally experienced.

This became evident to me when, rather half-heartedly, I went out as a participant to observe the Norwegian colony's celebration of the 17th May in Lund.[4]

Norwegian Conviction

The reason for my half-hearted attitude was due to my preconceived idea that the celebration of Norway's national day in the Scanian university town Lund hardly could be anything other than a pale shadow, bordering on the corny. My idea was to join the procession and make observations.

At Lundagård, the park by the university, about a hundred people are gathered; children, the middle-aged and above all students. Norwegian flags of different sizes are here, there and everywhere. Many people are dressed in *bunad* – national costume – and nearly everyone is dressed much smarter than usual. The exception is the Swedish student orchestra that has been hired to play the music, an indispensable element in the parade. The atmosphere is relaxed. Many people seem to be acquainted. They greet and exchange a few words with each other, or stop and talk a bit longer. Most of them speak Norwegian. I walk around on the fringes and take photographs. A man in shirtsleeves, with a megaphone over one shoulder and a little Norwegian flag in his hand tries to arrange us into something that can be said to resemble an organised procession. The musicians begin to play and take the lead, followed by six girls in national costumes that between them carry a large, horizontal Norwegian flag. Occasionally, as we walk, they lift the flag in a wave-like motion at the same time as they cry "Hip, hip, heigh-ho HURRAH!!!" Many of us join in with the shout.

Slowly, almost strolling, the parade moves out through Lundagård into the shopping streets of Lund. My own feelings are still dominated by a somewhat distanced isolation. On my lapel I have again attached a cockade, but this time in the Norwegian colours and as expression for an affiliation I experience as genuine. I end up beside a man in his fifties and we begin to chat

Slowly, almost strolling, the parade moves out through the shopping streets of Lund. It ritually creates an island of national pride by flag waving and the shouting of Hurrahs.

a bit. He in Norwegian and I in Swedish. Suddenly I feel a need to justify my right to participate in the celebration and to wear the Norwegian colours – despite my language. To prove to him that I have the right to participate. That my claim to affiliation isn't feigned. I quickly try to depict my background.

As we turn into one of the narrow, central shopping streets the conversation dies out. The street itself, together with all the inhabitants of Lund that go about their ordinary, daily business, jostle us that parade together. We are a group that is seen as the sort that wanders about. We make our affiliation visible and establish it as something obviously present in the centre of Lund. Suddenly I am a part of something. I intensively experience that I am Norwegian.[5] An experience of joy and pride. To belong to something that is bigger than I am. I join in with the cheers and wish that I had had a flag so that I, like many others, could have waved it in time to the music and the shouting. Affiliation is not something that I seek, but rather something that takes hold of me, that sucks me into the whole. In the constantly cheering group, which moves through Lund, a bit of "Norway" is re-created, constructed from nostalgia and memory. Obviously it is an idealised picture and it is hardly one that can bring about directed actions. But it represents a transformation from a vague and undefined affiliation, which I carry with me daily, to a condensed, almost physically tangible experience. One of the silent spaces of the life-world has suddenly been induced to speak (cf. Kirschenblatt-Gimblett 1998).

After a while we come to the city park where we stop by the flagpole. We sing the national anthem, listen to the speech of honour – that pays tribute to the constitution and democracy – and movingly watch the Norwegian flag being hoisted. Afterwards there are games, picnics, and the sale of (Danish) beer and hot dogs.

On my way from the park the experience of participation disappears. In its place, a vague and nostalgic emptiness comes that I long to fill. Ten minutes later all is normal again. The cockade has vanished into the inside pocket, my Swedish has ceased to be stigmatising and reverted to being an asset. The experience of participation is replaced by the everyday and the Norwegian Diaspora was only make-believe.

Playing with Time

The immediately experienced roots of an abandoned background can be seen as an expression for the production of cultural intimacy, the longing for proximity and primordiality at a national and regional level that the anthropologist, Michael Herzfeld observed (Herzfeld 1997). However, it is doubtful whether it is accurate to claim that the experiencing of roots primarily is used to create a fixed point of authenticity in an uncertain world, which many modernity theorists seem to claim (see e.g. Giddens 1991; Ziehe 1989). Roots ought not to be understood as a safeguard in an age when many feel suspicious of globalisation and multinational forces and movements. This is the interpretation of the historical project, focusing on time as flow, on variability and on changing social and cultural relationships. The experience can just as well be interpreted as a genealogical play of time and history. One can argue that, in its extreme consequence, the genealogical project aims to create a fixed point in the constant flow of time, in some sense to halt time halfway between before and after. The articulation of roots is telling us a story of stillness. The roots are there, spatially fixed in childhood or the family realm, on the steps of the National museum or on a small field in Lövestad. In this way, national days and fairs are indications that make ordinary, local life clear.

The play becomes clearer if we focus on fairs that, more than buying and selling, deal with playing with time. As events, fairs as well as national celebration days are parts of an immediate "now". This "now" takes place between the event's opening and closing rituals respectively and have their expression in the strong feeling of immediate presence that characterises participation: in a literal sense it can be too late tomorrow. But on closer inspection much of this focusing on the now is seen to be pointing beyond itself. Here is a strong element of repetition; both fairs and national days are regularly recurring events. By this, they create a crossing from within the course of time to historicity (cf. Ricoeur 1991:107–115).

By way of us both remembering and being reminded of how the event at hand repeated itself earlier, it becomes a confirmation that history is there. This type of event is often also expressly directed towards the past through allusions to cultural heritage, materialised in goods as well as rituals, even if it is also incorporated in the immediate of the now. Ultimately, both fairs and national days allude to the future. We are enticed to buy things to be able to satisfy future needs, national days are celebrated to safeguard and confirm the nation's continued existence. This play with time is illustrated in several of the features that Paul Ricoeur (1991) has discussed on how the narrative becomes both a model of our experience of time and a model for how we can learn about it. In Walter Benjamin's view, festivals can be said to have partially the same function as "narratives", i.e. they have their strength and legitimacy in the allusion to, but not the explanation of, a past community (cf. Lash 1999:312–321). The experience of a shared Norwegian community affiliation in Lund is for example dependent on the fact that it cannot be explained in detail. Because then everything that separates us out would appear with a clarity that would repress the experienced fellowship. Festivals are expressions of affiliation as an experience, not as shared knowledge. At the same time, they tend to suffer from the present society's focusing on immediate experiences – which we recognise as "gimmickry".

Yearnings in Jämtland

Thursday the 9th March was cold and windy but there were still quite a lot of people at the Gregorius Fair in Östersund, a centre of Jämtland, a region in inland northern Sweden. In my first stroll through the market area it becomes obvious that there is a type of zoning in the marketplace. In the main square there is a children's funfair with carousels and a lottery stall. There is also a mixture of various stalls: ordinary market goods (toffees, CD's, postcards, cosmetics), foodstuffs (with quite a large assortment of "regional specialities": smoked sausages, flat unleavened bread, goat cheese), handicrafts (mainly made from wood but also with a good selection of leather and textiles). The stalls continue along one of the main streets with a similar selection as those in the main square. The street ends in a park by the big lake, and there the fair takes on a more distinct profile: Jämtland's yeomen, grill-huts, Lapp cots, the Norwegian neighbouring district's big tourist drive. It is possible to ride a dog-sleigh on the ice. Not many make use of it during the course of Thursday. Also on the ice are "traditional" games for children: swings, a snow-castle, and a snow-sculpture of the lake monster. Even a little hockey field has been ploughed out. One can hire curling bowls. There are more children here than at the fun fair.

The fair stands out as being clearly defined and with that, a restricted event. It appears in a clearly defined place, with a "start " and a "finish ". Outside the fair's own area it is as if it doesn't exist. For visitors, the fair is first of all an *event*. One meets friends and acquaintances here. From the various greetings exchanged, I understand that there are people that one doesn't meet very often. People stop and talk a bit. Move on. Putting plugs in the movement. They belong. It is important that the fairground is cramped. One glance rests on the stall's selection of goods and at the same time another is hunting for a familiar face. Slow movements. At random – in addition one must peek at everything. The fair stands out principally as a frame around the visitor's own projects. Saunter. Look. Feel. Be jostled. Buy. Compare. Meet acquaintances. It is common to come across someone that one hasn't seen for a while. This is what the fair really is about. But the frame isn't empty and isn't casual. It isn't replaceable. The market's constitution can be described with cue words such as stall, crowd, sound and contact. They indicate that we, at least partially, are somewhere other than in everyday life.

The fair was covered by the TV Channel 4 local news. It showed pictures of the market visitors as we usually recognise them. Besides, the news feature informed that this year's Gregorius prize had been distributed. About half of the 2–3 minute long excerpt was taken up with this. Pictures of the dog skin clad trio that received the diploma out on the ice. They represented the mountain-museum of a small town in a neighbouring district some 200 kilometres to the southwest, which is a combination of both museum and tourist information centre. The museum was inaugurated by the King Carl XVI Gustaf a year ago and has since had about a hundred thousand visitors (that was roughly what was said – besides that it was an injection for the district). The three who took the prize were very happy (they said) and thought partly that it was fantastic in itself, partly that it was nice that someone from another region was allowed to come to Jämtland and win a prize. The feature emphasises culture. Certainly it is also sympto-matic that the prize giving took place on the ice and definitely not a coincidence that they were dressed as they were. Suddenly – in this arrangement that didn't seem to be anything – something became visible: "the culture" seems to have an obvious place. And it deals with activities that are aimed towards the cultural heritage! It was not an innovative artist who got the prize. But some people who had succeeded in combining the cultural heritage with place and with that had created a site for visitors. In their visions the prizewinners underlined exactly the nature of cultural heritage. Almost hidden as they were in their fur coats.

The icy lake develops into a distinct symbol. Important and significant events took place on or in close proximity to the ice. The fair's "ideological pointers" were there in the park, by the lakeside. Yeomen came across the ice with their horses and sleighs. The horses and yeomen were a significant element. Like the prize giving they justified the fair through representing the past here and now. Of that which was on the ice, only the sleigh rides with horses (to come up during the Saturday) and the dogsleds were specifically connected to the fair. Everything else – the snow castle, swings, warming cot, and fireside stool – is always there, throughout the winter. The ice expands the town. In this way the town's winter character is underlined. When one comes from a grey and rainy but above all freezing Scania, the contrast becomes very distinct: the very presence of the ice-covered lake becomes a statement of the otherwise: Here we walk on the water! – And so do our horses.

I suddenly heard *"That they may keep up such tommyrot!!"* when I walked round the area on the Friday morning. Some peddlers – standing around one of the carts that sold doughnuts – discussed Thursday's accident, when a bolting horse ran loose in the market area and injured a woman. They thought that it was bad in general terms, but yet lucky that it happened early in the day when there weren't too many people around. Above all they thought that the presence of yeomen was unnecessary. The final remark – "That they may keep up such tommyrot!!" was followed by a concurring mumble. The fair rests heavily on tradition. As well for someone who associates it with the historical market that goes way back in time and that ceased some years after the railway came to Östersund. As for the market that was revived in the middle of the 1980's, where history itself became an actor, a living presence.[6] That the fair rests in the tradition does not imply, however, that the different actors necessarily do so. For some, like Jämtland's yeomen, it is probably the main point as such. For others, like the doughnut sellers, it is the riffraff. Others make more or less clear connections to their cultural heritage, e.g. those that sell Indian gadgets. Or the key ring seller. But also the sellers of knitted sweaters, leather caps etc. A further group connects to the activity that characterises those people from sparsely populated areas – sellers of fishing tackle and sports socks. An assessment is that a good half – perhaps 2/3 of all the peddlers operate in a sphere without, or with very vague, connections to "the cultural heritage" (toys, kitchen gadgets, CD's, clothes etc.).

One might say that in market sales there are a few dominating themes or criteria: Cheapness, authenticity, and to quickly be able to yield to impulses from the stomach, the eye, imagination … The fair is clearly not there to deal with cultural heritage. But it makes itself felt in different ways. The thin rounds of unleavened bread become genuineness wrapped in a bag. And by "the stud-farm"[7] stand two women who contemplate whether they will eat or not. Talking about it they establish their own private and personal cultural heritage: "Last year I ate such a salmon-stud as that." The sale of sausages with different foreign heritages fits into this: If it isn't one's own cultural heritage it is in any case someone's cultural heritage.

In the crowds one can see people dressed up. A dog skin fur coat. A 19th century uniform. A folk costume. But those who wear the clothes make nothing of it – they do nothing in particular. They only stroll about like all the other fair visitors. But there are also some young women, dressed up and advertising something – I don't know what. They meet so many acquaintants that are more interesting than giving out information. The talk is a very typical, almost theatrical, local dialect. My thoughts go to the creative anachronists, people that actively and deliberately play with time by enacting some past.

Acquaintances meet and greet each other: "Have you been to the fair?" "I have had a stroll around and looked." The Gregorius Fair isn't a big event, but rather something that one pops into – and just as quickly pops out of. But for a few days Östersund is a kind of centre. Something happens in the town that makes it something more than it is on ordinary weekdays.

Festivals are events that produce an excess of significance. They do this by being collections of staged and moulded signs, that give the visitors possibilities to choose not only between obvious phenomena like market toffee or unleavened bread, between demonstrating or listening to a speech. They also create options as to which interpretations one will allow to appear. But all these choices have, as a basis, a reservoir of shared implications. Those who produce the symbols as well as those who read them have to recognise the symbols that can have importance. The symbols have to capture recognisable experiences and at the same time be interpretable, i.e. understandable. That which is conveyed is thus not the symbol producer's – the speaker's or the peddler's – experiences, but what these experiences signify in a certain context. But for this to be understandable it has to appeal and connect to the readers', or listeners', experiences. These experiences are, in turn, the result of how we act in the everyday. It is exactly in this moment that fairs as well as national days can relate to the elusive Europe. They are opportunities when everyday experiences are condensed and elucidated, when fairs and national days stand out as discourses that make experiences public. My argument here places festivals as political expressions within the framework of a triangle of relationships. A localised lifeworld, a public event and a global or European shade. By that every festival becomes a potential comment to the political situation in Europe as seen from a fixed point and characterised by its own power constellations.

Accordingly, places are at the same time elastic – they release and accept influences from outside – and coherent enough to be recognisable. They have permeable borders, i.e. it is possible for both objects and people to move between places, but they also have a diachronic dimension written into past events. To know the local, to have local knowledge can, therefore, as the American philosopher, Edward Casey, pointed out, be said to be about understanding what is generally true and valid in that which is locally obvious. To have a feeling for the place has to do with what is true for places in general, as it is expressed exactly at *this* place (Casey 1996:45). Places materialise in 'now-time' the past as well as the conceivable future, and festivals emphasise this. But even if the boundaries are elastic and penetrable they are in any case demarcations against what is outside and different. The place's peculiarity is precisely that it is separated from all other places (cf. Hall 1991). In the case of the nation there are more devices available to make uniqueness credible: education, museums, politics, monuments, armies etc. But in the small place, which can be confusingly like other small places, the authenticity of uniqueness rests rather with intimate relations than in big gestures.

One of the most important characteristics of every fair is its aim to accentuate the unique. And in most cases this is done through creating a definite local connection. The simplest way to do that is through the name, by designations that refer the event to a determined place and through that associate the place to the event. It becomes a bit more advanced; i.e. offers several associations, with a name that alludes to history. Through the name continuity is first alluded to, but also, at a deeper level of resemblance, to the local and the distinctions to everything that doesn't belong to the local.

One might wonder why festivals seems to be such an important element in the indication of spatial affiliation. Perhaps it can be said that it is exactly the increasing similarity between places in terms of architecture, road design, trade, education and employment – such things that allow us to say that we can no longer separate one place from another – that make us more attentive to *other* ways in which places are separated from each another.

Perhaps it is simply so that festivals give us an opportunity to appropriate the place? The appropriation that is present in the establishment of direct, immediate, sensory relations to the world that makes up the place. Or rather that the appropriation implies creating a feeling for the place in which our recognition is made up of the sensory impressions that festivals offer? It is through relating to the world around us, materialised not only in other people and social/cultural institutions, but also in physical objects, that we are constituted as social beings.

The main issue is about how we take in the world – and about how it appropriates us. It is about the significance of the events when we are absorbed as a mobile, surging mass of people, with sounds, sights, smells and feelings. The issue is about the immediate appropriation that is part of feeling, of buying, of eating.

In ways that seem trivial, but yet obvious, every fair may take a position in an international, regional and local place. It is positioned – more or less distinctly – in proportion to the other symbolic and practical activities that constitute local life, which more than ever today is characterised by the interplay between mobility and coming to a halt. The local places are not only spots to find oneself in, they are as much places that one can leave or return to (Olwig 1997). Places are no longer given points of affiliation – a topic that not least is present in all those places that are marginalized as thinly populated areas. They are constantly the subjects of comparison with every other real and depicted place. This comparison makes the place itself visible as a particular unit for its inhabitants. The place becomes the object for reflections on the distinctive character and gives rise to ideas on local distinctive character. It is the insistent presence of other places that gives grounds for celebrating that we, after all, find ourselves right here (cf. Ardener 1987). Local narratives, as festivals, localise these connections between the local and the global through placing them in a distinct historical context, materialised as cultural heritage (Sørensen 1997).

The Legacy of Museums

Like festivals, museums are opportunities when residence can be celebrated, when the roots can be put into focus and celebrated. They are each in their own way displays in what could be called nostalgic representations of a vanished past. But while the fair is regarded as being trivial and solely for enjoyment, many have maintained that museums are places where identities are substantiated. They have, as the ethnologist Birgitta Svensson (1998) has pointed out been turned into places where we are supposed to come to terms with ourselves through understanding that we have been. This becomes clear in a visit to e.g. Jämtland's county museum's multi-slide presentation, which introduces the county's history. One had to ask at the reception desk to see the slide presentation and the friendly staff set it in motion for my colleague and me when we visited the museum one afternoon during the fair. Two people were already sitting in the auditorium. Not to see the slides, but because they had found an out-of-the-way place for their own private conversation. Apart from them we were the only ones there.

In the dark, sitting in comfortable armchairs and far away from the fair's overabundant crowd, and sensory impressions, we let ourselves be captured by cultural heritage as seduction: The beautiful opening pictures and mystifying music pulls us into something different. Here Indians and settlers are alluded to and compared. Landscape views. Roving hunters. Here were (are) free men. Strong. Self-sufficient. A little talk about the mythological first settler. The slide presentation calls forth a feeling through its extremely beautiful pictures. Jämtland is described as an island in the wilderness; a barren climate in which a settled district was created. Here the mantra was launched: "INVENT! PULL IN! BITE HARD!" The voice tells how life is set back (plague and unrest) but "we" constantly rise up. Cling to the district. "INVENT! PULL IN! BITE HARD!" Prosperity grows. Freedom grows. Norwegian – Swedish – Danish. The land is ravaged. Hunger, destitution and poverty for 200 years. Surviving all the same. "Free people can't be suppressed". The cartloads draw towards the western sea, towards the eastern sea. The yeomen draw wealth back to the land. New times are emerging. The forest gave freedom, protection, pasture and timber. But then the private companies came. Farmers who sell their forests. Freedom is lost. The railway comes. The city. The forests are sold and the waterpower. The furniture vans hauled. Prosperity was to be found somewhere else. The old age and the longings were left behind. "We want to go home to the free country" "INVENT! PULL IN! BITE HARD!" Sure we can. "It is what we have longed for. Here we want to be." A Jämtland song is quoted at the end. The last text dies away while pictures of happy, hopeful children zoom up.

In relation to this the fairs stand out as the cultural heritage's disordered fringes: Places that have a broad set of props at their disposal but hardly any guiding manuscript. Everybody can create their own variant of the heritage – with or without Indian elements. The museum contrasts with this. The slide show's well-produced speech moralises on the reasons and consequences of the decrease in population. The migration from the countryside appears as a movement that arises without being created. Through its connection to the progress of society, what drives people "on the run" remains secret and unknown. Migration becomes an expression for society's development and with that linked to an abstract "time walk" that transforms movements in space to movements in time. Migration from the countryside can be considered as a movement in time, from the traditional to the modern (cf. Hansen 1998:46–52).

Another image is displayed at the open-air museum. Here the houses are neatly restored to almost their original state. Here is an antiquarian authenticity, but also an arrangement. Small information signs explain what we see. Careful geographical and temporal attributes metacommunicates with a world of knowledge rather than experience. But the museum does not really stand out as a pedagogic way into a time-embracing experience of history. Rather the open-air museum stands out – at least a winter's day when the visitors are conspicuous by their absence – as a park of monuments. A place that brims with the panegyric, with no other function than to give individuals a feeling that it was there before they came and will still be there when they have gone away. The houses in the open-air museum are outside the actually present world. It is this that emphasises and gives them characteristics of being monuments, unlike the commonplace nature that characterised them in the reality they were brought from. The open-air museum's recontextualisation signifies that continuity and the commonplace are replaced by ceremonial marking of the discontinuities of history. Accordingly time becomes distinct and the object of reflection. The narrative that *is* the open-air museum will make us pay attention to the differences between "then" and "now". Through this narrative the museum separates itself from the fair's moulding together of "then-now-later", from its mixture of high and low, new and old, into an immediately experienced "now". This difference becomes clear in the differing places that are used, for the various scenes for the celebration of one's own community (cf. Augé 1995: 60).

Those houses and environments that are in the museum are representations – something that will give a picture of something else and more than they are. The buildings become symbols that replace what they once were. The crucial moment here is that the symbolic *representation* of the past at the same time is a part of the museum's *presentation*. It can be said that it is when the museum does something with the houses, when the museum presents them to its visitors, that they also can act as a representing symbol. The open-air museum's houses are made to stand out *as* something, not by virtue of some inherent symbolic power, but by what the museum staff *has done* with them (cf. Thrift 1996:7). The authenticity that is associated with the houses is safeguarded by the museum as an institution. The genuineness of the representation is warranted through the whole context that the museum provides, as an institution of society. In this sense the houses become what they are, not by representing what they were earlier, but by representing them as museum pieces. What we have is thus a situation of "double representation". First of all, the buildings as representatives for a clearly marked off past, in a realistic sense. Secondly, the representation of the houses as exhibits and thus as something marked off from the past as a kind of general representation of history. The experienced genuineness is warranted through the second representation but is legitimised through the first. The problem can be said to be that the historical purport is, to a high degree, dependent on its context – i.e. the surrounding landscape, houses and people – as by its own contemporaneity.[8] In a completely different connection, the American anthropologist, Sidney Mintz (1985 (1995)), has in a striking way, underlined the context's meaning: "I don't think meanings inhere in substances naturally or inevitably. Rather, I believe that meanings arise out of use, as people use substances in social relationships" (cf. Thrift 1996: 29).

Cultural Mobilisation

In the cultural mobilisation that festivals represent, experiences of the local, national and international surroundings are dealt with. But it is not articulated. The surroundings represent no "case". Rather the festival practice confirms a spatial affiliation. Local cultural identities are chiselled out by actions, by emphasising and making the folklore that is presented as a characteristic, local cultural heritage. It can be seen in different forms of handicrafts, in food, or commemorative sites of local heroes and historic events. The past is mobilised genealogically to create purpose and belonging. A longing for roots, for spatial affiliation, leads to a redefinition of places and of material culture, a vitalisation that expresses the politics of distinction.

It is striking that marginality is brought out in these activities. In Jämtland, one's own life on the fringe, low technology, the proximity to nature, "rusticity" is brought out. In Hungary, a picture of the small, but proud and indomitable nation on Europe's fringe is conjured up. And in Lövestad the most indistinct picture is created, since the event's scale is such that those that take part in an obvious way, form part of the place. In this way the countryside also stands out as more genuine than the world around (cf. Ardener 1987, Shields 1992).

To many local actors the overall aim is, through one's own actions, to counteract marginality and depopulation, or to bring about incorporation and modernisation. The concrete aim of the place markings is thus not evident, but the work on the cultural heritage is making up some part of the project irrespective of what purpose it has. In this context the cultural heritage becomes a kind of "mobile monument", which makes up a reservoir of the past that can bring political power to the fore (cf. Augé 1995: 60–65) But this is not an invention that has its origin in consciousness, but rather in the material world around. One might claim that the celebration's participants become what they are through being observed in their social and material context (cf. Heidegger 1977:131). It isn't man that creates his world around him; rather man is the image of his context. The rules and routines of fairs and national days have a

The icy lake develops into a distinct symbol. The ice expands the town. In this way the town's winter character is underlined.

power that lies outside the control of those involved. The same goes for the place as a whole: We find ourselves not only in place – we are of place (Casey 1996:19).

There is a strange duplicity in events of folklore. On the one hand handicrafts, the cultural landscape and historic buildings are "genuine", i.e. representations of cultural heritage, an experience of belonging to some (fixed) where. Our native district is part of us in the sense that it is through that that we have got to know our world. On the other hand, festivals are clear exponents for the commodifying side of globalisation. The two sides mutually legitimise each other. Fairs as well as national days are easily recognisable irrespective of where one faces them. They are played out according to what could be called a transnational matrix. At the same time they are representing opportunities that strongly focus on the experiencing of genuine spatial affiliation. In this a part of the interplay between Europeanised and localised processes is also implied. A good European ought to have a local affiliation, but it ought to be shaped in a recognisable way, even when it is a tool for distancing him/herself from centralising processes.

To Become European

The increased interest for regions in Europe can be seen as an expression for how places now, as perhaps never before, serve as a reference point to people that seek affiliation. This can seem to be a paradoxical statement in a time said to be characterised by mobility as well as time and spatial compression. But regions are not unambiguously localised. Instead they appear in situations and exist in between as a possibility and potential (cf. Boissevain 1992). The new feature today is that there is a strongly increased possibility to change place affiliation. From the perspective of the individual possibilities have been opened up to maintain conflicting and competing spatial identities. The hierarchical order of places has become a field where people, to increase their influence, quarrel about definitions (Feld & Basso 1996, Lovell 1998) and no longer represent some finished "readable text".

Spatial affiliation instead becomes a way to take an attitude to the wider context from an idea of local conditions (cf. Stewart 1996: 40). "Culture", in this connection, becomes an expectation, a way to question or accept the world, a continuous searching for something that constantly escapes. In such processes the conceptions of affiliation represent important reference points and "Europe" represents such a possible reference point for people's actions, what they do in different situations. "Action" also includes the use of language, as fairs and national days

Local fairs strive to accentuate the unique, but are simultaneously easily recognizable, no matter where they are held.

very well also can be regarded as activities of speech. Every argumentative move is designed as an answer to earlier moves and an attempt to control the future. Activities are always carried out in relation to other actions, which gives the activity a persuading character or function, a potential ability to be materialised as the influence on somebody else's actions. Actions and activities are understood not only through their visible and material consequences, but also through the immediate categorising that they become subject to. Words arrange and structure the actions, by which they also get a social and cultural content. Festivals may be regarded as part of a continuous argumentative context, where actions and activities are the targets for criticism and justification. What is shared in a society becomes, in this perspective, not so much agreements about meaning and content as access to a set of argumentative positions. "Europe" and "the local" can be seen as two such complementary positions (cf. Shotter 1993).

At the same time as the meaning of, and interest for Europe increases, there exists a series of different opinions associated with this Europe. In Jämtland it implies bureaucratic control while in Budapest it can be seen as the free world's Garden of Eden. At a local level we can observe how regions, municipalities, cities and the countryside are deeply involved in celebrating their own distinctive characters.

Here we can understand how cultural heritage is used to mark distinction and establish new cultural borders inside Europe. These processes of becoming European and becoming local respectively are more than only parallels, they are also directly related to each other. We understand, approach and act in relation to the world from cultural categories. But it is participation in the world that not only gives us knowledge about it, but also the cultural categories (cf. Schutz 1970).

A Europeanised connection is shaped in linguistic and other everyday activities at definite places. The rhetoric over Europe provides the situated activity with a frame of interpretation, which give starting points as to how we reshape our own sense of our own everyday. In such contexts it can be said that the presence of that outside the local, of Europe, also makes the local connection more present, converting it from something obvious to a project. Unlike globalisation in general, to become European implies however, through the influence of the EU, also that new common rules for a number of different daily activities have been introduced. Such rules transform people's daily scope for activity but also make relative that which is understood as being an obvious way to do things. New sets of rules and regulations do not only change the possibilities for activities, they also create a discursive background for comparisons. By this

"Europe" becomes both something that structures daily connections and an expression for determined local everyday interpretations. The emphasis of local or national contexts problemises the preferential rights of the men in power and the media's obvious preferential right of interpreting Europe. The rhetoric over Europe provides the situated activity with a framework of interpretation that can be said to form a starting point for how one reshapes one's own commonplace. The political charges that can be tied to "Europe" will then be seen not as lying beyond or behind everyday activities, but within them, as structured conditions and as the actors' own ambitions. With "Europe's" increased presence we can also suppose that awareness about spatial multiplicity has increased, as a result of a compound process between all the positions where a group's identity is defined (cf. Hansen 1998:184–191).

With that a feel for place is created that integrates it into daily practise but that also establishes it as a separate space (cf. Stewart 1996). In a world that, among other things, is characterised by the globalised media, images of the genuine and the immediate are associated with the feeling of local affiliation (Peters 1997). Despite an increased element of intersecting communications between different environments, awareness about and expression of the differences have become more and more obvious (cf. Paasi 1996).

The Regions of Europe?

In the tension between local and global one plays with dichotomies between traditional and modern, the remote and the immediate, slow and fast, peripheral and central in ways that makes the place both a tangible and a uniting entity. But the new regional identities break up previous local boundaries. They are of places but at the same time they exceed the boundaries of place. The regional rhetoric supplies the local activity with a frame of interpretation, while the local supplies the regional order of communication with the legitimacy of the commonplace (Hansen 1999a). Regions are created in many different arenas, locally but also in Brussels, in the lifeworld but also through the mass media, in actions but also in speech. Regions find themselves in a field of tension between local cultural mobilisation, the national defensiveness and the European offensiveness. Less today than ever before, they can be understood without consideration to activities outside the region; political, social, economical, cultural. At the same time the region can, since it is so concentrated in itself, neither be understood outside its own limitation. The region sets its own agenda and emphasises its own uniqueness in the world. These processes are naturally parts of a movement that has become public in Europe, but this parallel can only be understood if we understand that its driving force is the idea of being unique.

In fact most regions are not one but many, fighting with themselves for a reasonable identity. Here you find the imaginations about the unique cultural heritage that captures the region in time and space. Here are transnational openings and niches, and there are claims in relation to the national state, which is the unit that the region measures itself against. In a wider European perspective we can see that regions relate in several different ways to the nation states. There is disassociation and autonomy of language, conflict avoidance and coexistence, presentation of alternatives and a search for authenticity. To take the essentialising discourse seriously – to look at it as reality – is to take the regions' cultural mobilisation out of context. Instead, the existing orders of discussion becomes more important to the extent that they constitute materialised social relations and through that conditions for action. By being understood relationally regionalisation takes a clear political dimension (cf. Brubaker 1995). Regions may indeed, at one level, be said to constitute a politically discursive field, where qualities are culturally constructed in a continuing argumentation (cf. Shotter 1993). But every cultural construction has to have a credibility in order to convey meaning. This credibility is achieved in the moment the discourse expresses experiences. In this way the experience is established as primary in relation to the discussion about it.

Accordingly, regionalism doesn't mean that the national vanishes – but neither that it unambiguously becomes something to dissociate from. On the contrary, in many cases we can see how the national is made regional, and how the regional is nationalised. Naturally people do not become defined by the surrounding space. We constantly try to take control over our own identity and the transnational, national, regional and local streams that are constantly met by active efforts to create one's own affiliations (Sørensen 1997:161). Festivals become a set of spatial, time bound and material opportunities to try out one's own experiences. "So every fair, festival, spectacle or masquerade is positioned; it has a location within international, regional and community space; it has a setting relative to the other symbolic and practical activities that make up local life" (Smith 1999:136).

Fairs and national days can be seen as materialised expressions as to how experiences are tested. But they do this in very different ways. National days are almost exclusively symbolical displays where cultural heritage turns into a monument. Contrary to this, the things that are sold as "genuine" products on the fair often lack an explicit symbolic force. Here the handicraft rather appears as an event in focus, irrespective of whether it concerns traditionalistic, modernistic or local handicraft (Hansen 1999b). The museums' presentation is something in between these extremes in its strive to create monuments of a popular, activity based, cultural heritage. To go to the museum, be jostled at the fair or to celebrate the national day accordingly becomes a kind of ceremonial activity. In a time of high mobility and strong ideas about "Europe" these events become expressions about how we seek an anchorage – even if only for a short while – in a fixed and determined place.

Translation: Sue Glover

Notes

* This paper has earlier been published in *Fönster mot Europa*, Studentlitteratur, Lund 2001.
1. Here there is naturally also an opposition to "Islam", anchored in national xenophobia as well as in right-wing populist politics but without officially being accepted as politically correct.
2. Throughout this article I use "cultural heritage" in a general and deliberate imprecise sense that above all aims to designate what in everyday speech is often referred to as cultural heritage. The term accordingly reflects a general use.
3. I use the terms like market, fair and festival without distinction both for fairs and national commemoration days. Where it doesn't disturb the logic too much I'm also allowing museums to be included in these sweeping terms. In the cases where I refer to the phenomena in general, the terms are used as synonyms.
4. The celebration was organised by ANSA, Association of Norwegian Students Abroad.
5. A similar experience is discussed by the ethnologist, Barbro Blehr, in connection with the 17th May celebration at Skansen in Stockholm (Blehr 1995).
6. It is a regular recurring feature before every fair that the local newspaper publishes culture historical articles about how the market used to be "in the past".
7. This is a pun. The Swedish word for stud ("stut") is also used as a name for a sandwich made out of unleavened bread with a filling. Thus, the little stall selling such sandwiches has named itself "stud-farm" ("stuteri").
8. This refers to the lack of knowledge about the future that people in the past had, but that today's museum visitors cannot liberate themselves from because this future is our present, or sometimes actually our past.

References

Anderson, Benedict 1983: *Imagined Communities: Reflections on the origin and spread of nationalism.* London: Verso.
Appadurai, Arjun 1997: The Production of Locality. In: *Modernity at Large. Cultural Dimensions of Globalization.* Public Worlds vol.1. Minneapolis & London: University of Minnesota Press.
Ardener, Edwin 1987: "Remote areas": some theoretical considerations. In: Jackson, Anthony (ed.): *Anthropology at Home.* ASA Monographs 25. London & New York: Tavostock Publications.
Augé, Marc 1995: *Non-places. Introduction to an Anthropology of Supermodernity.* London: Verso.
Bauman, Zygmunt 1993: *Postmodern Ethics.* Oxford & Cambridge: Blackwell.
Blehr, Barbro 1995: "... Og føler intenst et eller annet." 17 maj i Stockholm ur en deltagares perspektiv. In: *Gatan är vår! Ritualer på offentliga platser.* Barbro Klein (ed.). Stockholm: Carlssons.
Boissevain, Jeremy 1992: Introduction. In: Boissevain, J. (ed.): *Revitalizing European Rituals.* London: Routledge.
Brubaker, Rogers 1995: National minorities nationalizing states and external national homelands in the new Europe. *Daedalus* 124(2).
Bringslid, Mary Bente n.d.: *Bygda og den framande. Ein studie av det lokales de- og rekontekstualisering i ei vestnorsk bygd.* Doktorgradsavhandling, Bergen: Institutt og museum for antropologi, Universitetet i Bergen.
Casey, Edward 1996: How to Get From Space to Place

in a Fairly Short Stretch of Time: Phenomenological Prolegomena. In: Feld, Steven & Keith H. Basso (eds.): *Senses of Place*. Santa Fe: School of American Research Press.

Cohen, Abner 1993: *Masquerade Politics: Explorations in the Structure of Urban Cultural Movements.* Oxford: Berg.

Ekman, Ann-Kristin 1983: "Det är för jaktens skull vi jagar och inte för köttets." Älgjakt som kollektiv ritual och ekonomisk resurs. In: *Svenska livsstilar.* Anders Hjort (ed). Stockholm: Liber.

Feld, Steven & Keith H. Basso (eds.) 1996: *Senses of Place*. Santa Fe: School of American Research Press.

Giddens, Anthony 1991: *Modernity and Self-Identity. Self and Society in the Late Modern Age*. Cambridge: Polity Press.

Goddard, Victoria; Llobera, Josep R.; Shore, Cris 1994: *The Anthropology of Europe. Identity and boundaries in conflict.* Oxford: Berg.

Hall, S. 1991: The local and the global: Globalization and ethnicity. In: K. D. Anthony. (ed.): *Culture, globalization and the world-system*. New York: MacMillan and Binghampton: SUNY.

Hansen, Kjell 1998: *Välfärdens motsträviga utkant. Lokal praktik och politisk styrning i efterkrigstidens nordsvenska inland.* Lund: Historiska Media.

Hansen, Kjell 1999a: Det föreställdas politiska makt. In: Damsholt, Tine & Nilsson, Fredrik (eds.): *Att ta fan i båten. Etnologins politiska utmaningar.* Lund: Studentlitteratur.

Hansen, Kjell 1999b: Försäljning, vandrarhem, servering! Om kulturarvet och 1990-talets landsbygdsutveckling. In: O'Dell, Tom (ed.): *Non Stop! Turist i upplevelseindustrialismen.* Lund: Historiska Media.

Heidegger, Martin 1977: *The Question Concerning Technology and other essays*. New York: Harper Torchbooks.

Herzfeld, Michael 1997: *Cultural Intimacy: Social Poetics in the Nation-State*. London: Routledge.

Kirschenblatt-Gimblett, Barbara 1998: *Destinction Culture. Tourism, Museums and Heritage*. Berkeley: Univ. of Cal. Press.

Lash, Scott 1999: *Another Modernity, a Different Rationality*. Oxford: Blackwell Publishers.

Lovell, Nadia (ed.) 1998: *Locality and Belonging*. London & New York: Routledge.

Malkki, Liisa H. 1997: National Geographic: The Rooting of Peoples and the Territorialization of National Identity among Scholars and Refugees. In: Gupta, Akhil & Ferguson, James (eds.): *Culture, Power, Place. Explorations in Critical Anthropology*. Durham & London: Duke University Press.

Mintz, Sidney 1985 (1995): *Sweetness and Power: The Place of Sugar in Modern History*. New York: Viking Penguin.

Olwig, Karen Fog 1997: Cultural sites: sustaining a home in a deterritorialized world. In: Hastrup, Kirsten & Olwig, Karen Fog (eds.): *Siting Culture. The shifting anthropological object*. London & New York: Routledge.

Paasi, Anssi 1996: *Territories, boundaries and consciousness. The changing geographies of the Finnish-Russian border.* Chichester, Brisbane, Toronto, Singapore: John Wiley & sons.

Peters, John Durham 1997: Seeing Bifocally: Media, Place, Culture. In: Gupta, Akhil & Ferguson, James (eds.): *Culture, Power, Place. Explorations in Critical Anthropology*. Durham & London: Duke University Press.

Ricoeur, Paul 1991: The Human Experience of Time and Narrative. In: Valdés, Mario J. (ed.): *A Ricoeur Reader: Reflection and Imagination*. Toronto and Buffalo: University of Toronto Press.

Schutz, Alfred 1970: *On Phenomenology and Social relations*. Edited and with an Introduction by Helmut R. Wagner. Chicago and London: The University of Chicago Press.

Shields, Rob 1992: *Places on the Margin. Alternative Geographies of Modernity*. London & New York: Routledge.

Shore, Chris 2000: *Building Europe: The Cultural Politics of European Integration*. London: Routledge.

Shotter, John 1993; *Cultural Politics of Everyday Life-* Milton Keynes: Open University Press.

Smith, Susan J. 1999: The Cultural Politics of Difference. In: Massey, Doreen; Allen, John; Sarre, Philip (eds.): *Human Geography Today*. Cambridge: Polity Press.

Sørensen, Birgitte Refslund 1997: The experience of displacement: reconstructing places and identities in Sri Lanka. In: Hastrup, Kirsten & Olwig, Karen Fog (eds.): *Siting Culture. The shifting anthropological object*. London & New York: Routledge.

Stewart, K 1996: *A Space on the Side of the Road. Cultural poetics in an "Other" America*. Princeton: Princeton University Press.

Svensson, Birgitta 1998: The Nature of Cultural Heritage Sites. *Ethnologia Europaea*, vol. 28:1.

Thrift, Nigel 1996: *Spatial Formations.* London: Sage Publications.

Tilly, C. 1995: *Popular Contention in Great Britain, 1758–1834*. Cambridge: Harvard University Press.

Wagner, Helmut R. 1970: *Alfred Schutz on Phenomenology and Social relations.* Chicago and London: The University of Chicago Press.

Ziehe, Thomas 1989: *Kulturanalyser. Ungdom, utbildning, modernitet.* Stockholm/Stehag: Symposion.

Exhibition and Experience of Cultural Identity

The Case of Bergen – European City of Culture

Eva Reme

> Reme, Eva 2002: Exhibition and Experience of Cultural Identity. – Ethnologia Europaea 32:2: 37–46.
>
> In the year 2000, Bergen, the second largest city of Norway, managed to get the status of European City of Culture. The new won position provided opportunities to profile Bergen as a modern city and prove its rank at the national and international stage. However, results did not measure up to ambitions. Looking back, it seems that the year turned out to be dedicated to a rural and regional self-celebration. In a way Bergen might be regarded as an example of how pre-modern culture heritage get actualised and rediscovered in an urban setting. This raises questions regarding the intentions of emphasising the past and how people respond to such efforts. In answering these questions, focus will be directed towards how place not only is an integral part of social, economical and political processes, but also the way it constitutes essential elements that touches upon the inner landscape of the individual.
>
> *Eva Reme, Dr. phil., Department of Cultural Studies and Art History, Ethnology Section, University of Bergen, Nygårdsgaten 6, N-5015 Bergen.*
> *E-mail: Eva.Reme@ikk.uib.no*

The routes that take you to a place can be many. They might go through longings, dreams and logged memories, or through actions, experiences and discursive practices; they even follow the streams of thought and the touch of things. In etymology, place references are marked by both permanence and immanence, by the fluid and changeable as well as the stable and fixed. Places are the spawning ground for the activities of our everyday lives, and as such they may be regarded as immovable points on the great and unfathomable horizon of reality. Thus we relate ourselves to places out of habit, and based on contemplation and strategic considerations that involve identity formation as well place marketing. This paper will be focussing on these issues as I look into the questions of how we charge places with meanings and use them as repositories for storing these meanings, and how places may touch us and talk to us. My point of departure will be specific and close to home: Bergen in the year 2000 – when it was awarded the status of European City of Culture.

Bergen – a Place in Norway and in Europe

The European City of Culture is a project initiated by the EU, and the intention is to bring the multiplicity of European cultural heritage to the attention of its population. The Cities of Culture therefore take on the difficult task of transforming the variety and intermixtures of culture into a shared feeling of unity. The strategy involves exporting and importing cultural impulses which are intended to yield a result both local and European at the same time. This is not only a question of identity and creativity, but of economy. Drawing up the programme for a City of Culture, is therefore often considered a national responsibility, as the focus awarded to the specific city will inevitably draw attention to the nation.

This was, however, not the case for Bergen. Financial support from the central government was held at a minimum. Bergen's budget for its City of Culture programme amounted to no

Hanseatic warehouses – *Bryggen* – in the harbour of Bergen.

more than 10 to 20% of the funds available to cities of culture in other Nordic countries. Much of the criticism that Bergen's cultural programme appeared homespun and insufficiently challeng-ing, may very well have been caused by the lack of financial assistance. Still, Bergen is a town with many stories to tell, many places to show off, many activities for people to take part in. The question I want to raise, is why Bergen – as a modern city – chose to present its profile against a background dominated by pre- and early modern coastal culture?

On reading the programme and catalogues for the various cultural events, we find it is the traditional culture of Bergen and its surrounding area *Vestlandet* – or the western Norway, that dominates. This literature may in fact be read as guidebooks to Vestlandet, its cultural landscapes and its cultural heritage. If we browse through the programmes from other Cities of Culture, we will find themes relating to the urban complexities of technology and art. This would have been an option for Bergen as well, as the city is happy to view itself in the light of the modern and urban. Its university and colleges, commerce, technology, and maritime industries are distinctive features of its urban tapestry. Also, Bergen's cultural life is varied and variegated, with established institutions of music and fine arts. In combination with new artistic talent and experiment, these account for an exciting and progressive cultural scene. With its 250 000 inhabitants Bergen is far from a metropolis. Nevertheless, many of its features are typical of larger cities across the world. In short – Bergen is a city in motion and transformation.

So why did the Programme include so little of the modern and urban? Why was it dominated by the past and the regional? On studying the programme, we find it carries a range of different potential purposes. For instance, it may be seen as an opportunity for self-celebration, a chance to show off the ancient buildings and material remains of the medieval crown seat of Norway. Also, it is an opportunity for the city to remind itself and the rest of the country of the Hanseatic Era and Bergen's international roots as a locus for trade, which tied the northern and southern regions of Europe together. Trade, shipping and seafaring represent the basis for the Bergensian with artistic achievement and richness of cultural life. Grieghallen, the large concert hall with its modern glass facade, speaks of a city, which by tradition is an established member of the European club of fine arts. History, and Bergen's status as European City of Culture, thus carries a potential for making the city stand out as something unique and special in a national context. As a Swedish newspaper put it, Bergen is "a cosmopolitan city, in contrast to the rest of provincial Norway, with an ancient and international view to the rest of the world" (*Dagens Nyheter* 26/3–00).

On the other hand, the "City of Culture" status can be seen as an opportunity to define the city as part of a national landscape and folk culture. In this context, Bergen's contact with Hardanger – the surrounding fjord district – is emphasized. The mountains and the fjords, the orchards and the embroidered national costumes, the fiddles and the folk music make up a setting, which is considered to be essentially and traditionally Norwegian. Bergen likes to market itself as "the gateway to the fjords", the point of departure for those who want to experience "Norway in a Nutshell". The programme for the City of Culture 2000 was no exception in this respect.

In other words, Bergen has long held authoritative local as well as national reference points. As such, Bergen was able to consider itself a cultural city long before it was awarded status as European City of Culture. Perhaps this was precisely what the organisers of the Year of Culture wanted to show? Was it their aim to display a pre-ordained self-portrait? A portrait, which would receive a spruce-up of its cosmopolitan colours thanks to its European cultural city status? On studying the programme it is obvious that Bergen's ties to the outer world are important, in terms of the old and traditional roots between Bergen and the North Atlantic region, as well as the city's participation in our contemporary global world. Thanks to partnership schemes with the other cities of culture, the programme did include events and exhibitions which focused on international issues: nomadism, hybrid culture, technology and gene manipulations could serve as key words in this respect.

The programme includes references to the local, the regional, the national and the global, if to varying degrees. Perhaps this is why cultural anthropologist Thomas Hylland Eriksen sees the City of Culture programme as an onion made up of numerous layers of place connections. He further argues that the programme reflects an experimental attitude to the various meanings of the concept of culture, providing space for the formation of new constellations of "high" and "low" culture. "Here there are projects that draw parallels between Norwegian, European and non-European art and literature. Projects that accentuate the essential features of local life, a multitude of cross-over-projects where the mix of impulses is easier to eye than any search for roots" (Eriksen 2000:82).

It is tempting to agree with this conclusion. Abundance and variation are present; there are events that activate contrasting concepts of culture. Nevertheless, it is reasonable to question whether the onion metaphor is in fact the best way of illustrating the programme structure. Even though different layers and dimensions of culture, place and time can be identified, many factors point to the existence of an essential core – a core which is in touch with absolute roots and which are also meant to touch the public. An alternative interpretation of the programme may thus involve formation of identity rather than artistic and cultural experimentation. The City of Culture programme could be read as a programme for testing and adjusting Bergen's relationship with the rest of the nation and for investigating and reconstructing its bonds with the rest of the world.

Bergen and the Local Culture

Looking more closely at the City of Culture programme, we may find reason to see it as part of a strategy to emphasize regional identity and a search for distinctive roots. It might be interpreted as an attempt to disassociate Bergen from its former local image were either towns people or fjord-based farmers would play the leading part. A new front figure seems to recur in exhibition after exhibition, re-appearing at

Coastal farmers – *striler* – in town.

one event after the other, whatever the genre: the coastal peasant, the so-called *stril*. One of the more original manifestations, the *Naust* (boathouse) project is worth a special mention. A group of Nordic artists were invited to set up exhibitions and installations in old boathouses on the shores outside Bergen. The intention was to unify international contemporary art with local tradition and history. Another noticeable project focused on maritime food in art, featuring food-related installations in various passenger boat terminals along the coast. A third example worth a mention is *Mass for bad weather,* a project, which set out, no less, to poetically, reflect the sensuality and potency of coastal culture. However, most elements in the series of regional displays were based on the traditional coastal peasant, who appeared as part of innumerable more conventional museum exhibitions, shows, market days, crafting festivals and fish festivals. Through music and drama, folksongs, craftwork and traditional foods, a wide range of artefacts from coastal life and meagre rural existence were elevated and transformed into West Norwegian cultural heritage – worth conserving, worth passing on. This accentuation of coastal culture can be seen as an effort to legitimise and extend the culture of western Norway, for which Bergen is a focus and natural centre.

Many critical voices claimed that the Year of Culture was too colloquial and too parochial. Media researcher Jostein Gripsrud found in his project evaluation report (2000: 59) that the programme typically concentrated on small-scale producers, voluntary cultural contributions and just about anything that could be associated with the western Norway. As a result, the true "light houses" within the programme tended to disappear from sight. The endless series of events would generally involve activities with a somewhat mundane and parochial profile. Artistic expressions of urban life, with all its industrial and global aspects, were conspicuous only through their glaring absence. The national newspaper *Dagbladet* voiced similar comments (9/10–01). Unlike other Cities of Culture, Bergen's events came across as regional branding. We are living in a global era and are witnessing weakening national sovereignty. According to the newspaper, the result is the emergence of an arena where the battles between different cultures are not necessarily of a national nature; self-assertive regions like western Norway can just as easily be a party to this fight for further symbolic and economic influence.

Perhaps, then, place marketing was in fact the main project for this special year of culture. In this context, the long and varied range of local and regional activities was transformed into tools for highlighting Bergen, not only as a town, but also as a regional centre. If so, the rediscovery and recreation of that which was seen as traditional coastal culture must be understood as a core element in a renewed identity project based on a revised concept of place.

The Flexibility of the Coastal Culture Programme

The City of Culture 2000 programme received mixed reviews in the media, ranging from outright slaughter to great praise for a programme, which incorporated a multitude of cultural expressions. However, how was it possible for pre-modern coastal culture to attract this level of attention and enthusiasm?

Firstly, the traditional fisherman farmers, or coastal peasants, appear to have rid themselves of their former stigma, now enjoying more of a neutral status in social and cultural terms. This has turned the coastal peasant into a cultural icon, which comes in useful for locating and logging old and renewed traditions. Secondly, the coastline stretches to the very head of the innermost western fjords, thus tying the whole region together. Consequently, coastal culture is an extremely useful label for a programme seeking to establish networks and profiles to be shared by the entire region. Through this process, the various communities are linked to each other in new ways as new connections are estab-lished between the centre and the periphery. One of the positive comments following the City of Culture year was in fact that Bergen at last had recognised its hinterland as worthy of esteem.

The coastal culture also appears important in making western Norway specific and distinct. The director for the City of Culture put it like this: "The Coastal culture of western Norway is a significant element of our programme. Our aim is to bring coastal cultural into its European context. Norway has long neglected its boathouses while celebrating the traditional inland larders. The cultural institutions that focus on traditional inland Norwegian culture and building traditions are sufficiently many. However, there are numerous exciting dimensions to the boathouse – the building where the sea meets the land – and so far these have largely been ignored. Coastal communities need to strengthen their identity and legitimise their culture. We have an important job to do"(Gloppen 2000:17).

Furthermore, coastal culture may serve as a link between a heroic past and an industrial and prosperous future where Bergen takes on a leading position, both politically and economically. Its status as an international city is not a fact of the past; on the contrary, Bergen demonstrates a "natural" connection to the outside world. Seen from a regional viewpoint, the concept of "local globalism" is exceedingly appropriate. In this context it is possible to stress a cultural openness implicit in local traditions and cultural heritage.

The focus on Bergen as a West Norwegian centre rooted in rural, coastal culture carries many positive implications. The city may well uphold its position as "Norway in a Nutshell", but while appealing to the recognisable, Bergen's reconstruction of coastal culture is also an invitation to something wider, different and more challenging than the established image of the national culture. In this way the City of Culture programme may be seen as a project of identity formation, where Bergen and its surrounding areas appear as a unique place in

Boathouses symbolising the identity of Western Norway.

Europe. The programme stresses the opportunity to experience Norway in new ways, precisely because the emphasis on tradition has made Bergen a city where modernity appears to have touched the landscape unevenly. The different ages are still palpable in the spaces left behind, providing a sense of contrast as well as synchronism.

In this process the cultural heritage and cultural landscape carry political potential. Local culture can, for instance, be exploited so as to disrupt the balance of the national self-image. In the aftermath of the Year of Culture, the media debate included numerous calls for Bergen to be launched as the cultural capital of Norway. In national opinion polls, for instance, close to 50% felt that Bergen was the cultural city of Norway, whereas a mere 19% referred to Oslo in a similar way. In discussions and publications, it was pointed out that Bergen, in contrast to Oslo, was able to accommodate its surrounding countryside. Bergen allowed people from out-lying areas to feel at home. As a matter of fact, even if they were not from western Norway they would be able to recognize familiar features and feel at ease. Oslo, on the other hand, had been reduced to a centre of bureaucracy where feelings of alienation were tangible. In other words, Oslo is a city where the majority of the population is thoroughly urbanised, offering no familiar links with the countryside (*Morgenbladet* 10/6–00). These claims are clearly rhetorical in nature, but there is a message to be read between the lines, a message of cultural hegemony, which was never there before.

We could easily stop at this point and draw the conclusion that the City of Culture 2000 was a success. Rather than showing off an established, frozen and nationally constituted picture, Bergen was transformed into a movable landscape, which regardless of national ties, was marching to its own drummer-beat. But was this really a breakthrough in terms of Bergen and western Norway as a place for unique experiences? Coastal culture is a highly versatile concept, particularly because it carries such a large number of associations on individual as well as collective levels. Nevertheless, it is in fact this very versatility which gives rise to the problems. The coast encompasses the whole country. Last summer, another series of coast cultural events were staged in Bergen. One of them was officiated by the Minister of Petroleum and Energy. He gave voice to many of the points previously made by the City of Culture Director; only this time coastal culture was linked to the Norwegian nation. "It is unfortunately the case that in Norway, inland rural culture is called to our attention at every opportunity. It is now important that we focus on the coast. Most people live on the coast anyway" (*Bergens Tidende* 5/7–01), the minister claimed. In saying so, he readjusted the focus of our national cultural heritage, a result of which may well be found in many of the recent presentations of Norway, especially those intended for an international audience. Norway is here promoted as a modern coastal nation where industries such as oil, energy, underwater-technology, marine research, shipping and fishing are key features. The rural past of the coastal peasant is important in this context. Boathouses, traditional seafood, boat festivals etc. provide historical weight and legitimacy to this new national reconstruction. It is perhaps not without reason that the National Archives chose the year 2001 for directing their efforts towards the build-up of coastal culture.

Coastal culture thus appears to be an elastic concept, readily available for many different modes of exploitation. Returning to the question of why pre-modern coastal culture appears to flourish in an urban setting, we may perhaps find that the answer rests with the versatility of concept, in local as well as national and international terms. It expresses something about times past and present; it articulates something specifically characteristic about a certain place, yet without setting definite and fixed boundaries. On an official and collective level, it may be utilised as a hallmark; on an individual level it may give scope to private imagination and experiences.

The Experience of Coastal Culture

This raises the question of how most people perceive the phenomenon of coastal culture. The highlighting of a place is not a process under-

From the North-Steam Festival.

taken in an individual or emotional space. Personally, I have lived on the coast all my life, yet does not see myself as part of a coastal culture with long unfaltering traditions. On the contrary, I consider myself as a human being influenced by the lifestyles of modern urban Norway. But what happens when a more or less urban individual meets the past and the coastal culture?

If we pay one of the events of the City of Culture programme an actual visit, the *North-Steam Festival* might illustrate some of the potential experiences that the phenomenon of coastal culture give rise to. This event was largely organised and staged by voluntary organisations working for the enhancement of vintage boats and coastal culture. Its spotlight was on the recent past, when steam and diesel engines made the boat the most important means of transport, linking outlying coastal areas and the fjords with Bergen and the rest of the world. As such, the event was easily grafted into the Cultural City year, and to noone's regret, as the event was considered one of the most successful.

The North-Steam Festival represented one of the events I more or less by chance happened to become part of it. It was therefore with a certain sense of detachment that I walked onto Bergen wharf one Saturday morning, joining over 50,000 other people – if we choose to believe the newspapers – who had gathered to watch more than 50 vintage boats depart at the same time, all heading once more for their old destinations. Climax was reached at two o'clock. The boats were preparing for departure, many members of the public climbed aboard, while the rest stood waiting ashore – like tinned sardines. Children sat on their parents shoulders, people pointed, discussed, told each other stories and explained what they were watching: that boat over there was built in ... that one was used during the war ... this one sank at ... we always used to go on that one when we went on our summer holiday ... my granddad helped build it ... my neighbour was the engineer aboard this one ... do you know him? ... my aunt was a waitress ... was she the one who ...? There were monologues, dialogues and heated debate, and suddenly many found they were talking about the same boat, the same crew, the same episode from times long past. In an instant, people on the wharf were no longer strangers. Familiar

43

people, places and references made everyone feel acquainted, there and then.

The boats left the harbour, with steam rising towards the sky and engines gaining pace, accompanied by a multitude of choirs and bands in colourful period garments, all drowning each other out, yet at a volume which never managed to rival that of the hooting fleet of boats. They greeted one another and their passengers, while saying farewell to the people left on land. The air was filled with noise and smelled heavily of coal and diesel. Passengers waved and were greeted in similar fashion by the crowd of spectators. People smiled, some laughed – but as I looked around, I saw just as many weeping.

What is happening, I wondered. What is this? Then – suddenly – I heard the beat of a familiar engine. I recognized the sound, and turned around – to see the boat of my childhood years. This was rather unexpected, because this originated from further south than most of the other boats in the Festival. Its familiar beat went straight up my spine. Distant places and times came back to me, faraway faces came close, and I remembered the smell of the lounge – oil, damp clothes, cigar smoke mixed with newspapers, stories and gossip. It was perhaps not overwhelming, but nevertheless I did have to wipe a tear from my eye.

So what happened? The stir and hustle round the boats, the confusion and tangle of smells, sounds and colours in different shades rendered the senses alert and sensitive, thus bringing the past to mind and enabling the recollection of things forgotten. Bergen became a bigger city, transformed into a gateway to other places and other times. For a moment even I became part of coastal culture.

This episode may help illustrate some of the reason why coastal culture as a concept is useful in a drive to experience and market places. On the one hand, coastal culture can be related to specific artefacts, places and periods. On the other hand, the concept is so wide that it will evoke personal associations in most people. When Anthony Cohen (1996:807) writes about how national symbols become effectual and powerful, he claims it depends on how the symbols are constructed and what opportunities they offer for individual and collective interpretation and action. We examine the material of tradition and watch the rituals connected to them, and as individuals "we interpret and remake them in the sense that *we* are able to make of them" (ibid.). We listen to the rhetoric of government agencies, but mobilise our own common sense to understand its meaning. Abstractions such as nationality, and by default we could add concepts such as local and regional belonging, would become too slippery and lax if individuals were unable to process them through their own experiences. Instead the concepts like nationalism and regionalism are personalised.

These phenomena are of interest to Gaston Bachelard (1994). By using the concepts of "resonance" and "reverberation" he describes our approach to places and things, and our ability to grasp them as "poetic" pictures and movements. This occurs when we transform the expressions of a place into personal impressions so that the place not only becomes a part of our lives but also takes root within us and triggers our personal re-creation of our own selves. This process establishes a "reverberation" between the individual and the place, making us co-poets of our own lives. In this way, the sense of belonging to a place is never forced on us from above – it is a feeling we all help generate.

It is highly uncertain whether coastal culture founded on a pre-modern way of life might attain such "poetic" significance to the Bergensians. It would in any case need to take place through modes of recognition that point beyond themselves, beyond the world of stereotypes and clichés. However, I hold the view that pin-pointing a specific taking on the phenomenon of coastal culture is not all that important; perhaps it represents merely one of many opportunities for evoking past experiences and glimpses of recognition – like the North-Steam Festival did for me. To others, coastal culture may represent an interlude, or perhaps a different landscape where the pulse and trains of thought move at another pace than usual. Perhaps it unveils or releases a past filled with more magical and mythical yarn than what we spin in our everyday lives. The culture becomes a dig for an "archaeo-logy of experience" (Turner & Turner 1995), which allows us to peer backwards in time through our own senses

There are clearly numerous reasons why coastal culture in a pre and early modern disguise now seems to be integrated in present-day urban Bergen. It is a highly pliable concept with scope not only for cultural, political and economic meaning, but for an existential dimension as well. With traditional coastal culture integrated in the urban, modern city, we may draw the conclusion that the promoters of the City of Culture managed to create a programme, which made Bergen and western Norway visible on the national and European map. In doing so, the programme organisers addressed existing expectations amongst the public. Perhaps, then, the focus on coastal culture was a success because it helped highlight the sense of place, and the public joined the organisers in making this happen. In this process were we might observe a shift or better, an intermingle between a "constructive authenticity" based upon stereotypes and clichés and an "existential authenticity" where experiences and emotions are understood first and foremost as echoes of our inner selves (Wang 1999).

To conclude, it appears that the concentration on coastal culture directed the focus onto Bergen and Vestlandet – western Norway – as a unique place, brought to life by the organisers as well as the public. In this manner the region as a place turned out to be an eventful and specific happening. As the geographer Mike Crang (2001) put it: place "is more to do with doing then knowing, practice then representation, less a matter of 'how accurate is this?' than of 'what happens if I do it'" (ibid. 194). In other words, Bergen and western Norway turned out to be a place for acting out, for doing, a place where things and thoughts happen.

The Limitations of a Rural Past

The North-Steam Festival was a success in terms of spectators as well as participants. People were enthused; the past came nearer, people felt close to one another because they came close to their own feelings. In this way, dialogues were initiated with memories, which perhaps were not normally as intensely present. The triggers may have been many – the crowd, the noise, the smells, the visual impact of the old boats, the architectural surroundings with the old quays and ancient buildings. Through the experiences taking place here, the present was lived in an unspecified future. The boats, chiefly from between 1930 and the 1950s, and the ancient Wharf with its Mediaeval, Hanseatic and early 20th century buildings, represent the city's highlights in terms of history and cultural heritage. Through the material surroundings the past made itself tangible and thereby showed its capacity to become a "memory-place" were the power of the place it self marks our minds (Andersson 1996). As such the place constitute a potential storage room for various small and anonymous events as well as those we celebrate officially and recognise as our collective memory.

Perhaps it would be appropriate to say that the various material elements form some sort of punctual axis of time, which provides the place with its identity. However, the exciting thing about events such as the North-Steam Festival is their capacity to dissolve this axis of time and blend its elements with personal recollections about lives lived and the expectations associated with what is happening just there and then. In this way, bridges are built between the representations and stories about the past on the one hand, and the actions and experience of it on the other. Perhaps this is the key to the success of this type of events, i.e. the opportunity to experience a place in times present as well as past while perceiving ones own life in an extended continuum of time. The place, is transformed into a form of virtual reality where multiple times are on show, yet it is up to the individual to utilise his own senses and experiences in order to stage manage his impressions and the context they appear in. In this way, the place generates experiences, which in turn become new narratives about the place, continually charging it with new meaning and significance.

Consequently, what makes events such as the North-Steam Festival important is not the celebration of coastal culture in itself, but the fact that it reminds us of the deeper layers of our existence. These events show us that we are not only living in the present, but in a reality where different times and temporalities are overlapping, because our experience of the present moment is based on recollections of the past and expectations of the future. These are dimensions of experience, which are not stored in well-defined or closed files within our consciousness. On the contrary, they have deposited themselves in different ways within our memory and sensory systems through the lives we live and have lived. In this way, we exist not only within but also by virtue of time and space; our bodies link and incorporate these dimensions (Crang 2001).

However, the Bergen Wharf and harbour where the North-Steam Festival was based, is but a single place in Bergen. There are a multitude of others: streets and squares that carry associations with entirely different times and horizons of expectations. There is the Torgalmenningen Square for instance, which carries a resemblance with the wharf by virtue of the age of its surrounding buildings. Through being a commercial centre as well as a venue for various events and meetings, be they public or private, this is nevertheless more of an ambivalent place where the hustle and bustle exist side by side with leisurely strolls and relaxation.

Were we to continue our stroll into side streets and alleys, we would have found cafes which through minimalistic architecture, espresso coffees and music from other corners of the world, would signal a reality far removed from coastal and peasant culture. It would be possible to continue endlessly. Like any other city Bergen is a place with many squares, streets and alleyways, a place with many different speeds and intensities, a place with scope for numerous rhythms and times. This may well be what characterises modern communities and the people there. The challenge facing a City of Culture where locality and identity are central themes, could therefore be to grasp the place with all its multitude of intertwined times and places. Obviously, the practical implementation of such a scheme would be far from straight forward. However, it might be a good starting point to introduce a cultural concept which focuses not only on recognition, but which provides scope for the unexpected, unfinished and surprising. This would direct the focus not only to the 'intervals' in the temporality of everyday life or to the larger and more abstract lapses of time. On the contrary, there will also be possibilities for including speed and noise of the still unsettled and unfinished. The result might accentuate how both memories and imaginations mark the place and simultaneously link past and future to a continually altering present.

There is nothing wrong about coastal culture, but we might perhaps have incorporated other dimensions worthy of preservation – dimensions that are not necessarily founded on a more or less rural past. It would at any rate have been interesting to investigate this potential during Bergen's year as City of Culture as the city clearly wished to see itself as a European meeting place. Instead, the programme – whether intentionally or not – provided a venue for Norwegian culture to *meet* European culture. Understanding ourselves as part of what is European is perhaps too complicated a task when identity so often appears in the singular in a more or less one-dimensional past.

References

Andersson, Dag 1996: Erindingens steder. In: *Vinduet* 50.
Bachelard, Gaston 1994: *The Poetics of Space. The Classic Look at how we Experience Intimate Places*.
Cohen, Anthony P. 1996: Personal Nationalism: a Scottish view of some rites, rights, and wrongs. In: *American Ethnologist* 23/4.
Crang, Mike 2001: Rhytms of the City. Temporalised space and motion. In: May, Jon & Nigel Thrift (eds.): *TimeSpace: geographies of temporality*. New York.
Eriksen, Tomas Hylland 2000: Bergenske veikryss. In: Hazell, William R. (ed.): *Kulturby Bergen 2000. Det offisielle kulturbymagasinet*.
Gripsrud, Jostein 2001: En kulturpolitisk vurdering. In: Hazell, William R. (ed.): *Kulturby Bergen 2000. Norges europeiske kulturby. Prosjektrapport*.
Hazell, William Robert (ed.) 2001: *Kulturby Bergen 2000. Norges europeiske kulturby*.
Turner, Victor & Elisabeth Turner 1995: *Image and Pilgrimage in Cristian Culture: Anthropological Perspectives*. New York.
Wang, Ning 1999: Rethinking Authenticity in Tourism Experience. In: *Annals of Tourism Research,* Vol. 26 No. 2.

Bergens Tidende 5/7 2001.
Dagbladet 9/10 2001.
Dagens Nyheter 26/3 2000.
Morgenbladet 10/6 2000.

Place for Something Else

Analysing a Cultural Imaginary

Jonas Frykman

> Frykman, Jonas 2002: Place for Something Else: Analysing a Cultural Imaginary.
> – Ethnologia Europaea 32:2: 47–68.
>
> The importance of place and material culture for identity-construction in contemporary European regionalism is here brought up in an investigation of the region of Istria in Croatia and Slovenia. Theories of modernity tend to regard place either as disappearing in a time-place compression or as a compensation for the uprooting in a world of globalisation and insecurity. A slightly different perspective comes to the fore when focus is being put on how regions actually are used in a contemporary praxis: as basis for people's culture building and identification. Not as a place to defend or escape to, but as an "opening", a possibility. From a phenomenological point of view the imaginary potentials of things and heritage are being discussed, arguing that lived experience and agency must be studied in parallel to narrations and cultural constructions. Regions also could be seen both as outcomes of micro-nationalism and as cultural imaginaries where something different is formulated.
>
> *Professor Jonas Frykman, Ph.D., Department of European Ethnology, Finngatan 8, SE-223 62 Lund. E-mail: Jonas.Frykman@etn.lu.se*

Such will things always be for us:
the focal point for poetics.
(Gaston Bachelard 1992:28)

At the start of a new millennium, the Europe of Regions is emerging as the other face of transnational culture building. What does it actually mean to perform on the European arena at this time? Which regions are selected, and which of their characteristics are emphasized? Starting with the province of Istria in Croatia, which attained the status of a Euro-region in 1995, I will discuss two characteristics which recur repeatedly: multiculturalism and the soulfulness of place and things. Several of the features displayed in Istria have their counterparts in Swedish regions like Skåne or Jämtland, in Vestlandet in Norway or Carinthia in Austria, and so on. Yet it may be strategically justified to exaggerate the contours and the blackness of the pictures and tone down the similarities between the places. On the one hand, regionalization makes certain areas in Europe concordant precisely because they emerge as culturally significant at the same time in history. On the other hand, the distinctive local features in each area are placed in the developing tank. If distinctive local character is to be visible, then comparisons are necessary. The Swedish experience of cautious, low-key regionalism contrasts so dramatically with the tendencies to rebellion against an excessively bossy centre that are making themselves felt in Istria. In this essay I want to let a different world provoke the Swedish experience, allowing it to serve as a relief to what is happening "at home".

Cultural Imaginaries

Regions have, generally speaking, grown up as a kind of cultural interstices or imaginaries, in-between spaces of experimentation which make room for something different. They are at once virtual and real, for fun and in dead earnest. In today's debate they tend to be used to highlight something reprehensible and to hold up hopeful alternatives. In a similar way, social groups – women, coloured people, ethnic minorities, the working class – were used in the twentieth century as concrete points of departure for criticizing society and searching for functioning models to copy (Stewart 1996a). With the aid of the regions, a broad spectrum of issues has been raised today. These range from the criticism of globalization and the levelling out of differences to the abuse of political power and the technologization of life. When regions emerge, they thus bear the impression of contemporary unrest while simultaneously offering a cure for it. Yet the questions that can be articulated are different from the emancipatory ones of the twentieth century. The regions foster misty ideas of closeness, authenticity, mystery, and a way of life adjusted to nature within a micro-nationalist frame (cf. Harvey 1996). Unlike the dreams of utopian social communities, the fantasies produced by the regions mostly concern material phenomena – the place and its things.

When social matters are mentioned, it is in the form of experiments with post-national identities. New groups of professions such as computer operators, information officers, architects, publishers, and craftsmen appear in the regions side by side with the local population, minorities, and people in folk costume. Syntheses of old and new are created, culture building takes place using local features as crucial components. The hope that the borders between nation states in Europe will disappear seems to be more obvious in places like Istria or Skåne, where it is much more credible that the established national identities might be replaced by something new – at once common European and locally rooted. The tolerance of diversity appears to be greater than in national centres. One's own country gives contours to collective and personal identities. When Europe – especially the European Union – launches its motto *In Uno Plures* ("Unity in Diversity"), it is therefore easier to embrace the programme in the regions than at the centre. The European rhetoric that emphasizes multi-culturalism as its distinctive feature is thus most explicit here (cf. Shore 2000).

When, for example, the Norwegian anthropologist Thomas Hylland Eriksen writes an article about the European Cultural Capital for 2000 – Bergen – he stresses its cosmopolitan character and shows how the population has a multicultural heritage going back to the Middle Ages. The town was founded and governed by Dutch merchants and Germans from the Hanseatic League, and this has been reflected in its distinctive character ever since (2000:68f). Today this orientation towards the multicultural goes hand in hand with the tendency of the internationalist city – with its oil industry, its university, its shipping lines – to create an image distinct from that of the peasant culture of the surrounding countryside. On "Stril Days" (*stril* is the term used for the rural populace around Bergen), the city is occupied by people in imaginative folk dress alluding to the peasant culture of the turn of the century. What unites them all is that they are folksy and antiquated (cf. Reme, this volume).

When regions take the stage, their character is thus as much a dreamed as a factual geographical unit. They have something that the rest of the country presumably does not have: personality, life, and "soul". To give the soul a necessary anchorage, cultural heritage and ancestry have been put on the agenda. This may crudely be linked to the general European aspiration for distinction: it is by virtue of its civilization and its long history that the continent shapes its image (chiefly as a counter to the USA). And this is a strategy of which people are more aware in these vigilant cultural interstices. The cultural heritage undoubtedly functions as a kind of local charter, giving legitimation. The regions take pride in being more genuine, original, and ancient than the nation state. In Croatia the state as a national construction has a brief history going back no further than 1991 – although the declaration of independence was a "thousand years old dream" coming true, whereas the history of Istria started before the Romans. In this intermediate space there is not the same requirement for the state as an administrative unit; instead, people can experiment freely with long genealogies. Similar alternative genealogies, reinforced with the aid of the cultural heritage, function in most regions. Skåne and Jämtland, although long since parts of Sweden, invoke their Danish and Norwegian roots. Back in the Middle Ages, Vestlandet in

Norway was the seat of the Norwegian kingdom. These examples could be multiplied from the many parts of Europe where regionalism is strong: the Basque country, Catalonia, Brittany, Wales, Flanders – and they are growing in number and strength.

The Life of Things

The focus on the cultural heritage repeatedly highlights material culture. This has nothing to do with material circumstances in the historical materialist sense, but instead the concrete but far from dead material objects. The past becomes visible through its traces and artefacts, through houses, monuments, memorials, individual objects, art and sculpture. Things are truly living testimony to the cultural continuity and distinctiveness that people also search for elsewhere. And then something strange happens: the objects increasingly take on the character of subjects – acting of their own power. Of course, people use them to reason about identity and interpersonal relations, and for this they are ascribed the character of messengers, meaning-bearing objects. But surely they are something more than just what people around them want to read into them? Are they merely the *thoughts* they materialize? Are they not also surrounded by their own unique "aura" – the radiance that testifies to their strength and their power to invoke (Benjamin 1969)? Do they not also possess a poetic ability to give rise to new ideas, to activate people's ability to dream and fantasize (Bachelard 2000:187)? To be parts of the dialogue of the present with the past, they must be proved to be something more than objective testimony and remains. How could we otherwise understand why people in Istria constantly speak of the *ambience* of places and buildings? Why would there otherwise be such an obsession with trying to understand the magic power exerted by Illyrian settlements and votive sites, by fortresses or chapels dedicated to the Virgin Mary, by churches and relics, by places where ley lines and fields of force are visible, by medieval wind instruments and ancient live-stock breeds? Things like this – and many more – have become something more than symbols. They bear secrets and have to be induced to speak.

The study of *the life of objects* therefore comes naturally to the fore if one wants to understand how regions at the turn of the millennium are shaped. To obtain interpretative tools, we need to extend the scholarly perspective beyond the functional, the symbolic, or the communicative – perspectives which have hitherto formed the interface between researchers and things. To acquire ideas for new perspectives, one can turn to the extensive literature describing how other artefacts in our high-tech society act: microchips, computers, the Internet, mobile phones, surveillance cameras, implants. The objects of the new technology have been ascribed agency, the ability to act on their own (Latour 1998). They appear as subjects, as active transmitters of memories, as actors with discrimination and the power to speak and seduce (Lash 1999:342). Yet it would be short-sighted to regard that ability as being restricted merely to the things with which technology has provided culture at the end of the millennium! Surely everyday things and remains of earlier eras can also be understood according to similar principles? Things appear to have an ability to collect and retain, even without batteries and electricity.

Here I am going to examine how the interstices, the regions, speak and think through their landscapes, cities, and beaches; through their material remains of previous and contemporary eras. For the phenomenologist and philosopher Gaston Bachelard, for example, the house is as much a physical body as material construction which thinks and stimulates dreams. Its potential lies not in the function but in its incredible ability to give substance and life to imaginary worlds. The house exists in us as much as we live in it – it arouses a response, strikes familar notes, and sets our imagination in movement. A child has no problem with the idea that toys have a life and that they are merely concrete objects with which to start fantasizing. Becoming an adult, however, means that one ceases to dream, learns to stop being open to the potential of things and instead considers only their usefulness and function. As a researcher one should expend more effort on studying how imagination is slowly suffocated to make room for rationalism.

The house has the ability to do something to us, just as much as we do things to it. Its most distinctive characteristic is thus not just that it encloses us and grants us shelter and rest, but that it makes the world open up, that it actually functions as a sensory organ through which we investigate life. There is scarcely an idea about the world that is not mediated through open and closed windows or doors, by protective roofs and cosily furnished rooms. Every house is a possibility; it can be the start of a new voyage of discovery. It invites us on a journey where we can see one dreamed house after another rolling past before our eyes – to be examined, approved, or rejected.

When viewed in this way, materiality becomes a place from which our dreaming can derive nourishment and where our imagination can blossom; it has the ability to contain secrets and transcendence (2000:98). It can be seen from the point of view of its poetic, generative qualities – a cultural imaginary – as much as its utilitarian aspects. What story does it tell, what associations does it arouse with other buildings in other places (cf. Stewart 1996b:181)? Failing to see the life that proceeds from things would be like looking at sheet music but not listening to the music it denotes.

What has been said here about the house can be applied to much wider fields. High technology certainly involves something new for culture, but in this context it is justified to point out how it has made us sensitive to the power of things. We have once again become alert to the meanings that reside in buildings and home interiors, in beautiful objects and things with a past. From this point of view it is no coincidence that today's interest in design runs parallel to the new IT society. There is something more to things than social distinction.

Things have always spoken, but people have not always paid the same attention. Today we listen. Can we find here an explanation why buildings, monuments, and other expressions of the cultural heritage have emerged from the prison in which museums and historiography

The city of Motovun. Photo: Sergio Gobbo.

have placed them? If so, then material culture is not so much a testimony about as an entrance to the past. This in turn takes on the character of something semi-mysterious, living and contemporary.

Things thus appear to play an important role in the shaping of the imaginary, the regions that are "happening" today. In theoretical terms, this means opening up to the inspiration of phenomenology. This means that things should not be understood on the basis of what we have invested in them in a rationalistic spirit, or how they have been constructed. Instead it is a matter of understanding what they can create and give rise to – the diversity of resonance that arises in us in our encounter with them.[1] Or, as Bachelard says using a metaphor from the field of poetry: the wealth and depth of a poem are not revealed by tracing its motifs and composition but in the response it arouses in the reader (2000:23f). For ethnology and the cultural sciences this means keeping a sceptical distance to the otherwise so predominant perspective of modernity. That is an outlook grounded in social psychology. It makes it possible to understand people's relation to things in the light of deeper drives such as desire, compensation, and security. People's relationships to things are then mediated by human needs.[2] For Bachelard, on the other hand, it is more interesting to ask what *happens* in this encounter than to try to clarify the obscure reason for the occurrence of the encounter in the first place.

In several regions and "interstices" the liberation of local patterns of culture has taken place parallel to a series of political convulsions. Regions have risen in opposition to centres and asserted their distinctiveness on the grounds of cultural difference. When people begin to imagine that it is possible to make direct contact with the past through the place, the land, and things, it can give them a dangerous certainty about their own excellence. Things are so palpable, they do not argue, and they can therefore be used as evidence that we really have something genuine of our own, in contrast to the complexity of the surrounding world. "We have lived here since Roman times!" as the Italian-speaking population of Istria can be heard to say. In the Austrian province of Carinthia, peasant culture and the *Heimat* have been a similar power centre for Jörg Haider's FPÖ. In Vestlandet in Norway, Viking Age and medieval remains reflecting the conversion of the country to Christianity have been cited as evidence that this is a much more authentic land than the rest of Norway. The region easily becomes a place where micro-nationalism is confirmed by the things to which it refers. It is then important to bear in mind that materiality is much more ambiguous than political programmes and scholarly discourses. It can also serve as a strategy for bridging over history, liberating the place for communication with contemporary people. Material things are more accessible than memories of everyday social life. Just as it is possible to build a fortress against the outside world, so it is possible to open the local for free experimentation in a time of dramatic upheaval. Each region displays its own pattern in this respect. The pieces that people use to create something of their own are the same from place to place, but the outcome depends on local historical and economic conditions.

The role played by materiality in Istria will be discussed on the basis of the film festival in the little mountain town of Motovun in the summer of 2000. Perhaps more distinctly than in any other place, it shows the crucial role that things have come to play. The people here have actively repressed the self-identity built up of memory and narrativity. Instead they have used towns and landscapes and blended the magic of the place with technologies for communication and picture making. Local narratives and existing history were considered less interesting than the aura proceeding from things. Or to put it another way: If the past was to be made to speak, it had to be freed from memory, tradition, and history. In their stead came myths, fantasies, and volitional ideas. Reality became virtual more than real, and for this purpose materiality was needed, things which could bestow both mystery and concreteness. How this came about is the example used for showing the importance of material culture in contemporary European regionalism.[3]

From the Coast to the Heart of the Province

From my field notes from "The Second" film festival in Motovun, Istria, 1 August 2000. This was the second year the festival was held. It has now become an important film event.

"The day when the festival begins, we park below the town in the place to which we are directed. There are hundreds of other cars parked together. It turns out to be a mistake. When we want to head for home at midnight, the cars are parked so close that it takes me half an hour of steering and swearing to squeeze the car out. Along the road down the mountain there are vehicles parked on either side. Only one car and a thin sheet of paper can pass at the same time. It seems as if half the country plus Slovenia and adjacent parts of Italy and Austria have chosen to park here.

Like pilgrims we had walked the last steep slope up to the town. All private traffic was banned. This has become a *place* to which people come on pilgrimage, striving upwards. At the Venetian gate in the town wall there is a temporary ticket office where we queue to buy tickets for the evening's Chinese film and afterwards go to the opening party. An enterprising seller of Chinese food envelops Serenissima's winged lion of Saint Mark and the armorial bearings of the noble families in an aroma of sweet and sour sauce.

Inside the gate, the narrow terrace is lined by outdoor cafés which grant visitors the peace to regard three gigantic propellers cheerfully painted in red, green, and yellow, which rotate invitingly – a reminder of the power of the imagination. Some 150 years ago an engineer tried to drive boats up the River Mirna by means of propellers. Now they evoke wind and air, the landscape below seen through an element.

We crowd through the next narrow doorway, where signs saying "Pazi, klisko!" warn us that the stones are slippery. Centuries of soles have polished each stone smooth and shiny. The central square is thronged with urban youths: "hard blacks", beatniks with Jesus beards and headbands, who seem to have been resurrected from the seventies; slender girls with bare stomachs, constantly smoking Zagreb intellectuals and perfectly ordinary young people from the surrounding towns of Pula, Poreć, Pazin, and Umag. Their dress evokes other times, other fashions, other places. The articulation has been carefully chosen to be distinct in its expression. Sitting under the chestnut tree in front of Hotel Kaštelet gives you the crucial experience of being here and simultaneously being somewhere else. Here, beside the assembly place, is where the specially invited actors are staying: Bibi Andersson and Erland Josephson; the greying director Vatroslav Minica and his wife, visiting from Los Angeles, are sitting here. He is actually here retrospectively since he has stopped making films; he has come to receive the festival's special "award for lifetime achievement".

In the little square outside the church, an enormous screen has been stretched, and white plastic chairs are awaiting the evening's showing. Strolling around in the balmy twilight are artists and cultural celebrities, ministers from Zagreb and 136 accredited journalists from national and international media. There are cameras, video cameras, and mobile phones everywhere. Sixty volunteers from Croatia, Holland, Denmark, and England walk around with yellow walkie-talkies in their hands. On their black t-shirts one can read *Staff*, *Motovun* and (*the second*). The brackets are the region as much as they are a production of fantasy; as much phenomenology's demarcated world of differentness – *époché* – as the time allocated to a film festival in a place that is off the beaten track.[4]

This is the day for the potentiation of Motovun. Overnight the town has become a stage where a drama can be enacted, dealing with how something local becomes a touchdown place for – and harmonized with – outside worlds. A majority of the films, to be sure, come from the former Yugoslavia, but it is Lars von Trier's phantasmagoria *Dancer in the Dark* that wins first prize. Short films from the USA, Israel, the Czech Republic, and Sweden are blended in a highly international mix. All the short films could be viewed via the Internet. Visitors to the site came from the whole of Europe and beyond, and the voting for the best film was done at the click of a mouse.

People come here just as much for the ambience of the place as for the event. They also seem to be viewing things from a suitable distance. They are obviously present in a world of mobile telecommunications, a pictorial world, a world of celebrities. This is the place where expectations are to be translated into practice, where something that has been created far away in space or time is renegotiated. The production is both local and global, contemporary and from a dreamy past – virtually tangible like a computer game or a fantasy game. High-tech apparatus and ancient local artefacts help to convey and create this alterity. The medieval scene, in all its striking unreality, interacts with events in other places. A contemporary modern Europe makes itself felt, while its most cherished historical period, the Middle Ages, simultaneously helps to intensify that presence. Twenty thousand people visit a town that otherwise has room for only a few hundred inhabitants. It is still absolutely jammed when we drive away through the night."

The choice of the little mountain town of Motovun as the venue for an international film festival was in no way random. In post-war Yugoslavia there were annual national festivals in another place, one that better met the needs of festivals in those days – ostentation, swimsuits, palm trees, and culture – namely, the old naval town of Pula. This Istrian coast has long been famous for its bathing and tourism. The coast is the truly international place where hundreds of thousands of visitors every summer come from all over Central Europe to occupy the beaches. On one of the islands in the Brioni archipelago just off the coast, Tito had his famous summer residence to which he invited foreign heads of state. Officers and sailors from all over Yugoslavia gathered in Pula, to train and to serve in the republic's most important naval base.

With the breakup of Yugoslavia in 1991, a festival for Croatian production alone felt truncated. This is a small country with limited resources for filmmaking. Festivals are still held in Pula. This year's winner, among a small number of starters, was the farcical film *Marsala*, which portrayed what happened today in a little coastal community when Tito's ghost suddenly manifested itself. It was also one of the few films worth seeing that year, and the festival attracted little attention. No, if you have to choose an international place in contemporary Europe, it is obvious that the half-forgotten little mountain town in the heart of the region exerts a much greater attraction. The coastal city may be allowed to go on holding the national in an international setting. At the same time, that is its limitation. Mystery, imagination, and dreams gain an easier foothold up on the rocks. This is a place that is in harmony with its time, it is able to conjure up a material culture which is as full of unspoken and secretive things as the films they want to show.

When the functionaries in Motovun wore the message "*(the second)*" on their t-shirts, it was thus not just a reflection of an alternative flair for making oneself visible in an age that demands something imaginative. The Istrian interior can entice people with something that have hitherto been in brackets, something *more* that appeals to people's quest for transcendence. Just as things urge people to explore, so too does the place.

The Return of the Past

At the start of a new millennium, people's linkages to places have changed in character. The local is seen as something more than the place where one works, lives, sends the children to school, and reads the newspaper. It is also expected to answer questions about identity and is ascribed an ability to create stability. What people search for is not something general and easily accessible but something unique and specific. The cultural heritage, for example, is supposed to help to highlight distinctiveness. There is scarcely a county museum in Sweden today which does not say that it wants to communicate knowledge of what is called "local and regional identity". There is scarcely a place that does not claim to be able to point the way forwards by looking back. At the Istrian Ethnographic Museum in Pazin, an exhibition was staged in the summer of 2000 about the things which – in the form of souvenirs – are currently defining what is distinctive about Istria. These things had little to do with the flows of tourists or the busy beach life; they were taken from the peasant culture of the interior.

For places to be able to answer questions about identity, they have to be equipped with a biography, a life story, a question that is constantly open to new interpretations and surprising insights. We thus see how something local is once again populated, filled with revived narratives and mysteries that suit our own times. It is not the history of the place that is sought, but its ambience, its soul, and its ability to accumulate memories and dreams.

The British-American geographer David Lowenthal has pointed out in several works how the past is now found everywhere, how it has been bent in such a way that it can be used as references in political argumentation as easily as in people's everyday lives. It has, he says, assumed the dimension of something resembling religion – something that can constantly be awakened to give explanations, something to which one can confess collective guilt as if it was a matter of personal sins. Public personages, from Pope John Paul to the Swedish Prime Minister Göran Persson, ask forgiveness for the injustices committed in the past against outcasts and victims of persecution. The past that is brought out in political work and in people's everyday lives is not taken from the studies of historians and scholars. It is a moral history, one which can be used to tackle urgent questions. At a personal and collective level we see something that resembles *memory* much more than *history* taking the stage – or rather imagination more than actual memory (Lowenthal 1985, 1996).

Just as the biography is something that is constantly alive for the individual, the past of a place is not finished; it is a process extending into the present and reaching into the future (Marcus 1992, Bendix 2000). The past bestows an intention on the place and becomes an actor. It has an explanatory value rather than being something to be explained. Instead of appearing as the complex weave of politics, economy, and culture that always shapes the context in which events take place, the past is given intention and meaning. And this can be read in the places where events happened.

This development has opened up the well-known opposition between those who work professionally with the management of the past and those who need to make it speak; between those who want to honour the place and hence themselves, and those who have to weigh it against other places, other events. In every museum or archive, researchers never cease to be astounded by the interpretations of history that they see emerging within the framework of regionalism. This is particularly the case in Sweden, where established historians have for generations claimed the privilege of formulating the problems and questions. The "vitalization" of history that is taking place in Skåne or Jämtland has been met by academics with sneers rather than rebuttals (Hansen 1998). Yet the situation in Istria has been radically different. The mythical has acquired an explanatory value because there has hardly been any dominating master narrative.

A Multicultural European Region

The depiction of the past that is taking shape in Istria today is intended to make the place a contemporary partner in dialogue. Alongside the fascination with the material – to which I shall soon return – the politically marketable term multiculturalism has increasingly come into the foreground. This means that people have successfully repressed history, traditions, and the collective memory in favour of myth.

Like several other areas in Central Europe and the Balkans, Istria through the ages has experienced dramatic conquests with the ensuing brutal movements of ethnic groups. Both Bosnia and Vojvodina are spoken of today in highly euphemistic terms as sites of multiculturalism, whereas occupation, persecution, and genocide would perhaps be more adequate descriptions. Lying at the intersection between Europe's great empires has made life fragile here.

Istria is criss-crossed by boundaries, constantly challenged and always movable. This was where the Roman Empire fought against the Illyrian tribes; the power of Byzantium, the Eastern Roman Empire, extended this far; it was invaded by Celts, Visigoths, Croats, and Slovenes. During the Middle Ages, the boundary between the urban civilization of the Mediterranean and the feudal Central Europe – between Venice and Habsburg – cut through Istria. The hostilities between them swept over the province. All through the ages the inhabitants have had to get used to new lords coming and going. The population as such became mobile and mixed.

In the twentieth century alone, the inhabitants changed capital city no less than five times. From the fall of Venice in 1797 until the armistice in 1918, the whole of Istria was under Austria – apart from the brief but culturally significant interlude as an Illyrian province under Napoleon. The town of Pula was the home port for the Austrian Mediterranean fleet. After the First World War, Istria came under Italy. The region was then transformed into a real province, homogenized as a part of fascist Italy. From the Italian collapse in 1943 until peace came in 1945, Istria was for a short and terrible period directly under the Third Reich. As a result of the peace treaties of 1947 and 1954, the border between socialist Yugoslavia and the West was drawn just south of Trieste. Istria was now crossed by yet another boundary: the Iron Curtain. Under Tito, Istria became the place *par excellence* for in-migration for citizens of Yugoslavia, since this was the window on the west; the capital was Belgrade. With the dissolution of Yugoslavia in 1991, Istria's capital was moved to Zagreb – and to some extent Ljubljana. In a few years the Schengen border will divide Istria into a Croatian part outside the EU and a Slovenian part inside the EU.

Being a sandpit for conquest, campaigns, guerrilla wars, and changing loyalties can of course be regarded as centuries of deliberately cultivated multiculturalism. It can also be described in terms of the inhabitants of the region having been mistreated without interruption by various European powers. Closed, conservative, and suspicious are adjectives that could likewise be used in this context.

The traces that this varied history have left behind, according to today's historiography, are tolerance and openness. Both Croatian and Italian are spoken in the region today, along with Slovenian in the Slovenian part. Among Istrian intellectuals today there is a discourse, not just about the favourable influence that "Europe" is expected to have on the province, but just as much the reverse: an "Istrianization of Europe". This means that they believe that they are able to contribute a knowledge of how to find solutions whereby people can live together in a changing multicultural world, how different languages, religions, ethnic groups, and their traditions can live side by side in a limited area – while simultaneously supporting distinctiveness (Rakovac 1998). They have thus embraced the idea that the local is not just an application of general patterns, but more a place where patterns are renegotiated and from where something new and different is spread.

The regional political party, IDS, has put tolerance, multiculturalism, and orientation to Europe high on the agenda. Its slogan in the last election was in English: *Yes IDS!* And the leader of the party, Ivan Jakovčić, was Minister for Europe in the Račan government.

Repression of Memory

This interpretation of the past can only be kept alive if history is repressed, rewritten, and adjusted to the current situation. Istria has all the conditions necessary for allowing this discontinuity to gain ground. The people here are used to negotiating with the past. This seems due in no small measure to the fact that it would be a good thing if real history were forgotten. And there is a rich material culture to invoke and revive. The many lords have left numerous splendid traces. What is the process whereby the place and the material acquire the status of subject, something that is believed to have the ability to act while memory is repressed?

In the town of Motovun it is really only the things, the place, and the landscape that show continuity. This place is poor in memories. Of course, there is rich documentation from archaeological and historical sources. There are monuments from the Roman Empire and Drug Tito's workers' state in the 1950s. And of course there are descriptions of the church, chapel, loggia, town wall, well, and other historic buildings. (Descriptions like these are the very prerequisite if material culture is to acquire the aura that will let it speak.) But people have come and gone – or conquered and been expelled – on such a scale that it is the buildings and landscapes that have survived while the memories have been subdued.

When the author Stephan Vajda had visited Motovun he was touched by conditional and insecure nature of people's lives and their clinging to material culture. The variegated history forced people to be extremely open to what is specific to the place, since this was the only thing that represented continuity:

"Lords came and lords went, Motovun was stormed, given away, pledged, sold, eroded, lost, and proclaimed a sanctuary. It nevertheless remained an Istrian town up in the mountains: just as much Roman, Illyrian, Byzantine, German, Italian, and Slavic. Traces and remnants, languages and objects grew together into an imaginary whole which ended up appearing wholly European – completely unintentionally – and so it remained, through bad times more than good" (Vajda 1998).

History taught people the usefulness of "unremembering", actively acquiring the ability to forget. After the Second World War, as we have seen, Istria was regained from Italy. It was now important to forget quickly. What had been won could of course be lost. The nationalization process was therefore quick and summary. The war against memory became a continuation of politics by other means (Girode 1999).

The majority of the Italian-speaking population disappeared into voluntary or enforced exile. Collaborators, real or alleged fascists, were executed. After the definitive transfer in 1954, the abandoned houses were confiscated or subject to compulsory purchase – often at arbitrary prices.

"Motovun was a very Italian town. It had its own theatre, and there was a middle class which took an interest in contemporary issues and culture. Among the small population – a couple of hundred – there were families who had long traditions and profound cultural interests in the place. When the partisans took the town in the closing phase of the war, they found no less than nine pianos",

according to the local journalist Davor Šišković who works for the newspaper *Glas Istre*.

"After the war the inhabitants were forced to move. Hardly a single person from the time before the war is left in the town now. For natural reasons, the middle class was the main enemy, as regards both class and ethnicity."

Into the empty houses moved people from other parts of Yugoslavia, mostly rural people. Many came from the region of Medimurje on the Hungarian border. People who had seen their homes destroyed during the war were uprooted and moved about. Those who now moved in had their family ties and networks elsewhere; their loyalties were to the party and the state more than to the place and the past. In their everyday lives and habits, they bore with them patterns from home – along with a profound conviction that history was disruptive, that the past was not something that led up to the present; it was best unremembered.

The Swedish journalist Richard Swartz, who lives in one of the small towns of Istria, made a comparison in a personal interview with another area in Europe that was afflicted by a massive exodus after the war, namely, the Sudetenland, Bohemia, in the present Czech Republic. There it was Germans who were expelled. At one stroke, the people who had borne up the society vanished, and newcomers moved in.

"To describe the situation in Istria after the Second World War, you have to imagine Stockholm having been invaded by people from northern Sweden, half of the population put to flight, the invaders taking over their flats and jobs and dividing the benefits between their family members and friends. What memory of the past would we have had in Stockholm if the city had undergone such a fate? As a bastion of northern Sweden?"

The comparison indicates that it was not really a matter of the expulsion of an ethnic group; the intolerance was directed against those who were stewards of the narratives, the traditions, and the local expertise. Italian had been the language of the cultured class, the language one had to speak if one wanted a job, as a civil servant, primary school teacher, engineer, accountant, or doctor. That was how it had been, with few exceptions, during the Habsburg period. Many people took their education in Trieste, which was under the Habsburgs but where people spoke Italian. Venice was closer than Vienna. And so it continued to be, it goes without saying, under fascist Italy. Now the region was homogenized in earnest through an unscrupulous nationalist policy. Schoolchildren were forbidden to speak Croatian; street-names and place-names were Italianized; even the mountains and landscape formations were given new names. Oblivion appeared under Italian names. People in important positions in society were also forcibly enlisted in the local *fasca*.

Croatian speakers who refused to toe the line were expelled from the province, moving to the nearby town of Karlovac and the Croatian capital of Zagreb. A whole neighbourhood in that city is filled with street-names referring to previous homes: Oprtalj, Pazin, Labin, Buzet, and many more. The living memory of a past life in the town of Motovun was thus driven into exile, placed in a refugee camp in Trieste, or emigrated to the USA or Australia. After the war in 1991, there were several inhabitants of Serbian origin who withdrew from what had now been declared a foreign and hostile country. A well-established and dreadful pattern was repeated.

But the memory that was preserved in the diaspora quickly changed character from historiography to reproach. The Italian speakers who had a local family history in Motovun, who were able to retell the narratives from the past, were declared undesirable. Not only did the memory disappear; it was regarded as a threat to the new state of Yugoslavia. The Italian speakers' knowledge of the district and the town gradually merged with the claims to regain their lost homes. The memory and the local traditions became a matter of demands on the state of Yugoslavia.

In the city of Završje-Piemonte a majority of the houses are deserted. Photo: Sergio Gobbo.

Those who had been proclaimed ethnic aliens thereby became bearers of memories who could be constantly called into suspicion.

It was specific linguistic groups that were expelled. Among them it was primarily those who bore some form of official history – the intellectuals – who were the main risk that the past would return. The war against memory blocked the entry to the past. What was then left for people to rely on when trying to create an identity?

The Partisan Monuments and the End of History

After 1947, the struggle against fascism was invoked to gloss over the past and function as a bearing myth. That struggle had exacted sacrifices, leaving hardly a village without loved ones who had fallen in battle or been summarily executed. The names of the fallen can be seen today as material remains everywhere in the landscape; they are carved on memorial tablets, symbolized in sculptures and monuments. In every village and every town, at roadside crosses and in cemeteries, the party and the local municipality have raised countless partisan monuments. In their socialist realism they are explicit and easy to read. They preach a morality translated to the sphere of art. They make statements about what history should have been like. Time stopped when the liberation came. A new society – that of socialism – with no other history than that of its own origin, emerged. The message that was cast in steel and concrete said that future was almost there, that paradise was just around the corner. The Istria in which they were raised could be that paradise and could be united with other provinces and countries which were also but a short step from becoming the true paradise. Yet Istria as such, as a province and as a country with history and a long continuity, was not interesting compared with what it could become. The place as such was provisional. It was determined by the monument, not by its own potential.

The monuments in Istria were maintained in good repair, unlike other parts of Croatia. Since the latest war many have been subjected to vandalization and outright destruction. What was once the triumph of the Yugoslav state has been redefined as monuments to a dictatorial power. The link between the monuments and the now detested Yugoslav army, JNA, was all too clear. In many parts of the country, memory has caught up with the monuments and made them reveal themselves as demagogic attempts at persuasion. When people in Croatia needed to gain access to their history, they had to remove the monuments that were blocking their path. That is why they stand today as destroyed monuments. Access to history must be gained *through* them – not *around* them.

But here in Istria – which actually did not witness any hostilities during the fighting between 1991 and 1995 – there has not been any vandalization; people here have been schooled in living with a mythological history, a past to which they can relate relatively freely. Perhaps it is this training that has helped the population to close their eyes to the countless other "monuments" that were created at the same time and still stand today: memories without inscriptions.

The people who escaped or were driven away left houses which are still standing today. The Italian-speaking population owned most of them. These ruins, memories left behind by those who once belonged to the place but who cannot return, exert a poignant attraction. There is hardly a village that does not have boarded-up windows, crumbling façades. They are scattered here and there in the towns, like fossils from a bygone era, condensations of a history that is half-averted, promises from a world to which it is still possible to connect. Along some streets, one half of a house may be renovated and inhabited while the adjacent half is in decay. There are towns like Završje, Boljun, and Oprtalj where houses with inhabitants seem to be outnumbered by those without. These ghostly houses of grey stone are constant promises that the past is here among us, that the present has a depth that both attracts and frightens, that the bill for the past has still not been paid. "It makes me so sad to travel through Istria", says my Bosnian/Italian interview-partner who commutes each weekend between Trieste and Opatija and can hardly bring himself to stop along the way. "All these empty houses." Half-demolished farms, town houses, and small palaces have become training points for sensitivization, material reservoirs filled with the unspoken, something palpable but still not accessible to the memory.

Every memory, moreover, is filled with torment. A closer study of the past can tell us that today's society rests on the occurrence of a series of crimes – not just a victorious struggle against a fascist occupier. Ethnic cleansing was of course just as repulsive during the partisan fighting as it is now. If one starts digging in the past, one runs the risk that both evil and good will come spouting up in lumps and chunks. Houses without windows whisper that the past has not been cleared up; they make history force itself on us, asking questions about the present.

People in Istria had thus learned to live with a virtual world and with a history written in stone. At the same time, the many ruins have taught the lesson that the past is constantly round the corner, that the reckoning is still waiting to be settled. The houses have a life and the place is replete with an expectation of something more than today will admit. The possibility of recreating the present from the remains with which one is surrounded is thus painful, possible, and rewarding. The past that is now just around the corner contrasts so starkly with the socialist dream that history was completed, that paradise was at hand.[5]

The Magic of the Landscape

Istria as a region with a soul, palpable through its things and places, has found it easier to stand out by letting memory be repressed. Materiality has been a more dramatic, accessible way to come into contact with the past. In the general image of Istria today, things, architec-ture, landscape, and nature are prominent as artefacts full of life, much more so than society or culture. The words of the Swedish poet Verner von Heidenstam can be used to describe Istria's longing, "… but not for people! I long for the land, I long for the stones where as child I played".

Recent years have seen the publication of books about the region, especially the interior, with titles to fire the imagination, such as "Terra Magica", "Istria between Reality and Fiction", "Terra Incognita", and "Bewitching Istria".[6] In a short time the word "ambient" has risen from the pages of tourist brochures and become a frequently used adjective to show the life of the region. Places which were already rightly recognized for their beauty are now regarded from yet another dimension, one associated with the promise of personal reward – the exploration of the self. The poet Roman Latković tells in one of his books how he set off from nearby Rijeka in search of the elusive spirit of Istria; how during his trip through the landscape he tried with his pen to "reach the heart of Istria" and how he "constantly sends her love letters, tests the possibility of depicting the peninsula with a feeling that is ever new". He "worships her like a lover. Enraptured time and again by her slightest tremor" (1994:80). And the truth can be found in her existence outside history:

"This Istrian country, this Croatian country, has been devastated by primitivism, communism, state banditism, careerism, of spiritual dwarfs and by all the other 'isms' one can imagine and be disgusted with, and that spiritual vacuum, ugliness and debasement should be subjected to the resistance of the desire for something better, more beautiful" (1994:82).

And he finds it in castles, in villages, in the small towns perched on mountaintops; it lives in wells and in the peculiar white cattle, *boskarin*; in the wine and in the local dishes. This Istrian spirit or *genius loci* is as elusive as it is ever-present. It is in the place but it does not offer itself willingly.

"In Grožnjan everything seems to be just here, just around the corner, hidden in the glass of wine of the 'Al violina', right here, quite near to you but when you aggressively look around with a desire to grasp its illusive spirit, it vanishes…diabolically keeps out of your reach and disappears, right there, right around the corner. That's Grožnjan. And that is Istria Everything that is just around the corner, just a few metres away from the main road, and calls for a bit of effort on your part" (1994:42).

This ambience that is found in the earth and the stones, in buildings and things, becomes a con-

Grožnjan. The city-gate.
Photo: Sergio Gobbo.

crete recollection of a truer past which has an intention for the visitor. With almost religious zeal, Latkoviç sings of the beauty and mystery that ascends from the soil and the things. But now it is not emanating from any higher power or "ism". Istria has become the landscape, not of history, nor memory, but the imaginary.[7] What material things in the Istrian landscape can be described so easily in terms of subject? What ability does the place have to "hold" and contain so much and so many?

The Labyrinth

From the field diary, 2 August 2000: "We approach Motovun from the main road between Buzet and Buje. The River Mirna flows gently towards the coast in flatland between the hills. When the silhouette of Motovun is visible, we are already there. It is the recognition and Bachelard's "resonance" more than surprise exercising its magic. The pictures, fantasies, and interpretations call on each other. I believe that I have experienced this before, as a dream or a pristine memory. As if the really important images were already prepared and waiting to manifest themselves. The town wants something of me. The church tower crowns the town, striving upwards in almost Gothic fashion. There is a verticality and lightness which invites play and demands analysis. What a view there must be from up there! Although surrounded by other towns and with distinct boundaries, it speaks of solitude. Like a town among towns it reminds me of respectful community without intermixture as much as of melancholy and isolation.

The impression of recognition is reinforced when we pass through the gate. This is a town criss-crossed by the European Middle Ages and a provincial Renaissance. The buildings stick up massively out of the ground, communicating the same odd feeling as the stout town walls, that of brutal weight linked to lightness. This is after all a defensive structure.

The streets are irregular and labyrinthine, running between houses of two of three storeys. The alleys run like spirals in narrow passages from the central square. They seem made for slowing down rather than strolling. At the same time as one feels the place in advance, one is enticed to explore it. What lies round the next corner?

It is not possible to obtain any clear idea of the plan of the town; there is no street grid; no simple order to make the structure understandable. As in other medieval towns, there is nowhere but the church tower to offer an overall view. No one has taken any pains to impose a comprehensible pattern on the streets. The town grew up before linear perspective was established. Obviously, it should not be seen; it has to be experienced at close hand. What is within the walls delineates itself darkly, one meets it with the close-up senses: smell, touch, hearing. The houses have walls of cut stone, and the gaze catches and dwells on irregular angles, steps, ornaments, extensions. Rising from the cellars is a smell of centuries of damp and leaking sewer pipes. The street surface – comprising slippery, uneven cobbles – slows down the step and calls on our attention.

It is difficult to imagine that anyone could come upon the idea of strolling around to see and be seen, yet one feels that one is under constant observation from windows and through door drapes. In pure fascination and out of an instinct of self-preservation, one never takes one's eyes off the surroundings, while simultaneously one feels that one is penetrating a world which has seen so many other people pass by without taking any notice. Is this a town that is looking at you, or is it you looking at the town?

It is the world outside that invites the gaze to pan. The views from the town wall are dizzying. You feel you are in a painting or in the middle of a world where the landscape is in the present, in the *doing* form. The gaze explores it. The river, surprisingly far below, makes its way through the fields; vineyards climb up the slopes in terraces; roads coil through the landscape; they work their way up to other hills, to other small towns. Church towers point to the sky above another town, above a cemetery or a chapel of the Virgin Mary. The wind blows across the Mediterranean-blue sky, granting cool relief in the summer heat. Away on the horizon a gleam from the Adriatic Sea flashes to hint of its presence.

Everything is near and yet far away, infinitely beautiful as a picture, and alive as if it were making itself and had been doing so all through the ages. At the same time, it is heart-rendingly lonely, isolated, abandoned. The beauty also makes something else present. The view from the wall makes the destruction palpable. This really is a European miniature. How many times has it been destroyed? How many times has the small population been replaced? The location on the hill was not determined by a longing for beauty, but by the need for security.

Why do some landscapes become culturally productive? There are evidently qualities in them which evoke a response in everyone, but which have also been exploited at specific points in time. Istria today is in search of its soul. And it is to be found here in the interior. Virtually all ancient inland parts of Europe satisfied the longing of nineteenth-century nation builders for something genuine and materially full of soul. They were transformed into mental landscapes as much as physical ones charged with emotions (Löfgren 1993:96). Dalarna in

Sweden, Setesdalen in Norway, Zillerthal in Austria, Zagorje in Croatia, Karelia in Finland. The coast was more dubious, permeated by influences which spoke of an outside world. People arrived and departed from the coast; this was where commerce was pursued; the horizon was open. The world was always becoming different. The presence of something from beyond challenged the ability of the place to "hold", to be itself. It was easier to find a *genius loci* in places that were half turned away (Frykman 1999b).[8]

Istria, with its dramatic history of population movements and violent death, has a potential to let itself be filled with the imaginary and to offer the visitor a place which simultaneously is recognizable and gives observers a chance to get outside themselves. Material things stand out so much more clearly in the absence of memory and history and on the basis of qualities in the landscape as such. Other very small stone towns also beg to be seen again – Buzet, Grožnjan, Oprtalj, Boljun. It will also be said of them that people have lived here for thousands of years. Up here they have been well protected against hostile attacks and cattle rustlers, autumn damp and winter fog. The towns speak to us about the hidden continuity that tickles our curiosity.

This "something" that fills the visitor with wonder declares that the place is unfinished, waiting, challenging. The secrets are just the first step in staking a claim – on the landscape and on the observer.

My Country Which is Not

The film festival in Motovun in August 2000 demonstrated the presence of the international and the multicultural. People of varying backgrounds could easily occupy ground in a material environment where the "active things" – telephones, video cameras, and networks – were so obviously in harmony with the houses, the place, and its ambience. Both Erland Josephson and Bibi Andersson and the other celebrities who were interviewed in the media, stressed the attraction of the place. The concord between the place and the imaginary, the dreams, was also underlined by the art that was exhibited in connection with the festival.

Two exhibitions were opened on the first day of the festival, one of them in a newly built café annexe at the Hotel Kastelet, the other in the premises of the old museum, with its creaking floors and visible roof beams. The latter was beside the old town gate. Outside the window, the landscape billows far away and far down. The opening ceremonies were held within an hour of each other.

From the field diary:
"In good time before the first film, the first of the evening's two exhibitions opens. Vlado Velickovič has been invited by the management of the film festival and by the main exhibitor of the previous year, Edo Murtić. He is an artist of Serbian origin, who trained and got married in Zagreb but now lives in Paris. The dozen works that he chose to exhibit were grotesque portrayals of the convulsions that his country and people had undergone during the 1990s. The paintings repeated the same distorted man's body hanging from a rope, upside down, with blood, excrement, and sex painted in black, white, and red. Violence and war, physical suffering and ruthlessly exposed torment convey a message of a human tragedy that is difficult to capture. There is no reference to any country, nation, army, or other obvious organization.[9]

Velickovič named the exhibition "My country which is not". He regards himself as a relic of the old Yugoslavia in exile. The 1990s have made him homeless, cheated him out of place, homeland, and memories. The flaring nationalism in Serbia and Croatia has left him feeling "too little of a Serb to be a part of the new Greater Serbia and too little of a Croat to be a part of Greater Croatia." He mourns the memory, agonizes not only over the suffering but also over the dream that was not fulfilled. And he does this from a great distance. The artist himself was not present at the opening; a friend, an art critic from Zagreb, who has also lived in Paris for a long time, represented him. Only a small group has gathered for the opening: were there 25 of us?

Quite a different opening ceremony greeted the artist Karlo Paliska from the Istrian town of Labin, about fifty kilometres away. All the local dignitaries who were able to crawl or walk had assembled here. The former minister of culture

Who looks at whom?
Photo: Sergio Gobbo.

in the HDZ government, Vesna Girardi-Jurkić from Pula, now living in Paris as UNESCO ambassador, was there, energetically waving a fan in the heat under the low roof. The evening sun shone in through the windows, making the outside world highly palpable. Also there were the provincial governor, the mayor from the provincial capital of Pazin, hordes of journalists and all the visitors greeting each other in recognition. The perfume hung heavy in the air, the clothes were elegant and the jewellery opulent. It was obvious that this was a tribute to an Istrian artist.

Karlo Palinska stood silent, listening attentively to the speeches in his honour; a thin, thoughtful man in his seventies with a light-coloured jacket over his shoulders, perhaps to detract attention from his stiff right arm. He paints with his left hand. The exhibition was a retrospective, showing a long and active career in art. The contrast with Velickovic was striking. The motifs were mainly architectural: buildings, landscapes, street scenes, rooms, and more or less dreamed shapes. Not factual but poetic representations, conveying subtle impressions, like moods captured in ambiguous and enjoyable pictures. The observer had ample scope to fill the paintings with content and meaning. The depicted objects scarcely described reality; they rather teased it out. There were also some figurative paintings, portraits and self-portraits, but stylized, without distinct poses or explicit pointers.

The main speaker at the opening was the art historian Berislav Valušek from the art museum in Rijeka. In his speech, which we simultaneously received in printed form, he expressed his interpretation of Karlo Paliska's art, as not only provincial in that he lived in Istria, but also provincial in its relation to the Centre, to the national élite of intellectuals and arbiters of art. Paliska is a moderate, modest man, we were told. He has never striven for attention from those with influence or from the masses, and his art was thus still open for interpretation, rich in meaning, not yet defined or delimited. "He himself is as tranquil as Istria and just as withdrawn. Like Istria, he can be discovered time and again."

There are not really very many artists from the province, he said. But within the pleiad of Istrian artists or artists who have Istria as their motif, "who share the fascination with this strange part of the northern Mediterranean – Bassani, Kokot, Jasna Maretić, Milić, Diminić, Murtić, Prica – Paliska's contribution will be acclaimed as one of those which has helped most to shape identity in this part of Croatia."

At first the description provoked our surprise, since the paintings did not really contain any motifs whose provenance could be identified. It seemed to be going too far to inscribe him in the place, to let his art articulate an Istrian identity instead of something more transcendent. But of course, the art historian was right. This artist made the place and the material culture present in such a composite way that people really could bond with his works. The presence of the many and the influential at the opening was no coincidence.

Regions and Beehives

When a region like Istria emerges and "happens", it carries with it an impression of the present day just as much as parts of its history. The most striking thing is how much space is given to material culture and place-bound distinctive features, and that this happens at the expense of social contexts. The result is not so much a community to long for as a possible imaginary world to connect with. It will therefore differ crucially from other areas where the quest for cultural identity and home has taken root during the twentieth century. At the beginning I mentioned how ethnicity, race, gender, or class have functioned as important determinants in the latter half of the now finished century. They have functioned as redeeming utopias and monolithic explanations for those who have searched for identity. They have also functioned as political and societal labels. In the nation state, people have been able to demand justice, to claim attention by virtue of their age, their gender, and their profession.

Yet the strategies cannot be used without complications in a globalized – or Europeanized – society. Here the political intention is that people will be physically mobile and culturally flexible. Identity is then not something you always carry with you; it can just as much be attached to the place where you happen to be. "When in Rome, do as the Romans do." Asking for attention from Brussels is much easier if you speak from a place than from an ethnic, racial, or social position. To be recognized as an ethnic minority in the EU, you have the greatest chance of success if you can make your demands from a territory. Europe today has many more such acknowledged minorities than it has nations. By contrast, large immigrant groups have scarcely any chance of attracting the same attention. In Sweden, for example, the Sami, the Finns of Tornedalen, and the Roms are recognized as linguistic minorities, whereas the one million people who ethnically belong to other cultures merely have immigrant status. It looks as if the twentieth-century obsession with "the politics of identities" is slowly giving way to the twenty-first-century "politics of place".

However, the significance of place as wrapping paper around different groups not only has a political foundation but also a social foundation that is at least as strong. The sociologists Scott Lash and Mike Featherstone have pointed out how people's ties to society's institutions, workplaces, and professions has come to be perceived as far too rigid. The place, in their opinion, can then contain the flexibility that our time is crying out for, something that simultaneously gives scope for chance, contingency, and concrete palpability (Featherstone & Lash 1999).

If this is correct, it means a challenge to the research community to think again when it comes to interpreting people's relation to places. I stated in the introduction that researchers applying the modernity perspective have tended to regard the local as a source of security in a changeable world. The place has had a strong taste of mother, family, relatives, neighbours, and tradition (cf. Siikala 2000).[10] For many people, the place and the local became a backward-looking utopia to do with an undifferentiated life (Melucci 1991). This idea of the significance of place proceeds from metaphors such as *roots* and *belonging*. They become a dream of flight – but flight in the sense of escape, not aviation. The owls of Minerva fly at dusk, and place becomes important because people really are uprooted. This is an antiquated and static view of place as something closed, referring only to itself, yet the notion has paradoxically survived in the social and cultural sciences thanks to the powerful position occupied by the modernity perspective.

The study of Istria shows some of the potential of a place to be used for experiments in diversity, a world where the bonds between structure and culture, between social background and identity are stretched, and where people are open to the multifaceted effect that landscape and things can exert on them. It also indicates that the scholarly discussion of place is not a question of replacing one bunch of monolithic explanations with new ones. Place has no birthright in relation to other explanations. It is not more *primary* than anything else. What we are facing instead is "a polyvalent primacy", as the philosopher Edward Casey says. "The primacy of place is not that of *the* place, much less of *this* place or *a* place (not even a very special place) – all these locutions imply place-as-simple-presence – but that of being an event capable of implacing things in many complex manners and to many complex effects" (1997:337). In other words: place is where things happen.

When people begin to ask profound questions about a place, when they wish to be noticed for *where* they are instead of *what* they are, it is necessary that the place and the things should be given a dimension of actor and subject. What can give meaning is not unambiguous but complex, not predictable but surprising, not passive but active. When Istria emerges as a region, it is a process with many outcomes, with traditional peasant culture and European presence side by side. Above all, it happens by virtue of being a place where the imagination can gain a foothold, and from which it can take leaps forwards and backwards in time (Bachelard 2000). Places which have explicit definitions and demarcations are more difficult to think with than those which can bear a profusion of meaning. Landscapes which are to be used for a specific purpose and for attempts at ideological persuasion rule out surprises. The Istrian landscape that I have described is open to a series of elaborations.

Perhaps, says Casey, using a metaphor from the animal world, a new age forces us to see places not so much as dovecotes and more as beehives. He borrows this image from Gaston Bachelard's ideas about material things as a kind of beings, almost living creatures around which dreams assemble (Casey 1998:287). The dovecote is closed because it contains the idea of return, of a physical nest with its demarcations, security, repose after adventures in the outside world. It is a place in the sense of a container. The entrance to a beehive, on the other hand, is buzzing with images – information, interpretations of the smells, tastes, and directions of the surrounding world. Familiar aromas land outside the beehive; from here new flight routes are planned, and meaning is created. "Metaphors of the pigeonhole … give away to the spider's web or the beehive as we begin to appreciate what is at stake in poetic imagery: intense efflorescence" (1998:287). The beehive as materiality is in itself an actor, one that affects the world around it. It is like poetry, open to a multitude of interpretations, a point of departure for dreams and fantasies.

When regions happen in today's Europe, it is therefore part of a swarming culture-building activity which contains a large measure of today's political and societal reality. When the political phenomenon known as the Europe of the Regions exploits the capacity of these domains for mystery and romance and innovation, it holds a potential to generate new connections, to let artefacts join in the birth of new dreams, the creation of new productive forces.

The study of Istria can also give perspectives on how place – more than ideologies or national, ethnic, or religious identities – can serve as a basis for people's identification, something they can use for their own culture building. The place does not make the same demands as party, background, or ideology. It is more open to diversity than definitions which proceed from the nation or the group. As we have seen, there are historical precedents for this development. Through the ages, the place, the landscape, and the things in this region have represented a real continuity, provided room for people from different parts of Europe. One precondition for this is that the region has not been impregnated with interpretations or ideologies. There has not been any single grand narrative which has tried to bring people together, claiming to answer questions about whence and whither. This openness, however, has been bought at a high price.

Regions in Europe thus have a rich potential to function as new cultural growth zones today and in the future. Many of those, which have a long and well-known history, also contain a longing for a homogeneous and well-controlled world where the boundaries between the others and us are sharp and difficult to cross. Parallel to the openness, micronationalism is also growing. The friction between the two poles is of course not just a matter of one region against another. It takes place within every one of the regions entering the European stage today. Both possibilities are there. At the same time, the history and the materiality that are highlighted are not random choices, and, as we have seen, they affect the outcome. If one has a history which contains a wealth of diversity, it is difficult to use it as a foundation for provincial fundamentalism.

To sum up, the example of Istria teaches us a couple of lessons. It suggests something about the role the regions will have in Europe, and it shows the conditions whereby the beehive and not the dovecote will be the guiding model. It challenges us to fix our gaze on the things and the place. As a consequence of this, we can search for the research perspectives which can clarify how these become culturally productive.

Notes

1. My intellectual debt to the phenomenologically inspired researchers who, more than any others, have worked with place and culture – Michael Jackson (1998) and Kathleen Stewart (1996) – is much greater than the references suggest.
2. A rich array of analyses in this field may be found in such classics as Anthony Giddens's studies of self-identity (1991) and Ulrich Beck's explorations of people's relationship to risk in modernity (1996). Culture is analysed here on the basis of people's need for security and control. And their projects in life appear to be the conscious building of cultural identity as a response to the insecurity caused by various threats in the form of globalization and the dissolution of permanent relationships.
3. The study is based on extensive fieldwork by Maja Povrzanović Frykman and Jonas Frykman in the summers of 1998, 1999, 2000, and the spring of 1999. The fieldwork consisted of participant observation, interviews in English and Croatian, and video recording. The cooperation with Lidija Nikočević at the Ethnographic Museum in Pazin has made this research possible.
4. Epoché designates the possibility of putting everyday life in brackets and annulling its blinding taken-for-grantedness.
5. For the film festival, the municipal authorities had set up new street signs of blue enamel in two languages, Croatian and Italian. "It's just to attract the Italians," mutters one of the old partisans, Ernest Benčić, well aware of how easily the past can be erased in the absence of historiography. He is chairman of the local veteran club and of those in the surrounding towns. The memories he has represent today the past of local history which is not good enough for shaping memory from. After a generation of paying tribute to those who gave their lives in the struggle against fascism, the recent past is now about to fall into oblivion. Once again it is time to rewrite the history of the place.
6. In 1997 the cultural historian Branko Fučić published the work Terra Incognita, which in a short

time has become a standard source for the cultural history of Istria. The historian Miroslav Bertoša, who is a leading authority on the history of the region, refers to the rich occurrence of fictions in his *Istra izmedu zbijle i fikcije* ("Istria between Reality and Fiction") from 1993. *Terra Magica* has set the pattern for the presentation of Istria, and the book has been translated into English, German, and Italian.

7. Edward Casey points out the importance that place has acquired in religious thought, how place is no longer a location where God or the gods can manifest themselves, while remaining empty while he or they are not there. Instead, the places contain the god: "Particular places have taken the place of God and the gods: this is precisely what makes them divine" (1998:341).

8. And what identity project can manage without castles? They are symbols of power and self-determination. The castles in Istria have also attracted particular attention in recent years, being the subject of surveys and exhibitions. In the building of a regional identity, then, a series of familiar devices from nation building are reused. What is new about the regions compared to the building of the nation state is that material culture can be highlighted without any demands for ethnic homogeneity being raised.

9. Edo Murtić was much more explicit in his exhibition on the theme of Muerte "Death", which we had visited in Zagreb the week before. Here one could see military berets and insignia of rank. The suffering had an origin, and death had its own organization.

10. For a generation of scholars and politicians alike, the dream of "the local community" was to represent the utopia of a whole life, of solidarity and ecological adaptation. Local communities became alternative places in the maelstrom of modernity. In the last decades of the twentieth century it was considered rewarding to link up with Tönnies' indestructible dichotomy of Gemeinschaft and Gesellschaft. There was something secure about imagining that the contexts into which people were born were also the contexts in which they died. In the Gemeinschaft they do not need to negotiate their relations; economic activities are adjusted to nature, and life and thought make up a stable union.

* This is a revised version of the paper "Motovun och tingens poesi", in *Fönster mot Europa*, Studentlitteratur, Lund 2001.

References

Bachelard, Gaston 1992: *Jorden och drömmerier om vila*. Lund: Skarabé.
Bachelard, Gaston 2000: *Rummets poetik*. Lund: Skarabé.
Beck, Ulrich 1996: *Risk Society. Towards a New Modernity*. London: sage.
Bendix, Regina 2000: Heredity, Hybritity and Heritage from One *Fin de Siècle* to the Next. In *Folklore, Heritage Politics and Ethnic Diversity: A Festschrift for Barbro Klein*. Botkyrka: Mångkulturellt Centrum.
Benjamin, Walter 1969: *Illuminations*, ed. Hanna Arendt. New York: Schocken.
Bertoša, Miroslav 1993: *Istra izmedu zbijle i fikcije*. Zagreb: Matica hrvatska.
Casey, Edward 1996: How to Get From Space to Place in a Fairly Short Stretch of Time: Phenomenological Prolegomena. In Steven Feld & Keith H. Basso (eds.), *Senses of Place*. Santa Fe: School of American Research Press.
Casey, Edward 1998: *The Fate of Place: A Philosophical History*. Berkeley: University of California Press.
Eriksen, Thomas Hylland 2000: Bergenske veikryss. *Kulturby Bergen 2000. Det officielle Kulturbymagasinet*. Bergen.
Featherstone, Mike & Scott Lash (eds.) 1999: *Spaces of Culture: City – Nation – World*. London: Sage.
Frykman, Jonas 1995: The Informalization of National Identity. *Ethnologia Europaea* 25.
Frykman, Jonas 1996: Istrisk mosaik. *Lundalinjer*.
Frykman, Jonas 1999a: Hem till Europa. *Rig* 2.
Frykman, Jonas 1999b: National Identities: Between Modernity and Cultural Nationalism. In *Volkskultur und Moderne: Europäische Ethnologie zur Jahrtausendwene. Festschrift für Konrad Köstlin. Europäische Ethnologie* 21. Vienna.
Fučić, Branko 1997: *Terra incognita*. Zagreb: Krscanska sadasjnost.
Giddens, Anthony 1990: *The Consequences of Modernity*. Cambridge: Polity Press.
Giddens, Anthony 1991: *Modernity and Self-Identity: Self and Society in the Late Modern Age*. Cambridge: Polity Press.
Girode, Isabell 1999: Jeux de mémoires, jeux de miroirs: Récits historiques et construction de l'identité en Istrie. Christian Giordano & Johanna Rolshoven (eds.): *Europäische Ethnologie*, ed. *Studia Ethnographica Friburgensia* 22.
Hansen, Kjell 1998: *Välfärdens motsträviga utkant: Lokal praktik och statlig styrning i efterkrigstidens nordsvenska inland*. Lund: Historiska Media.
Harvey, David 1996: *Justice, Nature and the Geography of Difference*. Oxford: Blackwell.
Jackson, Michael 1998: Phenomenology, Radical Empiricism, and Anthropological Critique. In: Michael Jackson (ed.): *Things as They Are: New Directions in Phenomenological Anthropology*. Bloomington: Indiana University Press
Klein, Barbro 2000: "Folklore, Heritage Politics and Ethnic Diversity": Thinking About the Past and the Future. In: Pertti J. Anttonen *et al.* (eds.): *Folklore, Heritage Politics and Ethnic Diversity A Festschrift for Barbro Klein*. Botkyrka: Multicultural Centre.
Lash, Scott 1999: *Another Modernity: A Different Rationality*. Oxford: Blackwell.
Latkovic, Roman & Dokmanović, Ranko 1994: *Bewitching Istria: A Never Ending Story*. Rijeka: Carli.

Latour, Bruno 1998: *Artefakternas återkomst: Ett möte mellan organisationsteori och tingens sociologi*. Göteborg: Nerenius förlag.

Löfgren Orvar 1993: Nationella arenor. In: Billy Ehn, Jonas Frykman & Orvar Löfgren, *Försvenskningen av Sverige*. Stockholm: Natur och Kultur.

Lowenthal, David 1995: *The Past is a Foreign Country*. Cambridge: The Free Press.

Lowenthal, David 1996: *Possessed by the Past: The Heritage Crusade and the Spoils of History*. New York: The Free Press.

Marcus, George 1992: Past, Present and Emerging Identities. In: Scott Lash & Jonathan Friedman (eds.): *Modernity and Identity*. London: Blackwell.

Massey, Doreen 1994: *Space, Place and Gender*. Cambridge: Polity Press.

Melucci, Alberto 1991: *Nomads of the Present: Social Movements and Individual Needs in Contemporary Society*. Philadelphia: Temple.

Rakovac, Milan 1997: Die "Istrianizierung" Europas. In: *Istrien. Europa erlese*. Frankfurt: Wieser Verlag.

Shore, Chris 2000: *Building Europe: The Cultural Politics of European Integration*. London: Routledge.

Siikala, Anna-Leena 2000: From Sacrificial Rituals into National Festivals: Post-Soviet Transformations of Udmurt Tradition. In: Pertti J. Anttonen *et al.* (eds.): *Folklore, Heritage Politics and Ethnic Diversity A Festschrift for Barbro Klein*. Botkyrka: Multicultural Centre.

Stewart, Kathleen 1996a: An Occupied Place. In: Steven Feld & Keith H. Basso (eds.): *Senses of Place*. Santa Fe: School of American Research Press.

Stewart, Kathleen 1996b: *A Space on the Side of the Road: Cultural Poetics in an "Other" America*. Princeton: Princeton University Press.

Vajda, Stephan 1998: Abenteuer Abseits. In: Johan Strutz (ed.): *Istrien, Europa erlese*. Frankfurt: Wieser Verlag.

Violence and the Re-discovery of Place

Maja Povrzanović Frykman

>Povrzanović Frykman, Maja 2002: Violence and the Re-discovery of Place. – Ethnologia Europaea 32: 2: 69–88.
>
>Violence imposed on a place bears not only the implicit challenge to the identities associated with it, but it also provokes responses related to a sense of place. In the context of war, place suddenly matters in a more direct and more intense way. The uniqueness of the place based primarily on the social value it has for people becomes visible and reflected upon as concrete and at one with action and thought. In this article, personal narratives on war experiences in the 1990s by the civilians in Dubrovnik, are related to Edward S. Casey's propositions about every place being *encultured* and every culture being *implaced*. The tension is explored, between being "Europeans" and being "war victims" – two types of place-bound identity.
>
>*Maja Povrzanović Frykman, Ph.D, Ass. Prof. at IMER, Malmö University, SE-205 06 Malmö, Sweden; Outer associate of Institute of Ethnology and Folklore Research, POB 287, HR-10000 Zagreb, Croatia. E-mail: maja.frykman@imer.mah.se*

Whilst collecting war-related narratives for the purpose of a doctoral thesis on dealing with fear in the context of everyday life in war-torn Croatia in 1991–92[1], I talked to several people in Dubrovnik, a town on Croatia's Adriatic coast with some 60,000 inhabitants. My first question was about their most important war memories. The long narratives induced by this question were predominantly stories about air-raid alarms and shelters, about food, water and hygiene, about neighbours, friends and helpful strategies, about the importance of family ties and the care of children and elderly people, about obstinacy and courage. They outline a war-time politics of identity, based primarily on strategies of survival in the context of siege, military attacks, injury, death, and destruction. These narratives show that everyday routines were an efficient means of coping with war-provoked deprivation, fear and anxiety (see Povrzanović 1997).

Yet the unexpected part of the collected material – and it was its relative frequency that surprised me most – were the statements about people's love for their town, about the feeling of belonging to the region and about feeling like a family with all the people inhabiting the region ("In war, everyone is ours"; cf. Povrzanović 1997: 156–157). People that I interviewed explicitly revealed an awareness of their lives being anchored in the places of daily interactions: this awareness acquired in war was worth remembering and possible to talk about. The war-experiences mentioned above, that were reflected upon in the interview situations some years later, have been significantly embedded in the narration about belonging to the place. In this article, they are analysed in relation to the philosopher Edward S. Casey's claim that "however oblivious to place we may be in our thought and theory, and however much we may prefer to think of what happens in a place rather than of the place itself, we are tied to place undetachably and without reprieve" (Casey 1993: xiii).

Violence and Belonging

There is certainly neither a singular theoretical connection between place and identity, nor an univocal interpretation of any place characterised by a social and historical complexity and multiple links with the "outer" world. However, it seems that violence imposed on a place bears not only the implicit challenge to the identities associated with it, but also that it provokes responses "intimately related to a well-developed sense of place" (cf. Tangherlini 1999). A comparative reading of studies of such responses facilitates an understanding of their – as it seems – universal character.

Discussing the Los Angeles riots in 1992, the folkorist Timothy R. Tangherlini (1999) shows how the riots impacted a space that had been transformed into highly specified and culturally charged places by the people living and working in them. The story of the city had been forcibly rewritten by destruction: the landscape that had been defined by the spatial practices of people who worked and lived in it had been deeply scarred and, in some instances, reduced to rubble.

As shown by the anthropologist Michael Jackson (1995) writing about Australian Aborigines' concepts and practices of appropriating the landscape, it is the activity of those who "own" the place that gives it value. They "own" the place, but at the same time "belong" to it: the value of an inhabited place is embodied by the people living in it.

The Aborigines' mourning over their destroyed dreaming-places in the Australian landscape, the people whose dwelling and working places have been destroyed in the Los Angeles riots and the civilians trying to keep minimal everyday normality under violent attacks in the 1990s war in Croatia, have indeed been living in very different political, social, cultural and spatial circumstances. Yet, the reactions to the violence imposed on the places they define as their own seem to be similar. Together with the most obvious shock and anger, such violence intensifies the relationship between people and place and provokes a complex and very pronounced feeling of self being fused with the sense of place. Place suddenly matters in a more direct and more intense way; the uniqueness of the place is based primarily on the social value it has for people becomes visible and reflected upon.

Edward S. Casey (1993: 31) claims the truth of two related, yet distinct propositions: about every place being *encultured* and every culture being *implaced*.

"Implacement is an ongoing cultural process with an experimental edge. It acculturates whatever ingredients it borrows from the natural world, whether these ingredients are bodies or landscapes or ordinary 'things'. Such acculturation is in itself a social, even a communal act. For the most part, we get into places together. We partake in places in common – and reshape them in common. The culture that characterises and shapes a given place is a shared culture, not merely superimposed upon the place but part of its very facticity. (…) The time of cultural implacement (and the time experienced in that implacement) is that which informs a place in concert with other human beings, through one's bodily agency, within the embrace of a landscape" (Casey 1993: 31–33).

Taken as encultured, places are matters of experience (along with the bodies and landscapes that bound, and sometimes bind, them). We "make trial" of places in culturally specific ways. This principle, according to Casey, applies not only to the familiar places to which we are accustomed but also to faraway places that are visited.

It also applies to the places deprived of their peaceful familiarity. "If a position is a fixed posit of an established culture, then a place, despite its frequently settled appearance, is an essay in experimental living within a changing culture" (Casey 1993: 31). The experimental-experiential "trials" of the *places changed by violence* is the theme of this article.

A comparison of narrative presentations of such "trials" and the experiences and images framed by the concepts of *belonging to Europe* and *mobilising cultural heritage* might be seen as being too far-fetched. Namely, the newly raised awareness of belonging to the place in my examples indeed happened in an abnormal context. It happened in a situation of manifold reversed orders, in the context of restriction or annihilation of most peacetime and peaceful everyday coordinates of identity which imply preferences and choices.

Yet, while illustrating the re-considered, re-discovered and newly discovered relations to the place in which their everyday life has been situated, this article also relates the experiences

The Cathedral immediately after being hit, December 6, 1991. Photo: Milo Kovač.

of modern urban Europeans, for whom belonging to Europe has been an undisputed fact. It has been taken for granted not only by geographical location but first and foremost by inheriting, living with and taking care of some of the most distinguished objects of European architectonic cultural heritage.

The poet, Luko Paljetak, (web site http://www.dubrovnik.hr) expresses it like this:

"Like a sea-shell, full of the sounds of life, Dubrovnik lies on the shores of the Adriatic, in Croatia. (…) Without it, you will not be able to complete your mosaic of the world's beauty. (…) Dubrovnik's culture, literature, painting, architecture, music, philosophy, science and diplomacy are an integral part of the cultural heritage of Europe and the world. Dubrovnik is a cultural monument under UNESCO's special protection. (…) Dubrovnik will be just the way you are yourself when you come to it. And you will leave it the way Dubrovnik is. Unique. Perfect."

This quotation reveals an exalted insider's conviction in the power of the place "to direct and stabilise us, to memorialise and identify us, to tell us who and what we are in terms of *where we are* (as well as where we are not)" (Casey 1993: xv; italics in original). It is thus valuable to reflect upon the tension between two types of Dubrovnik inhabitants' place-bound identity, between being "Europeans" and being "war victims".

The War

When the war started in Croatia in Summer 1991 – in the regions with a considerable Serbian population – the people of Dubrovnik did not feel threatened since their region was indisputably Croatian with regard to the ethnic affiliation of the vast majority of its inhabitants. No claims on "Serbian territory" similar to the ones in Eastern Slavonia were imaginable (see Goldstein 1999: 198–238). Besides, the border between the Dubrovnik region and the areas that are today parts of Montenegro and Bosnia-Hercegovina dates from the Middle Ages. However, Dubrovnik was attacked a couple of months later.

As explained by the historian Ivo Goldstein (1999: 235), besides the strategic need to provide the future Greater Serbia with a suitable port, the attack on Dubrovnik was also motivated by the long-standing urge of the Hercegovinian and Montenegrin mountain dwellers to make this city Serbian. In 1991, the old propaganda which claimed that the citizens of Dubrovnik were never Croats, but Serbs who converted to

Roman Catholicism, was repeated in Serbia and Montenegro and among the Serbs in Bosnia-Hercegovina. The plan was to cut Dubrovnik off from Croatia and force it to join Yugoslavia. The defenders of the city environs were few in numbers and badly armed, so the city was completely surrounded after several days of fighting, from the land, as well as from the sea. Electricity and water supplies were cut off by the enemy in the whole area (for about 90 days in 1991 and again for about 40 days in 1992).

Almost the whole immediate area of Dubrovnik was plundered and set on fire; most of the inhabitants of the surrounding villages fled to the town and found refuge in the hotels. Some 34,000 people were banished from the area, 12,000 of whom were staying in the town of Dubrovnik by the end of 1992. Literally everything they left at home was either destroyed or taken away by the enemy. People talked about even the sockets being taken out of the plundered and then burnt-down houses![2] In 1991–92, a total of 7,757 dwellings (encompassing 1,353,501 square meters) in the area were damaged. 539 buildings were totally burned down, and 1,051 buildings suffered heavy damage (for the chronology of the wartime events in Dubrovnik, as well as for the photographs of the destruction see Foretić, ed. 2000).

Enemy soldiers positioned on the nearby hill were so close that some of the Dubrovnik inhabitants that I interviewed could see them from their flats through binoculars; and were therefore afraid of stepping out onto their balconies. Fear of snipers was even greater than the fear of shelling, which happened at irregular intervals. In the first months, shelling was directed at the modern parts of the city and to the hotels close to the town, but not at the city centre surrounded by the 15th Ct. walls and encompassing the most valuable historical buildings. Therefore, people were fleeing from the outer, attacked ring of the city to their friends and relatives living in the old centre. No one believed that the attackers would dare to harm it: they supposed that it was simply too exposed to the international gaze and too important to the international community.

However, in the fiercest and final attack on 6 December 1991, some six hundred shells fell on the old city and hardly any of the historical buildings were left undamaged. People were killed while trying to extinguish the fires that raged throughout the town. Twenty-two people were killed and about sixty severely injured (out of 92 civilians killed and 225 wounded in the Dubrovnik area in 1991–92). Luxury hotels in the vicinity were completely destroyed. The Inter-University Centre was burned to the ground, including the library with some 25,000 books. The headquarters of the Dubrovnik Festival – an international summer festival of music and theatre – together with documentation collected over a period of 43 years, went up in flames.

On the same day, the UNICEF representative made a dramatic plea from Dubrovnik, and international notes of protest were sent to the Yugoslav Army's general in charge. Only a day later a cease-fire was agreed under international political pressure. *Europe* stopped the destruction of its monuments. However, the city area remained surrounded by the enemy army and a significant part of Dubrovnik Commune remained occupied. In June 1992, some of the historical monuments were hit in new attacks. With irregular breaks, civilians in the Dubrovnik region were experiencing heavy artillery attacks until July 20, 1992 when another cease-fire was signed. Yet, Dubrovnik airport was bombarded even in Summer 1994, and the city surroundings shelled in Spring and Summer 1995: people being wounded or killed. On August 28, 1995, the main director of UNESCO "warned world public opinion that the attacks on Dubrovnik, which was protected by the inter-national convention, are a war crime" and "reminded the world of the fact that the committers of such crimes must be responsible to the International Court in the Hague" (Foretić, ed. 2000: 116).

The general danger alert remained in force for the whole region until the end of September 1995, three and a half years after Croatia was internationally recognised as an independent state.

So much for the historical facts and frameworks. If interest is directed to the personal narratives mentioned above, the tendency to situate one's own identity in spatial terms is striking. This was significantly intensified due to the lived encounters of war-violence. From the individual experiential point of view, the siege combined with military violence was indeed "nailing people down" to their dwelling place (the ones who decided not to leave; see Povrzanović 1997).

The phrase "down to earth" resounds here with its most literal implications.

On the one hand, military violence is, in a simple and very much down to earth way, about killing living beings and destroying buildings and natural landscapes.

On the other hand – and this is my focus of interest – people became aware of the importance of their physical position within the surrounding urban and landscape structure. They also became aware of their physical dependency on the surrounding nature (sea, plants and animals), but also on nature in terms of one's own bodily potential, most importantly health and physical endurance.

When the shells were destroying the town, the buildings were not really a cultural heritage to be proud of; they only served to protect endangered bodies. When the circulation of goods was stopped because of the siege, the palm trees – a tourist area symbol *par excellence* – were chopped down and used for heating. When all the taps were dry in the town, the surrounding sea was not something to be appreciated for its beauty and economic potentials, but for saving people from a humiliating stink and infections. Thus, when talking about *non-mediated experiences* of the place, I talk about bodily experiences of the material world in which places are not merely bare positions in space, but "concrete and at one with action and thought" (Casey 1993: xiii).

New geographies were established in terms of safety and danger: of landscape, of the streets that had to be used e.g. when going to work or to collect water, and even of one's own home, depending on a certain room's exposure to potential shelling. During the shelling, the distances measured in meters mattered. A bathroom could be a good place to sleep in if it had no windows. The shape of the nearby hill, from which people in Dubrovnik were shot at, became extremely important too. It did matter in which part of the town one's house was situated, and on which floor the flat was. It did matter if one lived close to the sea or not, because 25 litre canisters are very heavy. It mattered very much if one had a traditional water collecting well in the garden, for that water was possible to drink. And so on.

In peaceful normality these common and often trivial experiences of basic safety, water, food and shelter are taken for granted and not reflected upon. However, in a context of violence, people are reminded of their central, existential importance. The sense of belonging to a place is thus intensified by the insights into one's own dependency on the material qualities of the place. From the point of view of the civilian surrounded by danger, it is the physical qualities of place that are in the foreground, rather than the symbolic ones.

If violence happened to the people in Dubrovnik "by chance", simply because they were civilians physically present in a place enmeshed in war, I would argue that their reactions did not come about by chance. These reactions follow a cultural logic that seems to reflect the potentials generally present in the relations of people to their dwelling places. In the experiential circumstances defined by violence, these potentials are realised as a pronounced feeling of belonging to the place, and seem to turn into people's central emotional concern, next to the concern about survival.

Belonging to Europe

Violence is not only re-inscribing the place in physical terms, through material destruction and creation of local geographies of more or less dangerous places. It is also imposing an overall definition of a place as an attacked or occupied place, as a military territory – a definition that has nothing to do with any wished for, chosen or worked upon definitions of the same place by its inhabitants. Needless to say, the perpetrators of violence have the upper hand: that is why the underlying experience of all civilians under siege is one of humiliation. The choices made in active efforts to oppose the imposed victim-identity are manifold. They might be successful in keeping – in a minimised form – the established forms of urban community and culture (see Povrzanović 1997), but they are

Consequences of the shelling of the Old Town (Stradun), December 7, 1991. Photo: Božidar Đukić.

framed by the overriding definition of place as a military territory to be threatened, shelled, bombarded, set on fire, destroyed and/or appropriated, taken away from its "owners". To quote a Croatian author, Dubrovnik was bombarded by "those who have no affective relation towards it and nor intellectual understanding of it. (…). If they cannot have it, they show clearly, they can destroy it" (Maroević 2000:78).

Who "owned" Dubrovnik when the war started? Was it Croatian or Yugoslav? Was it a European or a Balkan town? To who did the cultural heritage in Dubrovnik belong? Was its protection the responsibility of the town council or UNESCO?

Dubrovnik developed from a city commune to an independent republic during the 12th and 13th centuries, and kept its independence until 1806, when it came under French rule. Later, as part of the Province of Dalmatia, it was subjected to Vienna. Until the 17th century the Dubrovnik Republic was renowned for its social, economic and cultural prosperity. Economic prosperity brought public standards of living similar to that in Western Europe. In the 14th century the streets of Dubrovnik were paved and it had sewerage and waterworks, the first system of quarantine in Europe for travellers to the city as a protection against epidemics, one of the first European orphanages, a hospital and a pharmacy (Goldstein 1999: 28f.). Dubrovnik was the first centre in which literature in the

Croatian language developed under the influence of humanism and Italian Petrarchan and Renaissance poetry. Many of the most important Croatian poets, playwrights and scientists came from Dubrovnik. Most of today's cityscape came into being in the 15th century. The famous walls and towers were built in the 14th and 15th centuries. Since the mid 1960s, when the tourist boom started on the East Adriatic coast, Dubrovnik has been the most internationally renowned tourist centre. The well preserved historical town is protected by UNESCO as a world cultural heritage centre.

Dubrovnik, sometimes dubbed Croatian Athens, is one of the key symbols of national identity: "the most complete and most distinguished model of civilisation, harmony and subtlety" (Maroević 2000: 78). The historical core of Dubrovnik is called "The Town" (*Grad* written with a capital G) even today, not only locally, but also nation-wide. The Dubrovnik Republic's flag with the word "Libertas" has also in the modern era been invested with pride. It is no surprise that the Croats saw its destiny in the 1990s war as one more – and internationally the most convincing – proof of their rightfulness in fighting for independence.

The popular image of Dubrovnik's history is well-captured in a letter to an Italian friend written by a Croatian art historian when Dubrovnik was under siege in 1991:

"It is a city with a long and rich Catholic tradition, the home of preachers and of the religious orders that promoted scholarship and architecture – Benedictines, Franciscans, Dominicans, Jesuits. Dubrovnik is a city – and expression – of the cosmopolitan, peaceful, maritime, hardworking, educated and cultured Croatia, the birthplace of great scientists and scholars, writers, sea captains, entrepreneurs, excellent cartographers, and engineers. And despite its historically justified cautiousness, it has always been a very open city, with a Mediterranean atmosphere, with excellent commercial and maritime communications, and displaying full religious and national tolerance. It was neither servile nor xenophobic. It was the home of German craftsmen, Greek and Spanish scholars, Italian physicians, lawyers and artists, painters and architects. It was the home of people coming all over Croatia and from many parts of Italy. It was also the Frontier: Light on the Borders of Darkness" (Zidić 2000: 62).

The 1990s "frontier" destiny of Dubrovnik was at the same time seen as proof for the accuracy of the existing metaphor of Croatia's current otherness/westerness/betterness in relation to Serbia, namely the metaphor of *Europe* as opposed to *the Balkans*. It became especially relevant and was charged with heated political meaning.

The concern about "belonging to Europe" is widely shared in Eastern European countries. Mattijs van de Port (1998) offered an anthropological analysis of this wish on the basis of Serbian material gathered from 1991. He explains the concern with *being good enough to belong to Europe* as a result of peripheral position and the century-long instability due to many wars. He also discusses that anti-civilisatory extremes like war crimes are not only committed by Serbian paramilitaries, but also openly displayed by the international media, and the discourse opposing Europe which he met during his fieldwork. In that discourse, summarised in the statement "we don't want to be a part of Europe; we know the truer truths, we know what life is really about", Europe is presented as decadent, to say the least, and thus not worth an effort. The same has been mentioned by the Slovene philosopher Slavoj Žižek (1999) – in regard not only to Serbia, but also to the whole of the Balkans. Žižek calls this anti-civilisatory, thus also anti-European attitude "reversed racism", for it is a reverse image of the one that "Europe" has about the Balkans, within what he calls "reflexive", European politically correct racism.[3]

The ending of all formal relations with other former Yugoslav peoples in early 1992 with whom they had been sharing two states since 1918, was perceived by the Croats – and here a general statement is accurate – as a welcome ending of all their connections with the Balkans. The notion of the Balkans – regardless of the variety of its possible meanings – most often became reduced to the opposition of *Europe* in an essentialised, only seemingly explanatory, dichotomy, which is first and foremost a value statement.

Europe in the dichotomy *Europe vs. Balkans* stands for high culture, wealth and freedom. Europe is urban, middle-class, civilised, controlled, economical, Western and modern (Port 1998: 61). [4] *The Balkans* is the negative opposite: it means primitivism, poverty and wars. It is rural, peasant, wild, uncontrolled, wasteful, oriental and backward (Port 1998: 61). In Žižek's (1999) words, "there is the old-fashioned, unabashed rejection of the Balkan Other (despotic, barbarian, Orthodox, Muslim, corrupt, Oriental) in favour of true values (Western, civilised, democratic, Christian)".

The military attacks on Dubrovnik thus easily fitted into the metaphors of barbarians attacking civilisation, (Serbian and Montenegrin) primitives destroying (Croatian) cultural heritage, the Balkans invading Europe. [5] The following example was written by a Croatian theatre director who was one out of many intellectuals trying to make "the world" (most importantly, politically influential Western Europeans) understand what was happening in Croatia in 1991.[6] The underlying civilisation-debate is obvious:

"I cannot supress my need to compare this siege with the conquering of Dubrovnik by Napoleon. It never occurred to Napoleon, that is to his Marshal Marmont, later "the Duke of Dubrovnik", to take the water away from the City. Because he did not come to conquer Dubrovnik in order to remove its cleanliness but to add another clean city to his large French Empire. (…) Dubrovnik could turn over the keys of the city to Marmont but it will not surrender to this army made up of 'dukes of *opanci*' (Serbian moccasins) because cleanliness cannot be surrendered to dirtiness, nor can harmony collapse before harshness. This is a collision between two mutually exclusive worlds, which are not joined in life or death" (Violić 2000: 19).

Such metaphors were not only adopted by the local people or Croats in general, but also by some Western intellectuals, like for example the Italian author Enzo Bettiza (1996):

"It is not by chance that this war (…) for the first time in European history united genocide and culturocide. The straightforward strategy of 'ethnic cleansing' is permeated by the straight forward doctrine of 'cultural cleansing'. (…) The Serbian attempts to distort more than conquer Dubrovnik, to disfigure its architectonic beauty, its renaissance and Mediterranean uniqueness, is the most obvious example of that project of destroying of cultural symbols of a disliked Slavic civilisation, cosmopolitan, maritime, far from Orthodox cupolas, from Byzantine icons and from sacred documents written in Cyrillic letters. (…) In the Athenian Dubrovnik the Orthodox Sparta has rightfully recognised an extraordinary victim of a new cultural Holocaust that is maddening over the Balkans" (Bettiza 1996: 21–22).

During the war, many Croatian authors and intellectuals wrote in similar vein. The following examples depict the widely adopted understanding of the recent war, for which the special symbolic significance of Dubrovnik is central. The town is presented as "one of the symbols of ancient Europe and one of the deep roots of our Mediterranean origins", as a "metropolis of Croatian culture", as a counter-point to "the disorderly chaos of the eastern, Byzantine-Serbian and Turkish, hinterland", as "a model of an ideal city" in contrast to "the obscure Balkan market towns and brigands' holes", as being "separated from the dark and threatening forests and wild gorges of the distant hinterland by a belt of Arcadian harmony", as "everything that Serbia is not" (Zidić 2000: 62).

"The beauty of Dubrovnik has been transformed into 'harmony' (*skladnost*). The word derives from Dubrovnik and it expands the meaning of beauty, the notion of beauty, enriches it and adds its own character. No language (as far as I know) has this word with the meaning it has in Dubrovnik. The Dubrovnik 'skladnost' means not only refinement but also the connection the people have with the scenery and architecture of the City. (…) When juxtaposed with harmony, I detect a subtext of conflict before the walls of Dubrovnik, a layered meaning. Harshness vs. Harmony" (Violić 2000: 17).

A Place in National Space

I could hardly expect people who experienced the siege and shelling to frame their narration by the metaphor of Dubrovnik as "Harmony" and "Croatia's soul" or by the claim that "the beauty of Dubrovnik is a sublime announcement of the spiritual integrity of the Croats" (Violić 2000: 16f.). As I discussed elsewhere (Povrzanović 1997), peoples' personal narratives about war reveal a multiplicity, diversity and complexity of experience that challenges the uniqueness of the national narrative. Their first-hand knowledge about the sufferings of war is retained as bodily memories. It gives them an authenticity that needs neither media phrases about their heroism, nor narrative frames of suffering for the nation.

The monovocal and unique national narrative on war makes use only of the generalised experience of war victims. Also, there is a cleft within the unified complex of the narrating about the nation as victim, since people from some parts of Croatia suffered terrible losses, while some other parts of the country were not physically affected by war.

Yet, with its cultural dimension and affiliated historical, social and political aspects that contribute to the "density" of a place (cf. Casey 1993: 33), for millions of people outside the town Dubrovnik was an important cultural space that was so easy to identify with rather than a physical space. This is not to say that no one was actively trying to help the civilians under siege, but the dominant media image (equal to the one used in international political negotiations) was not one of the town as a site of actual resistance, but as a crystallisation point of Croatian cultural identity. Culture indeed was put forward as the "third dimension" of place (Casey 1993: 31f.), that affords it a deep historicity and all the positive connotations mentioned earlier.[7]

The intensification of the idea of one's own cultural relationship to a place also explains the highly emotional reactions to the destruction of Dubrovnik by people throughout Croatia. Although their position was that of an outsider in physical/experiential terms, the manifold identification possibilities relativised the notions of inside and outside (and that holds for the general reaction of Croats to the 1990s war, regardless to where in Croatia or how far away from Croatia they lived). "Like 'place' and 'space', notions of 'inside' and 'outside' depend upon cultural and historical context" (Hirsch 1997: 13). Although relatively separate and detached, these notions, just like the notions of (experiential) *foreground actuality* and (political) *background potentiality*, are never completely disconnected (cf. Hirsch 1997: 4).

The "here and now-ness" of Dubrovnik shelled and besieged was of course not excluding the town's presence in the national narrative on the victimised Europeans expecting rescue. On the contrary, it was the very Europeaness of the town that was invoked as the ultimate reason for the hoped-for international political action.

Actual place was first and foremost a part of political space. The narrative of a victimised nation used in political representation was illustrated by visual images of destruction. The physical landscape being set on fire was heating the symbolic landscape of *Croatia in the flames of war*.

Within the political discourse on the rightfulness of Croatia's independence, Dubrovnik acted as a prominent piece of national soil. Within the discourse on cultural heritage, it was the most significant proof of Croatia's belonging to Europe. For the people within the besieged town, Dubrovnik was the site of civilian resistance, consisting of preserving the place's (minimal) *normality*. People who stayed in the town kept up their everyday routines – including the evening walk along the main street in the historical centre – as a means of not consenting to the violence-imposed transformation of *their town* into a "common" place of destruction (cf. Povrzanović 1997: 158).

Being aware of the importance of cultural heritage, the insiders perceived the historical centre as "protected". They firmly believed that *Europe* would not let the old town be damaged. As a reverse of the same coin, people also did not believe that the ones shooting at them would have the audacity to damage cultural monuments, for they would then "show their true face" to *the world*, and lose any political support. Yet, the "unbelievable" did happen: UNESCO flags denoting the world's heritage eventually served as precise demarcations of the most valuable objects to be destroyed. When crying a day after 6 December 1991 ("everyone was crying in the streets, men, women, elderly, kids"; "it really seemed as if The Town was turned into ruins"), people realised that the historical city walls guaranteed no protection from a common war destiny (Povrzanović 1997: 158). The illusion that their place could be excluded from war because of its cultural heritage was lost. They understood that symbols could not stop the war, that culture – neither in the form of heritage nor as an undisputed "belonging to Europe" – couldn't overpower violent force.[8]

In the international media, outstanding individuals called for help for the monuments being destroyed only "two hours from London" – to quote the title of a British TV-documentary. In the national media, the image of a "hero-town" was promoted, very much in accordance with Dubrovnik as a national symbol. People who faced the attacks on the town were thus either forgotten in the midst of Heritage, or turned into mute "heroes" inhabiting a place in national space, saturated with symbols which served as a trump card in political negotiations. (Indeed, the international shock provoked by the bombardment of 6 December 1991 seemed to be a decisive gain in Croatia's struggle for political recognition.) It made them step directly into history, their personal war experiences disappearing in symbols (cf. Povrzanović 1997: 161).

Being There

Experiences described by the already mentioned spatial metaphors such as position, location, situation, centre or margin, inside or outside, open or closed, change radically due to the *lived experience of violence*. In this context, to Casey's general claim that "what matters most is the experience of *being* in that place and, more particularly, becoming part of the place" (Casey 1993: 33) should be added a remark about an "essentialising" force of violent destruction, which makes place-related aspects of identities central (cf. Povrzanović 1997: 154). Simply, since people were attacked on the basis of their mere physical presence in the town, the physical position that a person or a group is occupying while being exposed to violence becomes an unavoidable and non-negotiable starting point (metaphorically, but also literally!) of any identity creation.[9]

In 1991–92, it was obvious that the division of people whose life was at stake and those whose life was not, was not necessarily a dichotomising division. It was possible to see it also as a matter of gradation, as a spatial continuum within which people were occupying a place more or less close to danger. Only the similarity of the lived experience made the bridging of different "grades" of exposure to violence and the probability of dying possible (e.g. the experience of hiding in a shelter was the same for all people, regardless of the fact that in some places that was what the lived war experience consisted of and elsewhere people had many other, more dangerous encounters with violence). In November 1991, the *others* for people in Dubrovnik were even their closest family members who had left the town only a month before; in the meantime, the violence escalated in a way that radically changed the place. So, the ones who were not there could not know what it was like.

The variety of war experiences was not only related to space, but also to time: the war was *coming closer*, slowly but steadily. It was *creeping* from Konavle, the village area east of Dubrovnik, but even from a very short distance, from Lapad, the modern town quarters west of the centre, to the core of the town encompassed by the walls. For months, people staying in different parts of the town had a very different experience of attacks. It is hard to imagine, because these are very short distances indeed. More importantly, many people had even been covering the distances on a daily basis, e.g. going to work in a more dangerous part of the town and coming back home to a less dangerous part. Thinking in terms of a *microgeography of danger* makes a lot of sense here.

"I called work; my boss asked me: 'F., how is it in The Town?' I told her: 'Listen, if Hell exists, then I am in it.' She sometimes mentions it today, because the next morning I came to work and told that The Town was burnt down, that the

Inter-University centre was burnt down, and she was hiding there in the shelter... She did not believe it she did not believe a word, nothing, not any thing – as if I was in one world, and she in another. Because they didn't hear it in the hospital. Because it's far away, so it wasn't heard all that much. They knew that the wounded are brought in and everything, but they did not know what was happening *in reality*, because they were as if in a bunker."

When narrating about meeting the war in *their town*, people did not talk about war as History, but about the experiences lived through in the shadow of historical monuments.

The Dubrovnik author, Feda Šehović, who spent the war in the town, wrote about the parallel existence and the uniting of Dubrovnik as a symbolic space and as the place of his own everyday life (Šehović 1994: 32). The care for cultural monuments is characteristic for Dubrovnik people but at the same time they were worried about their friends and relatives living with, in, or next to these monuments.

The already mentioned regular walk along Stradun, the main historical street, was a means of keeping up an important aspect of urban everyday life. It was not an active resistance to the enemy by means of weapons or political engagement; it was not even an expression of obstinacy directed to the enemy. It was *obstinacy for one's own good*, aimed at preserving integrity by keeping up the segments of everyday life. At the same time, it was an act of non-acknowledging/denying the fact that the symbolic and the physical space of the city had been turned into a war-ground, i.e. degraded to an object of destruction. This non-acceptance of the imposed new, non-cultural or a-cultural categorisation of their place, was realised by *being there* and thus making certain peaceful meanings of the place happen.

The running across Stradun to the dangerous south side (the attackers could not shoot directly at the north side of the street form the hill they were occupying) – done by some teenagers – was also a way of denying that the enemy had an upper hand in the situation. To be there and ignore the danger was not primarily a statement of bravery turned against the enemy, but an impetus for youthful competition within one's own physical and social space. In peace-time, a willing exposure to certain dangers could be called "crazy". In war, the weight of meaning is added, since the very lives of the competitors are at stake.

In Mokošica, the western, modern part of the town, as well as in the town centre, several teenage boys were killed because they went out of the shelter in order "to see where the shells are falling".

The places of suffering are spaces in isolation from the "outer", peaceful world or from places closer to peace. In narration, that experience of isolation is often expressed as an impossibility of communicating experience to the ones who have not been there: "it can't be told" (cf. Povrzanović 1997: 156).

"I was literally stumbling, like a drunkard. I look at the house: is it possible, it's my mother's colleague's, a teacher's, house – burnt down completely! The policemen standing there, sawing the tears in my eyes, and sawing me zigzag left and right, staggering, they were stepping out of my way."

"It was ghastly the day after, too (after *the sixth of December*). The day after we all went out, we all wept at Stradun. It really seemed as if The Town was turned into ruins. It really looked as if The Town was demolished."

Places containing one's material and cultural properties frame everyday activities. In the quotations cited here, if a place-based conditioning of perceptions is obvious, it might mean that it is indeed not possible to communicate certain traumatic experiences, for they are so significantly bound to place. That is also why the humanitarian aid convoy "Libertas" meant so much to people in Dubrovnik. Some participants of the convoy did not sail away after a short visit to the town, but remained in the place (cf. Lang 1997). Like the visits and stays by several people attached to Dubrovnik Inter-University Centre, their remaining in the town was very much a personal statement of emotional – and experiential – links to the place. The concert on 31 December 1991, performed by the National Orchestra from Toulouse had a similar function, although the presence of Croatian and international officials accompanied by international TV-crews pointed to another, more politically informed, kind of solidarity and the intention to make it public.

Regardless of these differences, it was *being there* that mattered. Seen from the outside, there was no better (no more efficient or convincing) way to express solidarity with those under siege, to restore their importance and dignity along with the importance and dignity ascribed to Dubrovnik monuments. Seen from the inside, the fact that someone came to stay in the attacked town (while many of its inhabitants were fleeing) was not only an expression of solidarity in suffering and enduring, but also an embodied hope in the restoration of normality (in which numerous people wish to visit Dubrovnik). This explains why many were irritated with the "hit and run" journalists who paid very short visits to the town, and angry when such journalists tried to feature them in war-photos from Dubrovnik.

Home, Town: Physical and Symbolic Destruction

"Buildings are among the most perspicuous instances of the thorough acculturation of places. *A building condenses culture in one place.* Even if it is more confining than a landscape, a building is more densely saturated with culture than is landscape (unless the landscape is a cityscape). As itself a place, a building is a *focus locorum* – indeed, a *locus locorum*, a place for places. It exists between the bodies of those who inhabit or use it and the landscape arranged around it. If it gives dwelling to these bodies, it gives cultural mission to that landscape. Within the ambience of a building, a landscape becomes articulate and begins to speak in emblematic ways" (Casey 1993: 32).

The Town has been structured by history; people's personal histories have been structured by the experience of war violence. Yet, the violence was experienced in a place consisting of cultural monuments – their material quality being the material surroundings of people's everyday life. Within the insiders' perception of monuments as familiar, everyday sites and objects, some spots in the town might be – more or less private – symbols of identity for the insiders themselves.

Dubrovnik is not only a famous stage scenery used during half a century of the Summer Festival; it is also a scenery for the historical and everyday, the national and local, art historians' and tourists', private and festive, war and peace plots. Calling the place "a scenery" here by no means implies any imagined character, any artificiality, falseness or un-realness. On the contrary, in all those plots the very materialness of the place is crucial.

As explained above, the insiders' *geographies of symbols* have been re-considered due to the lived experiences of war violence. But new symbols have been emerging from those experiences too. New meanings are ascribed to some previously a-cultural spaces; a hill or a wood where an armed conflict happened can become symbols of resistance and of the victory that is going to come.

In talking about a friend who died in the middle of Stradun, at a spot he stepped on every day in his daily business, a young man told me that that particular spot is a more important place of mourning than his friend's grave. He also said that he *has to* remember what happened there every time he passes. Death as the ultimate imprint of violence thus imprinted the street by rupturing its old, peacefully neutral, primarily material character. But, there is no absolute quality in this imprint: it is there only for the ones who are emotionally involved, *the ones who can see it* today because of having been there during the war.

Danger, disaster and evil create places of intense fears. This is why places defined as safe within a peaceful cultural order become deformed into dangerous places in war. Home, usually understood as a place of absolute private control and definitely a safe place, becomes a potentially dangerous place. It is marked by a fear that is perpetuated by the unpredictability of events, instead of being marked by the repetitiveness of daily routines. The contrast is total, radical and very powerful precisely because home or house is the most proximate and the most intimate place (in Croatian language "home" – *dom*, is often equated with "house" – *kuća*; so "at home" means *kod kuće*, "in the house").

"My sister couldn't go home any more. (…) Her house remained intact. Because they didn't shoot so much at that part by the border, they didn't burn it down. I suppose they counted in it becoming theirs. (…) One house, belonging to my nephew, burned down, totally. He lost everything. (…) And in my house, one part was on fire, but the house was hit by three shells, so the roof, the ceiling, everything was falling down, and everything was exposed to rain, to the winds, everything…"

"A bullet flew in through my neighbours' window. From three kilometres away, from some sniper. They were not at home. (…) The first day, it was a shell of eighty millimetres that hit; the other one was hundred and twenty millimetres; it pierced the roof, made a whole one-metre wide – the whole room in dust. The neighbour was in the kitchen with his child; he hid the child under a chair. He was lost, he didn't know where he was, and then, later, luckily nothing happened afterwards. It hit into his bedroom, some three, four metres from them."

One's own flat or house was easily turned into a place of fear and destruction. Yet, some people decided to stay in their homes not only during air raid or artillery attack alarms, but also during the actual attacks. For some the decision was based on a war-acquired fatalism. For others it was a minimal, very private, act of resistance. The same sort of resistance was mentioned when discussing the walks along main street Stradun. Those walks point to the fact that *the town is home* in both a metaphorical and in a literal sense: in Dalmatia people spend a lot of their time in the streets, it is a part of a cultural pattern. Keeping that pattern regardless of danger means – just as the act of not leaving one's own flat – not accepting the violence-imposed redefinition of the home as a place truly appropriated by the dwellers.

Some people said that they even felt safer in their homes than in the improvised shelters in the cellars. It was *the safety of normality* surrounding them, the familiarity of the place that could help them "forget" the danger. Refusing to sit in a public shelter was also a statement of resistance to the violence-imposed group identity, in which self-definitions or personally preferred social contacts and ways of behaviour simply do not count. Staying in one's own flat was very much a matter of keeping one's personal dignity (unless, of course, the attacks became so intense that staying at home equated suicide).

For an old man, an armchair served as the last resort of normality from which he stubbornly did not want to move (Povrzanović 1997: 157). The place he did not want to surrender to the enemy was reduced to just one armchair, but it was *his* armchair. It was the last material oasis of everyday life, and the only remaining *firm point* of his identity.

"It was a strange experience – we couldn't go to the shelter, because Granddad didn't want to go anywhere. It is a small house with a flat roof, very stupid… but he didn't want to move and he was sitting in his armchair, just like in his whole life, and Granny with him, and then the two of us (the grandsons) were squatting there, too. We couldn't move into the cellar, for we couldn't leave them up there… I mean, it was stupid. Until a shell hit the house at last. And he remained unharmed. After that… soon after, they both died one after the other. First her, then him, seven days later. Because he decided to die. It didn't matter to him any more."

In more common, locally shared geographies of safety and danger, some places have been perceived as places of rescue. Many people felt safe in the public shelters organised in the towers of the city walls. In one narration the feeling of security, peace, comfort and hope in St. John's tower is explained as an analogy of being in the womb:

"First – you are in a closed space; the wall around you, just stone all around, isn't it? Second – the water, the sea, it reminds you of water, womb-water. It is rustling all the time; you have a feeling… a feeling of security. However false it may be, you still have a feeling of security."

Let me end this chapter by another, very different, kind of example of re-considering the practical and the symbolic dimension of places.

It is well known that sacred objects, primarily as signs in the landscape, symbolised for the attackers cultural otherness of the attacked regions (that has to be annihilated, so they could claim those regions were *theirs*). If not destroyed by arms, numerous churches have been desacrified in the war I am referring to.

Another type of "desacration" was happening in the occupied places of everyday life. They were devalued by ascribing an offensive meaning. In Dubrovnik surroundings, peoples' kitchens, bedrooms, and living rooms have sometimes been used as toilets by those who conquered them. "They came in and did on the desk the same as they did in Konavle houses: they defecated" (Zglav 1995: 148).

Nature and Animals: Ecological Order vs. War Dis-order

As explained by Edward S. Casey, place as we experience it – and that goes for the landscapes including nature and animals too – is not altogether natural. "If it were, it could not play the animating, decisive role it plays in our collective lives. Place, already cultural as experienced, insinuates itself into collectivity, altering as well as constituting that collectivity" (Casey 1993:31).

The insiders (like numerous outsiders) see the nature surrounding Dubrovnik as beautiful. Still, they do not love it because it is beautiful, but because it is *theirs*. Casey's (1993: 31–33) concept of *implacement* explained above, helps to understand this claim.

In a similar vein, Nicholas Green (1997) argues against the idealist "landscape concept", most evident in art history but also in urban sociology and anthropology, which searches for universal or immanent meanings in landscapes. Landscapes cannot be adequately understood simply as a set of objects and themes that are ideologically loaded, claims Green. A landscape cannot be grasped as text. Rather, it involves a materially-located process of perception and identification, a two-way dialogue that works to shape forms of social identity (cf. Green 1997: 40–41).

Thus "nature", as discussed in this chapter, does not invoke "landscape" in a static gaze-defined sense, as something laid out before one's eyes. It is *the proximate nature* – the sea, the hills, the beaches, as well as the vineyards, vegetation and animals – included in daily experiences in peace time through seeing, touching, hearing and smelling.

In the unusual example that follows, nature has been recognised as *protection* for the possibility of hiding by mimicry!

Familiar *grounds* (here also in literal sense of ground as earth) have been physically protecting two sisters in their seventies from being killed in the occupied area east of Dubrovnik. One evening they were trying to reach another village in order to take care of a cow that had recently had a calf and was in need of help. They knew that the owners had fled and left the animal and they didn't want it to suffer. They planned to sneak through a wood, but to their surprise and horror it had been burnt out. Only ashes were left and enemy soldiers were approaching.

"It happened on the day they started to shoot at Cavtat. They started to shoot at Cavtat – they were less than thirty metres away from us. We hear them, but you can't go anywhere. And there are no big stones to hide behind. Only a small rock, just like that. So we laid down, both of us – we can't move, for they will see us. And she covered me with ashes, and I covered her – on the head, everywhere. To look like nature, for them not to kill us."

In numerous other examples, nature is seen as literally feeding people ("Everything was growing abundantly – it saved us!"), but also as predicting misfortune:

"I don't remember that she ever went to pick olives – that was the first and the last year that the two of us picked the olives at Babin Kuk. There… where God said good night (*Bogu iza leda*)… There is a hotel complex built on the olive groves, these are the olives that give shade. So, what I remembered was asking what is a war, what is it like: I remembered that (the people were telling that) in the year when World

War II started everything bore fruit in an unbelievable quantity. That everything was extraordinarily fertile. So, when that summer (in 1991) I saw how abundant the grapes were and how many were left unpicked in Konavle, how plentiful the olives were – I was stricken! Instantly it was all clear…"

This quote comes from a woman in her thirties. But all my interview partners who talked about nature claimed that 1991 was a remarkably fruitful year, that all the crops were abundant.

"A new house was finished just before the war; now it isn't there any more – just ashes. But in front of it – flowers, lemons, oranges, as much as your heart wants! As much as your heart wants! The fruit, the vegetables… it was bearing fruit where you could least expect it, everywhere."

This of course might be a *post festum* projection, a contrast to the later unfortunate experience of shortages, especially of the scarcity of fruit and vegetables. Still, the narration reminding of the well-known folklore genres should not *a priori* question the reality of the experience of *the feeding nature*. It is also certain that in the story about war people connect important details that otherwise might not be connected and may not even be perceived. People were aware of nature's abundance because later on they found themselves deprived – not knowing how long it would last. This was more serious and therefore also psychologically, not only physically, hard to bear.

Nature was also seen as a saviour in animals as being sensors of danger. In the context of an overall heightened sensitivity to one's natural surroundings, people were taking them seriously.

"I got up to see who was making a noise – is it a soldier, who is it… it's dark, but I might see something. I stepped out, when the dog jumped at me and started to bark – he would not let me go, he was barking and barking. That was strange, he would not let me go there. Well, animals have a sixth sense… So I listened to him, I thought: maybe he sensed something, I won't go. And I didn't."

"The cats were walking on the roofs when it was calm. If the cats are not up there, but down – run away! And the dog would sense it (the attack) in advance and start barking. So I behaved in accordance to the animals. The birds – the birds would fly high when it was calm. When you see them hiding in the walls (the city walls), you hide, too!"

Turning to nature – in the lived situations as well as in the narration about them – explains how and why nature is perceived as being an important part of peoples' physical surrounding. As the importance of nature intensified, the sea, crops and animals were re-discovered. People's dependency on nature has been re-considered. Nature has definitely been included in the life-world that people talk about. It is the proximate and familiar nature: *domaća* – "domestic", intimately appropriated, felt close to, and *zavičajna* – "belonging to the home region".

The relation to nature as culturally established has also been shown at another level – that of exclusion, incompetence, and lack of cultural understanding of (what has to be done with or done to) nature by those who do not belong to it and (thus) do not own it either.

In his war diary, Niko Zglav (1995: 148) writes with contempt and sadness about the unpicked ripe figs and the picked unripe grapes in his occupied village of Konavle.

The following quotation from another war diary unites the same perspective with the question of who has the right to enjoy the fruits of *our* nature:

"Who is going to pick my beautiful grapes? Are they perhaps going to rot unpicked? And the olives that are going to be ripe soon? Who is going to drink the wine made from our grapes and fill the wine-skins with the oil made of our olives" (Šehović 1994: 15)?

A direct connection to nature has also been expressed as the emotional relation to animals.

"We went to The Town, but our nephew brought us back. Because of our love for the house, for the animals."

The two old sisters mentioned above were brought to safety (The Town by then was considered to be safe) a few days before the enemy soldiers definitely occupied the region to the east of Dubrovnik. Yet, being peasant women who spent their entire life in the same village, they could not stand being away and returned after only two days.

In situations of total disruption of everyday normality animals are very often seen as members of the family. This is not only true for the pets. In an example from Vukovar, a rat sharing the shelter with people was eventually given a name and referred to as a "family member". In the narratives referred to in this chapter it was not only one animal that people were talking about, but animals as a living content of nature/the home-region (*zavičaj*). In talking about the fish in Dubrovnik aquarium that served as a public shelter, a young woman explained: "We all got attached to them!" The following story about communicating with a fish sounds almost fantastic:

"One fish – we were all surprised – she was recognising her! She was swimming in circles by the sides of the pool. My mother would sit on the rim, and the fish would open her mouth and let mother caress it, then make a circle again, open her mouth again, let my mother caress it again, and so on. My mother said: come here, look at this! And really, people couldn't have been more surprised: is it possible?"

The animals and the people were living beings inhabiting the same place defined by violence. In a very basic way they were all sharing the same destiny: they were all exposed to the same shelling. In Dubrovnik under siege, people have been "feeding everything alive" (the Croatian phrase "everything alive", means all encompassing, non-critically included; here it has a double – also literal – meaning). In the deserted streets, even the otherwise non-homely, non-domestic pigeon has been seen as *our* animal.

"As people were fleeing from Konavle, from Župa, so the animals fled with them. Some people had their dogs and were taking care of them. But some would take care of them to a certain extent, and then let them go... So, there were many stray dogs, also cats, right here in The Town. And somehow... you neither would kill them, nor... I don't know. I was giving food to all of them, for I was pitying them all. There are no kids, there is no laughter, there is nothing – sadness, grief, horror, so at least you can feed the animals, isn't that right? Half of your family is not there..."

Emotional reactions to the killing or any suffering of the animals I was told about, might seem surprising in situations where people are getting killed. Yet, the animals' victimisation as a part of an all-encompassing re-definition of a place imposed by violence is not the only reason for such reactions. The time of animals might be perceived as running parallell to human time; it may also be seen as a contrast to war. In perpetuating their habits in the same manner, animals *do not know* that a war is going on (although they might *sense* the abnormality of danger). Even if only symbolically, they might be seen as withstanding (or overcoming) war. The animals' existence is thus symbolically excluded from the war.

Nature in general is persistent in cycles that have nothing to do with human time and war destruction. The cycles of natural normality are perceived in war as a sharp contrast to radical ruptures of human normality. Nature "behaves" on its own accord, as if nothing strange was happening, as if there was no war. The "timeless" ecological order is a sound seed of hope in transience of war dis-order.

Body: The Last Resort

The body is the smallest and the most intimate physical space of human integrity. It is the last physical refuge of personal identity that – due to psychosomatic reaction to stress and fear – might slip out of personal control. The narration about the body that I am referring to is one about physical, unmediated, bodily experienced encounters with war. It is the narration about restricted mobility, shrivelling, freezing, smells, constant tension due to manifold fears, as well as the tiny pieces of shrapnel carried around in people's bodies, sometimes remaining there for their whole life as a physical memory of war (cf. Povrzanović 1997: 159). Also, the vicinity of death, injuries, blood and realistic possibilities of one's own body being (lethally) hurt, enable not only compassion, but also a direct identification with the victims of war.[10]

A soldier's live body, is physically opposing the attacker. Dead, it becomes a symbol that supposedly unites and fortifies a nation in war.

Victimized body can be a dead body, a wounded body, a cramped body, a body in pain, a stumbling body, a body that is falling, wavering in fear, a body falling into a deep sleep in order to escape from reality, a body somnanbulically ignoring danger when walking around in the midst of an attack, a body that hides, a body that runs away.

A body in war may also be a sick body. Illness – real and invented – could serve as a legitimate reason for not being called up or for leaving the town. Thus illness can be interpreted as a powerful means of controlling one's own war-destiny.

The ones who remained in the besieged town seem to have "chosen" extreme behaviour. Some became healthy overnight, leaving their chronic and other diseases for peaceful, normal times. They *did not have time* to be ill (having so much else to take care of), or they simply saw their physical difficulties as minor in comparison to the sufferings of war ("we all came healthier out of the war", Šehović 1994).

In contrast to that, some people became got fixated about their own health, and tried to make the people in their surroundings interested in their pain or simply in their own body as the focus of fears (as if saying: look at me, take care of me, don't leave me alone in this). One's own body is the last "free zone" in war, the last material value one can own. Indulging in worries about the body might also be seen as a way of keeping up one's own interest in oneself, of staying alive. Putting the body at the focus of attention means wanting to go on.

It is not difficult to understand the unease and fear coming out of physical weakness and dependency on other people's help, especially if these people are strangers meeting in a public shelter. All those interviewed confirmed that it was the old people who were most fearful. Although the feeble were "allowed" to fear, people strongly disapproved of those who panicked (since they were afraid of succumbing to panic themselves).

On the other hand, focusing on one's own body and its functions – the disturbed as well as the healthy ones – was a way of facing a situation in which people felt they were being "left to destiny". As already noted, one's own body was perceived to be the only remaining space of personal control in the context of reduced access to other spaces and of insights in the arbitrariness of danger. It was also a place of a personal – *bodily* – time measured only by one's own bodily functions.

"Pain dramatises, it forms a natural starting point for narrativity, and provides the framework around the individual, which can be filled with narrative zest". The experiences of bodily suffering may become "a biographical line around which identities are spun" (Frykman 1998: 15). It is therefore interesting how little I have heard about the physical difficulties that people went through; they were mentioned, but not dwelled upon. The person talking about them most was the oldest one. Although these difficulties were substantial and remembered very clearly, they are perceived as being less important in the context of the narration on war.

This bears witness to the interpretation that the *narration about war* as presented in this chapter, really (and truly) is the *narration about resistance to the war*. This resistance was also significantly realised by not succumbing to fear and lack of cleanliness – by keeping up the dignity of the body.

Zavičaj – the Home-region: Shared Identities of Feeling

What gives a region its specificity is not some long internalised history but the fact that it is constructed out of a particular constellation of social relations, meeting and weaving together at a particular locus. Instead of thinking of the region as an area with boundaries, it can – to paraphrase Doreen Massey (1994: 154) – be imagined as being articulated in networks of social relations and understandings, bearing in mind that large proportions of those relations, experiences and understandings are constructed on a far larger scale than those we can define in that moment as the region itself.

In the romanticising poetic expression of a theatre director – yet presenting a widely shared image of Dubrovnik's noble qualities, "(t)he special link among the three fundamental levels of life (so rare in the world) is still alive in Dubrovnik – the level of Man, the level of City, and the level of Nature. The People, the City and the scenery of Dubrava (Dubrovnik's nickname) are intertwined in harmony which is then transferred to the inhabitants of the City and leaves its marks on every Resident" (Violić 2000: 17).

Dubrovnik, *The Town*, is not only a national symbol, but also an experiential anchor of identity for all the people from the region. It is a point of reference in the landscape bearing the aura of lasting – "eternal" – value and beauty, but it is also the historical and the actual centre of the region. Peasant women from the region come to The Town every day to feed its inhabitants with their agricultural products sold at the market – and the same has been going on for centuries. Just like the intellectuals quoted earlier, they love Dubrovnik; it is theirs as much as it belongs to the people living within the walls. The Town is unthinkable in isolation from the surrounding region. Amputated and preserved only as cultural heritage, as an empty museum piece without life pulsating in it, it would lose all its current meanings except that as a historical *object*. In other words it would cease to be *a place*.[11]

In discussing Vico's theory of knowledge as opposed to the Cartesianism, Eric Hirsch (1997: 17) points out the central place of imagery, metaphor and "common sense". For Vico, knowledge is found in socially shared identities of feeling that people and their surroundings create in the flow of activity between them. The identities are what Vico calls "sensory topics" (*topos* means place). These identities give rise to "commonplaces", i.e. to shared moments in a flow of social activity which afford common reference. "Sensory" refers to the moments in which shared *feelings* for already shared circumstances are created (cf. Hirsch 1997: 17).

This can help to explain the strong sense of belonging to the home-region expressed by the people I interviewed. It is important to note that region here is meant in terms of *zavičaj*, which is Croatian for "Heimat", but defined strictly as local region. In Croatian language the concept of *zavičaj* cannot be extended to the national territory (which is called *domovina*, homeland).

"One should stay. Remain true to oneself, to one's own proper being. Remain a *gospar* (ancient term for a nobleman, today locally meaning a person from Dubrovnik region, who, precisely for living there, is noble; it's a standard local term for Dubrovnik citizens; MPF). Stay alive. Then live again. Freely. In dignity. For oneself and for the others. Openly. It starts in the ashes of the burnt down house. And like in a few places in the world, in this place, in this Dubrovnik, Croatian ashes, *the challenge of place as destiny* is being confirmed" (Nodari 1994: 224; italics MPF).

The challenge of place as destiny. Imagined and experienced belonging. The concept of *zavičaj*, connecting local landscape, animals and people. The importance of *being there*, not to be encompassed by military maps, but by the insiders' cognitive maps and emotional geographies of belonging in which moments, things and symbols are united in a concrete locality.

In a way that leaves no doubt, the paradox of *belonging to Europe* in terms of geography and cultural heritage, but not in terms of everyday experience, became clear to the people engulfed by violence aimed at territory and targeting civilians. For their perceptions of place and the definitions of concepts such as position, situation, centre, margin, inside, and outside (in their spatial but also political meanings), the lived experience of violence became crucial.

After the "pilgrimage" on the Stradun street full of broken glass, cracked stones from the historical buildings and smells of burning, a young woman washed and wiped her face: the towel was all grey from the ashes covering her face, her hair, her clothes. The body and the place melted into a single physical experience of war (Povrzanović 1997: 159).

Previously being used to take a peaceful life

in a modern urban European setting for granted, people enmeshed in war re-considered their links with the surrounding urban structure and re-discovered their essential dependency on nature. There was no relation to priority: spatial and social aspects were united in the violence-imposed intensified experience of the place.

Notes

1. Being a Croatian ethnologist, I was working on the dissertation entitled "Culture and Fear: Wartime Everyday Life in Croatia 1991–92" (University of Zagreb, 1997) in the capacity of research assistant at the Zagreb Institute of Ethnology and Folklore Research. I collected private letters written by people from Zagreb in late 1991, and interviewed women and men of different ages and of different social backgrounds (mostly Croats, but also Serbs) not only from Dubrovnik and the Dubrovnik region, but also from Vukovar, Županja, Vinkovci surroundings, Osijek, Zadar, Šibenik and Zagreb in the period from 1991 to 1996. See Povrzanović 1997 for an analysis of the processes of identity formation in war based on the same material. If not otherwise noted, the ethnographic details presented in this article come from the personal narratives about war by people from Dubrovnik and the Dubrovnik region collected in early 1996.
2. My interview partners have been united in recognising war loot in its classical form of material goods as being one of the reasons for the attacks. Many also feared that the irregular groups of plunderers that followed the Yugoslav Army to the occupied territories might pay night visits to the still unoccupied parts of the region. Ivo Goldstein shows that plundering was approved of by the Yugoslav state: "in the first days of the aggression Montenegrin television included in its news an appeal by Montenegrin school hostels to be sent several hundreds pairs of trainers from the Dubrovnik area" (Goldstein 1999: 235).
3. Slavoj Žižek (1999) defines "reflexive", politically correct racism as "the liberal, multiculturalist perception of the Balkans as a site of ethnic horrors and intolerance, of primitive, tribal, irrational passions, as opposed to the reasonableness of post-nation-state conflict resolution by negotiation and compromise. Racism is a disease of the Balkan Other, while we in the West are merely observers, neutral, benevolent and righteously dismayed". Because the Balkans are part of Europe, they can be spoken of in racist clichés which nobody would dare to apply to Africa or Asia. Political struggles in the Balkans are compared to ridiculous operetta plots; Ceausescu was presented as a contemporary reincarnation of Count Dracula. Slovenia is most exposed to this displaced racism, explains Žižek, since it is closest to Western Europe. He also points to "reverse racism" which celebrates the exotic authenticity of the Balkan Other, as in the notion of Serbs who, in contrast with inhibited, anaemic Western Europeans, still exhibit a prodigious lust for life (cf. Port 1997). Žižek claims that such reverse racism plays a crucial role in the success of Emir Kusturica's films in the West. "When Kusturica, talking about his film *Underground*, dismissed the Slovenes as a nation of Austrian grooms, nobody reacted: an 'authentic' artist from the less developed part of former Yugoslavia was attacking the most developed part of it. When discussing the Balkans, the tolerant multiculturalist is allowed to act out his repressed racism" (Žižek 1999).
4. *Europe* – in the Croatian public and vernacular discourse most often referred to in a personified way – is *good* also for its political stability and standards of living. Besides, liberal and left-wing politicians do not just want to be "considered European" and "given what is deserved", i.e. be valued as equals in relation to Western Europeans; they also want to establish "European" – democratic – standards in Croatian politics.
5. For a comprehensive insight in Croatian history see Goldstein 1999. For an analysis of the perception and active efforts in establishing cultural boundaries towards "the Balkans" see Povrzanović Frykman 2002.
6. See Ines Prica's "Notes on ordinary life in war" (1993) for an illuminated insight into the Croatian intellectuals' dilemma regarding the writing on and within the war, questioning the value of "fighting with the pen", as well as of the already ironized "writing for eternity". In one of the best ethnographic pieces about the war in Croatia in 1990's (for a complete bibliography see Povrzanović 2000), Prica analyses different kinds of letters and appeals sent abroad (always westwards), and the political conditioning of the (non)reactions to them. "The general point of these reactions is the priority of the grief over monumental and cultural richness before the misery of people", states Prica, claiming that such reactions were following the dominant Western official treatments of aggression as "culture-cide". "The most controversial is the case of Dubrovnik, which evidently was, with the help of the world, saved from total destruction as 'walls', not as a human settlement" (Prica 1993: 47).
7. Place becomes social because it is already cultural. For the same reason it is also historical. It is by the mediation of culture that places gain historical depth. We might even say that culture is the third dimension of place, affording them a deep historicity, a *longue durée*, which they would lack if they were entirely natural in constitution (Casey 1993:31f.).

8. A theatre director wrote about the conviction that Dubrovnik "would serve as a refuge from warfare, would exclude us, with our unquestioned pedigree, from the horrors which descended upon unlucky regions of Croatia. (...) Have we been able to perceive its soul, we would have understood that the refinement of its shape had to be hurt, the nobility of its structure maimed and the finesse of the carved stone, chipped" (Violić 2000: 16).
9. Paradoxically, the first civilian killed in Dubrovnik (by a shell that landed in his own flat) was a Dubrovnik poet who happened to be a Serb. At the same time, the attackers were aiming at their victims' ethnic affiliation (Povrzanović 1997: 160).
10. Therefore, many people from the Dubrovnik region talked about their own emotional affiliation to the towns undergoing war-histories similar to their own. They could very well imagine – or rather, they *knew* – what it was like to live in Sarajevo under siege. Interestingly enough, the Sarajevo situation, generally seen as much worse than theirs, was often a reason for embarrassment: their experiences were "nothing" in comparison to Sarajevans'; they were not worth telling, since someone else had it so much worse. Hence a double embarrassment for being called "heroes" in the national discourse on *Dubrovnik, the hero-town*.
11. Such a "solution" had been feared during the war in 1991–92, and bitterly criticised by the outstanding Croatian intellectual Vlado Gotovac: "Dubrovnik has been hit by the sentimentality of pragmatism. In the name of beauty, but in a trivial manner. Incapable of comprehending the whole, of comprehending its context and meaning, it ignores even the suburban landscape. (...) From a pragmatic point of view it is incomparably easier to save Dubrovnik in isolation than in a perspective and with the ties of its whole survival. Nobody's Dubrovnik is a toy for international safekeeping…" (Gotovac 2000: 10).
* This is a revised version of the paper "När våldet tar plats", published in *Fönster mot Europa*, Studentlitteratur, Lund 2001.

References

Bettiza, Enzo 1996: *Egzil*. Milano: Hefti.
Casey, Edward S. 1993: *Getting Back into Place. Toward a Renewed Understanding of the Place-World*. Bloomington and Indianapolis: Indiana University Press.
Foretić, Miljenko (ed.) 2000: *Dubrovnik in War*. Dubrovnik: Matica Hrvatska Dubrovnik.
Frykman, Jonas 1998: "Introduction". In: J. Frykman, N. Seremetakis and S. Ewert (eds): *Identities in Pain*. Lund: Nordic Academic Press, pp. 9–18.
Goldstein, Ivo 1999: *Croatia: A History*. London. Hurst & Company.
Gotovac, Vlado 2000: "The Defence of Dubrovnik". In: M. Foretić (ed.): *Dubrovnik in War*. Dubrovnik: Matica Hrvatska Dubrovnik, pp. 7–11.
Green, Nicholas 1997: "Looking at the Landscape. Class Formation and the Visual". In: E. Hirsch and M. O'Hanlon (eds): *The Anthropology of Landscape. Perspectives on Place and Space*. Oxford: Clarendon Press, pp. 31–42.
Hirsch, Eric 1997: "Landscape: Between Place and Space". In: E. Hirsch, and M. O'Hanlon (eds): *The Anthropology of Landscape. Perspectives on Place and Space*. Oxford: Clarendon Press, pp. 1–30.
Jackson, Michael 1995: *At Home in the World*. Durham and London: Duke University Press.
Lang, Slobodan 1997: *Dnevnik Libertas. Dubrovački ratni zapisi*. Zagreb: Pegaz.
Maroević, Tonko 2000: "Dubrovnik Besieged". In: M. Foretić (ed.): *Dubrovnik in War*. Dubrovnik: Matica Hrvatska Dubrovnik, pp. 76–79.
Massey, Doreen 1994: *Space, Place and Gender*. Cambridge: Polity Press.
Nodari, Maja 1994: Spaljena kuća – mjesto sudbine. *Dubrovački horizonti* 34:223–224.
Port, Mattijs van de 1998. *Gypsies, Wars & Other Instances of the Wild*. Amsterdam: Amsterdam University Press.
Povrzanović, Maja 1997: Identities in War: Embodiments of Violence and Places of Belonging. *Ethnologia Europaea* 27: 153–162.
Povrzanović, Maja 2000: The Imposed and the Imagined as Encountered by Croatian War Ethnographers. *Current Anthropology* 41(2): 151–162.
Povrzanović Frykman 2002: "Establishing and dissolving cultural boundaries: *Croatian culture* in diasporic contexts". In: S. Resic and B. Törnquist-Plewa (eds): *Cultural Boundaries in Europe: The Balkans in Focus*. Lund: Nordic Academic Press, forthcoming.
Prica, Ines 1993: "Notes on ordinary life in war". In: L. Čale Feldman, I. Prica and R. Senjković (eds): *Fear, Death and Resistance. An Ethnography of War: Croatia 1991–92*. Zagreb: Institute of Ethnology and Foklore Research, Matrix Croatica, X-Press, pp. 44–71.
Šehović, Feda 1994: *Dubrovački ratni dnevnik*. Zagreb: Bil Commerce.
Tangherlini, Timothy R. 1999: "Remapping Koreatown: Folklore, Narrative and the Los Angeles Riots". In: T. R. Tangherlini (ed.): *Built L.A. Folklore and Place in Los Angeles*. Special Issue of *Western Folklore* 58: 149–173.
Violić, Božidar 2000: "Harshness vs. Harmony". In: M. Foretić (ed.): *Dubrovnik in War*. Dubrovnik: Matica Hrvatska Dubrovnik, pp. 15–20.
Zglav, Niko 1995: Ratni dnevnik Nika Zglava. *Dubrovački horizonti* 35: 144–149.
Zidić, Igor 2000: "The Siege of Dubrovnik and the City's Wounds (Letter to and Italian Friend)". In: M. Foretić (ed.): *Dubrovnik in War*. Dubrovnik: Matica Hrvatska Dubrovnik, pp. 59–63.
Žižek, Slavoj 1999. "You May!". *London Review of Books*, March 18th 1999. http://www.lrb.co.uk/v21/n06/zize01_.html

The Politics of Cultural Heritage

An Urban Approach

Michi Knecht & Peter Niedermüller

> Knecht, Michi & Peter Niedermüller 2002: The Politics of Cultural Heritage: An Urban Approach. – Ethnologia Europaea 32:2:89–104.
>
> The paper addresses the performance and display of cultural heritage in context of late modern urban culture. Contemporary metropolises constitute core settings for the political and symbolic representation of cultural diversity and multiculturalism. One of the most important forms of such representation is the "ethnic" or "multi-ethnic" festival. The Carnival of Cultures in Berlin is analysed as an example and compared to the much more prominent Notting Hill Carnival. The paper concludes that "ethnic" cultural heritage has strong social and political components which should be made central in ethnological analysis.
>
> *Michi Knecht, Dr., Institut für Europäische Ethnologie, Humboldt Universität zu Berlin, Schiffbauerdamm 19, D-10117 Berlin. E-mail: Michi.Knecht@rz.hu-berlin.de*
> *Professor Peter Niedermüller, Dr., Institut für Europäische Ethnologie, Humboldt Universität zu Berlin, Schiffbauerdamm 19, D-10117 Berlin.*
> *E-mail: Peter.Niedermueller@rz.hu-berlin.de*

In his introduction to the volume "Detraditionalization" the English sociologist Paul Heelas provides a condensed overview of current research in the uses of tradition, history, and cultural heritage (Heelas 1996). He distinguishes two dominant stances in the way cultural and social studies tend to think about the forms and functions of tradition and cultural heritage in the global world of late capitalism we experience today. The *radical thesis* accentuates the erosion and decline of tradition, "the radical turn from tradition" (Giddens 1991: 175–176). Here, modernity is construed as the opposite of traditional order. Modern societies are per definition and characteristically seen as "post-traditional". The other perspective, the *coexistence thesis* does not talk about a ceasing of traditions so much but rather stresses the simultaneity of divergent movements: Detradi-tionalization in this view always takes place by way of a complex process which simultaneously involves the maintenance of traditions, re-traditionalization and the construction of new traditions.

From an ethnographic point of view this approach seems to come closer to what actually happens in European societies today. The re-writing of history, reconstructions of the past and the revitalization of traditions all over Europe go hand in hand with economic globalization and post-industrial modernization. The celebration of newly invented folk traditions as authentic, the display of regional identities and heritages by means of symbolic practices somehow related to an allegedly "common past", the production of legitimacy through languages and practices of conservation and essentialization and the notion that "old" or "original" is an equivalent for "good" – all these strategies have been problematized and more than once been described as practices specific to contemporary societies. In public discourses and everyday language, however, what Paul Heelas calls the *radical thesis* still looms large. Conceptions of cultural heritage as belonging to a certain group of people and as unproblematically referring to a distant past are widespread. Frequently, anthropologists and ethnologists working in contemporary societies are confronted with reflexive traces and implications of cultural heritage concepts that once were developed by disciplines like *Volkskunde* but are by now considered historic by contemporary ethnological disciplines.

Classical ethnological concepts which represented culture as overlapping with notions of group and space and which focused on a spatial articulations of cultural differences, have been abandoned by and large by ethnology and cultural anthropology – but in a variety of contexts they are readopted and obviously considered plausible and convincing. And the "bounded concept of culture" is well and alive in what Barbara Kirshenblatt-Gimblett has depicted as "the cultural heritage industry": a commodified and commercially oriented "mode of cultural production in the present that has recourse to the past" and that produces and promotes notions "of cultural distinctiveness" and "tradition" (Kirshenblatt-Gimblett 1998: 7). Such revivals indicate, that concepts of culture and cultural heritage are much more than just ethnological approaches or theoretical traditions. They might better be understood as politically and symbolically institutionalized inventions and fundamental fictions of modernity. In this sense, Eriksen (1993: 148) has demonstrated how the bounded concept of culture went along well with one of the most central and "mythical" principles of modernity, that "of the integrated and bounded individual, who is presumed to be a member of 'a culture' who lives his or her life as a continuous, directed person" (ibid.: 148). And Liisa Malkki recently painted a portrait of ethnological and anthropological discourses about culture that showed them to be direct reflections of the mental and cultural basis of the nation-state (1997). She referred to different symbolic constructions and metaphors – like 'roots', 'father-land', 'motherland', and 'soil' – which reflect a "metaphysical sedentarism" in scholarly and in political contexts, and convincingly demonstrate how these constructions and metaphors create a culturally coded cognitive system by means of which people categorize the surrounding social world, and divide it into 'home' and 'alien', 'ours' and 'theirs'.

To us it seems quite clear that dominant notions of "cultural heritage" today can and should be analyzed as a symbolic continuation to these older concepts. Like them, the contemporary concepts of cultural heritage must be seen as symbolic constructions which territorialize cultural differences and which play an important role in the symbolic formation of regions, nations and supranational entities like the EU.[1] But we also have to rethink the links between cultural heritage and the present. European ethnology and cultural anthropology today are faced with contradictory challenges and transformations that are constitutive for our time. Migration and new forms of mobility have created a social and cognitive field, which exemplifies the political effects and symbolic consequences of "multiple rooting", of simultaneity of distinct social and cultural times. What we can observe today, especially in urban settings, is not "one cultural heritage", but a multitude of "possible" cultural heritages in constant exchange and flow. In the context of current globalization and transnationalism, urban – or for that matter any – culture can't be simply defined or understood with reference to "heritage" or "tradition" (Hannerz 1992: 218).

We therefore suggest to think about cultural heritage as the social production of the here and now, the result of symbolic and political conflicts over the presentation or representation of minority and majority groups, the outcome of symbolic negotiations referring to self-definitions of different social groups, and a political process of exclusion and inclusion which turns cultural differences into social boundaries. Cultural heri-tage, in this perspective, is a social and political production emerging in particular social situations in order to be able to "respond to the changing material conditions, semiotic codes, power relations, and relations among groups shaping a specific time and place" (Smith 1992: 512–513). In this sense, we argue for an understanding of cultural heritage as a provisional, historically conditioned conceptual and symbolic space, in which divergent cultural pasts and cultural differences are negotiated.

In what follows, we will show how "multi-ethnic" heritage events have acquired specific meanings in the context of contemporary transformations of urban culture, city marketing and the politics of urban space. We shall argue that contemporary European cities not only

The Carnival of Cultures as key symbol of a specific "multicultural milieu". Float sponsored by the broadcasting station *Radio Multikulti*. Berlin May 2002. Photo: Michi Knecht.

give ample proof of the coexistence of de-, re- and neo-traditionalization, but also of the side-by-side existence of different cultures and "possible" cultural heritages, no longer exclusively or even predominantly defined as regional, local or national, but as ethnic, multi-ethnic and multicultural as well. Taking the Carnival of Cultures in Berlin as our ethnographic example, we proceed to explore how cultural heritage is construed as a marker for ethnic groups, and how, in the form of "multicultural abundance" it figures as an important resource in the city's economy. The display of "multi-ethnic" cultural heritages in the streets of Berlin-Kreuzberg is shaped by strategies of commodification and politicization that both have implications for who gets involved and who gets excluded. Finally, we will try to sketch how the production and display of cultural heritage in "multi-ethnic" urban settings can be understood as a mode of social reproduction of groups as well as group relations and as a specific form of social capital.

Cultural Heritage Projects in Contemporary European Cities

Contemporary metropolises are privileged places for the study of social change. Having grown through industrialization and migration and today often serving as coordination points in increasingly globalized economic networks, they cannot possible be symbolized as places of unbroken continuity or authentic simplicity. Turning to the specific urban ways of displaying and promoting cultural heritage, we suggest to locate them theoretically in what Sharon Zukin has called the "new symbolic economy of cities" (see Zukin 1995), an unprecedented expansion and commodification of the "culture-generating capabilities of cities" (Scott 2000:14). The historical context for such a new cultural economy in urban centers is marked by the transformation from fordist to postfordist forms of production and consumption. Its main implications for the relationship between culture and economy include "changing consumer tastes and demands involving a general aestheticization and semioticization of marketable products" and, related to this, changing identity politics; an increase in services and goods that "trade on the basis of short- or medium-term fashion, information, and entertainment value, and on their merits as social markers" (ibid.: 6) and "new possibilities for inter-city differentiation" as well as "vertical disintegration" (ibid.: 7). While traditional neighbourhoods and social milieus dissolve, cities get simultaneously engaged in the deliberate creation of cultural-historical packages and marketable pastiches in which a more or less playful arrangement of historical and cultural elements is used to produce what are supposed to be attractive, pleasant and uplifting environments (Kirshenblatt-Gimblett 1998: 155). This entails not only urban redevelopment projects and gentrification, but also spectacles and events

Sound system at Notting Hill Carnival, August 2002, getting prepared. Photo: Michi Knecht.

created with the intention to attract tourism, "one of the few growth industries in late capitalist coun-tries" which relies more and more on the "marketing of distinctive cultures to bring in visitors" (Welford, 1998: 5).

The role of cultural heritage in the pervasive processes of symbolic and economic commodification is an important and substantive one and entails two dominant forms of urban heritage production: (a) local/national historical heritage; (b) ethnic heritages. The local/national heritage is represented as "history" and "past" inscribed in the architectural and spatial body of the city. It sustains and monumentalises the alleged permanence of the nation state or symbolizes the particular flair of the local. Ethnic heritages, in contrast, are always performed heritages. Staged as aesthetic phenomena and activities based on the expressive capacities of ethnic groups, this form of cultural heritage is often displayed to symbolize the coexistence of diverse cultures and the heterogeneity of the city, simultaneously emphasizing difference and constructing "otherness". Both forms of urban cultural heritage practices work together in emphasizing the uniqueness and attractiveness of specific cities and in culturalizing social conflicts.

The last decades have seen a marked increase of public urban festivals or spectacles in which a diversity of cultural heritages or "multi-ethnic heritages" – specific musical genres and styles, dances, costumes, ethnic foods and arts, etc. – are displayed and celebrated. Multi-ethnic concoctions seem to have become a valuable asset of urban regions, promising fun, displaying the exotic and strange, ensuring the picturesque and the colourful. These spectacles are the place, where the different and distinct populations of a city can meet and where the growing and distinct multiculturality of a city finds an expression: "Global nomads" – businessmen, artists, intellectuals and tourists – who roam around the world, and represent the voice of infinite, pleasurable consumption, the "voice of exotic cuisine" (Hall 1994: 56) encounter migrants, their second and third generation offspring and refugees, all of whom looking for new geographical places and social localities free from exclusion and discrimination. At multiethnic festivals, migrants and "global nomads" celebrate with, or are watched by the "native" population of the cities, the people "at home" (Niedermüller 1998).

Often, "multi-ethnic" heritage festivals like the multicultural "Stadtteilkulturwochen" in the "Gallus", a former working-class district of Frankfurt/Main (Welz 1992, 1994, 1996) start in economically depressed periods or city quarters, in which social problems are conceived by the dominant discourse as "ethnic problems" or as generated through the presence of certain ethnic groups. The display of cultural heritage then functions as an instrument in urban renewal and gentrification. As such, it is directed at harmonizing social antagonisms and at the same time at transforming those parts of the city, in which these festivals are staged, into "symbolic urban landscapes", aestheticised for the consumer interests of old and new urban middle classes. Another important function of urban ethnic festivals is the reproduction and presentation of differences between cultural heritages – between "our" national and "their" ethnic heritage. Recently, however, there is a second symbolic construction emerging, which is closely connected to the new economic position of culture as a primary resource for production and to a shift in the public discourse about migration and migrants. Here, "multiethnic-cultures" are fantasized as a much needed and potentially unlimited raw material, which must be put to use for the revitalization and the future of cities. In spite of local differences and regional or national peculiarities a number of general features that new "multi-ethnic" urban festivals commonly exhibit, can be detected. In her research on the representation of cultural diversity in German and American cities, Gisela Welz has shown that the genre "multi-ethnic" festival operates with a set of standardized rules or strategies, all aimed at displaying foreign cultural heritages in the mode of "staged authenticity" (Welz 1996) The genre and its organizers select forms of cultural heritage particularly well suited for display. Expressive, demonstrable and colourful forms are preferred: moreover, they need to be unambiguously assignable to particular ethnic groups. A certain style of dance such as flamenco, or a musical genre like salsa or classical Indian music is thus equated with a specific ethnic group. That is arts, musical styles and genres, handicrafts all get constructed as belonging to the timeless, static and somehow traditional cultural heritage a certain ethnic group "has" and "brings with it".[2] A further strategy of display identified by Welz is the comparability of the diverse elements brought to stage. While, on the one hand, differences between single performances or performing groups are strongly emphasized – thereby maximizing the appearance of variety and diversity – the webs of meaning and cultural practices to which these forms normally belong are all made invisible and ignored. In this way, the display of "multi-ethnic" heritages as a colourful string or sequence of varied performances is achieved. It is dependent on a perspective "from above", Welz concludes, a viewpoint located beyond, rather than entangled in the experience of difference (cf. Welz 1996).

While the forms of display, which can be found in multicultural urban festivals, follow certain standards and genres, the motives of participants and organizers are heterogeneous and diverse. They might encompass a professional interest in the promotion of certain "ethnic" ways of dancing, music making or costumes; a wish to humanise the city and to create new ritual forms of being together and belonging; fights for recognition and demonstrations against racism, very self-conscious attempts to define "a local identity in the face of globalisation" and europeanisation, mundane economic interests or a love of spectacles, entertainment and partying (Welford 1998). But it is important to see what sets the limits to such motives and

"Our Heritage". Ironic ensemble of "Russian heritage" packed in sacks, on a float designed by the Cultural Centre *Club Dialog*. Karneval der Kulturen Berlin, May 2002. Photo: Michi Knecht.

goals: we argue that it is precisely the genre (which privileges the display of comparable entities and distinct ethnic heritages and selects only certain "traditions" and "cultural elements" as cultural heritage, repressing or making invisible others) and its rules of commodification that to a large extent confine the interests of social movements and specific groups in their struggle for visibility.

Karneval der Kulturen – or Urban Summer Carnival in Berlin

Walking along Gneisenaustrasse in Berlin-Kreuzberg on Whitsun Sunday, both sides of the street and the surrounding areas are densely packed with people watching the parade of the *Karneval der Kulturen*. The mood along the route is relaxed and orderly. The crowd on the street today – groups of young people, visiting and watching the carnival with friends, families with prams from nearby neighbourhoods, couples of apparently mixed ethnic background, tourists – appears to be even more diverse than on a normal weekday, with maybe one major exception: people from Turkish communities don't seem to be particularly interested in the event.[3] A few spectators have put on heavy make-up or face paintings, others display certain accessories – unusual hats, rhythm instruments, a feather – as signs of their carnevalesque solidarity, but they are clearly outnumbered by people with video or photo cameras and the most common visitor quite obviously wears no signs of fancy dress at all.

The parade – called "Karawane" by it's organizers – is basically made up of groups of dancers and live musicians in costumes, elaborating on a chosen theme or *"playin' mas"* as it is called in Caribbean carnival traditions, alternating with huge floats and decorated trucks on which sound systems with DJs or live musicians are installed. Roughly speaking, the parade presents three distinguishable categories of bands and projects: The first group performs or displays all sorts of "ethnic", sometimes also religious or regional "heritages" – for example, Anatolian fertility dances, costumes from the Peruvian Andes, Mexican Mariachi music, a Kurdish wedding, Fandango, Cumbia, Merecum-

Queen of the group *Burrokeets UK,* performing their 2002 *mas* theme *"So Dey Say"*. Notting Hill Carnival 2002. Photo: Michi Knecht.

bès and Salsa from Columbia, Voodoo rituals from Benin, a Hindu puja ceremony, Brasilian Capoiera and traditional Croatian folk music. Their organizers and sponsors cover a wide spectrum, reaching from private or corporate businesses to political or social minority organizations to professional dance, martial arts or music schools. Side by side with these, a second group of participants represents sociopolitical projects, queer initiatives, artists, theatre people and pedagogic institutions in the youth sector that identify positively and explicitly with concepts of multiculturality,[4] many of them publicly funded or subsidized. The third group – normally lumped together at the end of the parade – is made up of sound systems with a youth- und subcultural music orientation (Techno, Drum'n Bass, Reggae, Hip Hop, House, Djungle, Garage, Trance), sponsored by clubs, record labels or music agencies. While the parade is on, performers and audience are rather clearly divided with spectators, who might dance, clap their hands, wave or whistle to show their appreciation, being more static and the bands moving on. But that distinction tends to collide at the end of the parade, when the sound systems draw large followings into the parade and revellers might get ecstatic and wild.

The Parade on Whitsun Sunday is the major feature of the *Karneval der Kulturen*. It is accompanied by a children's carnival one week earlier, a costume and performance contest, a three-day street fair with four open-air stages (dedicated to "Euro-Asian", "Latin-American", "Oriental" and "African" music styles and traditions), pre and post-parade parties like the "Long Night of Sound Systems", and stalls where food (everything from *Döner* to *Bratwurst*), drinks (margaritas and beer) and handicrafts are sold and where different political groups, independent ethnic associations and social movement projects inform about their work. All in all, the carnival clearly is an occasion for entertainment and fun rather than politics or protest, it is musically dominated by samba groups and other "Latin" styles (also this might be debated), more popular with the young than with other generations and still slightly less commercial than comparable public events, like the street ravers' "Love Parade" or the gay and lesbian "Christopher Street Day".[5] For American anthropologist John Borneman, who describes the Carnival of Cultures as part of "Berlin's summer trilogy of parades", the overall atmosphere is marked by "public nudity", a "transparent exhibition of desires and political aims" and "a mixed display of sexuality and 'primitiveness'". Even though it declares to present a maximum of cultural diversity, he sees the carnival therefore as distinctly "Berlinian" (Borneman 2001: 8).

The very short history of the carnival in Berlin spans only seven years but it is already an object of contest and conflict. Several cultural and social projects associated with the alternative milieu of "old" West Berlin are lining up for the role of "inventor" or "founder". In 1996, the "Ufa-Fabrik", one of Berlin's largest and oldest collective resident communities and social-cultural experiments played an important role, but right from the start the festival was organized by "Werkstatt der Kulturen", a publicly funded multicultural project that describes itself as a "centre for Berlins various ethnic, religious and cultural communities" and a "culturally and politically undiscriminating platform for artists, intellectuals and independent associations".[6]

Since 1996, when the Carnival of Cultures in Berlin started as a rather small, Kreuzberg and Neukölln based community celebration, it has developed into a large urban festival, watched each year by several hundred thousand visitors, respectfully and in great detail attended to by the media, sponsored by the city as well as by local and global businesses and engulfed by broad public sympathy. But this "success story" is not specific or unique to Berlin. Rather, it is part and consequence of a remarkable expansion of carnival festivities since the 1960s (cf. Knecht 2002) that introduced a new form of summer carnival into cities in Europe, North America and Australia, cities that previously did not have any carnival tradition of their own. The new carnivals were inspired by Caribbean carnival genres and traditions that feature a number of distinct cultural performances, such as "*mas*" and "*playin' mas*".[7] They owe a great deal to two historical processes: "First the movement of populations, both European and African, across the Atlantic",[8] and second, the Caribbean migration to Europe, Canada and the United States since the 1950s. In the course of these movements not only populations, but also ideas, knowledge and customs "shifted across the world, mingled and hybridized".[9] The historic trajectory of the new Caribbean inspired carnivals demonstrates this intermingling and traveling of ideas and practices. Carnival elements, that were brought to the new World by French and Spanish settlers, got picked up and reinvented by black slaves during the 19th century, made into a symbol of black liberation and then moved back to European cities with the West Indian migrants after World War II (cf. Nurse 1999). The most well known and largest of the new Caribbean inspired summer events is the Notting Hill Carnival in Kensington/West London, which shows a very strong impact of Trinidadian carnival traditions and which is celebrated annually during August bank holiday since the early 1960s (Cohen 1993, Manning

Folk Dances performed on stage at the Children's Carnival of Culture, Berlin 2002. Photo: Levent Soysal.

1990, Welford 1998, Melville 2002). Comparable carnivals were approximately at the same time founded in New York, Toronto and Miami and they have since then spread to many regions of Great Britain,[10] and to other European cities.

In these context of these developments, the Berlin Carnival of Cultures is one of the most recent. It could be called a newly invented tradition after an invented tradition, because it is modelled after, or at least inspired by, the example of the Notting Hill Carnival in London. It is organized by two professional experts for the representation of cultural difference, one of them an ethnologist. Both came to the "Werkstatt der Kulturen" as trainees in a course of further education that prepared academics for jobs in the field of public relations and event management. "At the 'Werkstatt'", they state in an interview, "the idea for a carnival was already in the air. (…) We wanted to have a carnival in Berlin like the one in Notting Hill or Rio". The new carnival according to their concept was right from the beginnung supposed to represent "the diversity of cultures" in Berlin. "All migrant groups should unite in a big festival". (*Der Tagesspiegel*, 2. 6. 2001: 11)

While the Carnival of Cultures is advertised and marketed primarily as a "multi-ethnic" carnival, "a unique opportunity for ethnic communities to make their respective cultures – both traditional and modern – visible to Berliners and visitors alike"[11] – it simultaneously declares and practices an explicit openness towards new trends and styles in youth and minority cultures and subcultures. The potential to draw together different and often conflicting groups or positions seems to be a historical legacy of carnival as a cultural form. In cultural anthropology and folklore studies, there has been a long and rich theoretical debate on how to interpret carnival and other rituals in which authority is mocked or reversed (see, for example, Schindler 1984, Moser 1986, Hauschild 1994, Gluckman 1963, Turner 1988, da Matta 1991, Nunley 1988, van Koningsbruggen 1997, 2000, Miller 1994, Handelman 1990), as a privileged space for rebellion and change or as a – "safety valve" which ultimately always affirms and supports the power of those in power. For Cohen, "every major carnival is precariously poised between the affirmation of the established order and its rejection" (Cohen 1993:3). Herzfeld emphasizes the symbolic space that is provided by this contradictory structure: "It is here that people can explore the tension, inherent in the fact that they belong to a community, yet may not share equally in its benefits." (Herzfeld 2001: 211). Arnaud (2001: 2) is more sceptical: For him, carnival is "a place of negotiation where the positions of resistance are strategic and themselves enabled by the structures of power." Murray's advice, to refrain from positions that analyse carnival as structurally and universally determined, is plausible here (Murray 2000: 103). He agrees, that carnival generally is a site in which symbolic tensions are expressed, but sees its social impact as neither "inherently revolutionary nor repressive". What the carnival means and does for different people will in significantly different ways ultimately depend on specific cultural, political and economic contexts (Murray 2000: 104) and may remain symbolically open. However, as a site of symbolic tension and problematic politics, the new carnivals seem especially well equipped to evoke concepts of multiculturality. Notions of multiculturality should not only be understood as harmonizing strategies but also as attempts to redefine the social question after the end of the industrial form of capitalism (see Wieviorka 1998: 112). This double function may help to explain their success. Summer carnivals may themselves be understood as events that simultaneously evoke concepts of multiculturality, regulate and manage the complexities of urban heterogeneity (cf. Arnaud 2001), and culturalize social differences.

Multi-ethnic Heritage, the Politics of Place, and the Construction of "the Other"

To understand the meanings and functions of the Carnival of Cultures in Berlin in its political and commodified dimensions, it is necessary to re-conceptualize it in the context of what Sharon Zukin called the two main related "production systems" of the urban symbolic economy in late capitalist societies. "The production of space, with its synergy of capital investment and cultural meanings, and the production of symbols, which constructs both a currency of commercial exchange and a language of social identity." (Zukin 1995: 24). *Karneval der Kulturen* participates in the production and redefinition of urban space as well as in that of social identities. It infuses public space with new images of "multiculturality", incorporating them into the visual representation of the city. And it partakes – together with other practices and displays of order – in the construction of a public taxonomy, that defines membership in "ethnic" or "cultural" groups in terms of characteristics that can be performed or/and commodified in order to belong. In the Carnival of Cultures, both production systems intersect.

Like many other summer carnivals, *Karneval der Kulturen* ranks high among the public performances "that have injected new energy and interest into urban life" (Manning 1990: 20). The making of a place for it was framed by public discourses that remodelled not only the public image of Kreuzberg, but also that of Berlin as the new capital city. Kreuzberg, a "mythical" district (cf. Lang 1995, Lang 1998) in the shadow of the wall was until unification known as West-Berlin's laboratory for alternative and multicultural lifestyles, for a unique mix of sub-cultural opportunities and migrant cultures, but in no way as a place of interest for capital investment or politics. When the wall came down, the district suddenly found itself in the position of being very close to the new centre of the unified city. This reconfiguration of space led for a short time during the early nineties to a discourse of "symbolic gentrification" (Lang), forecasting an aesthetic uplifting and fast rising land prices. But this did not occur in any large scale until today. While intense waves of gentrification and property speculation have swept through the inner city districts of former East Berlin,[12] Kreuzberg is pretty much left to itself. With some of its former attractiveness gone, especially for the current generation of young and hip people who tend to flock to "neue Mitte", today the district is still unique in its mixture, but publicly talked about more for its social problems, high rates of unemployment and difficult school situation. In this context, the *Karneval der Kulturen* has had some significance for reconnecting Kreuzberg with images of youthfulness, dynamism and change. The broad media coverage of the carnival infused the district with pictures of a vital and abundant multiculturalism, which is applauded by politicians and admired by local and multinational business investors alike and which eclipses the district's long standing reputation as a stronghold of radical anti-capitalist politics.

But the carnival was not only used to renovate the image of Kreuzberg. From the very beginning it was also advertised – side by side with the Love Parade and the Brandenburg Gate – as one of the central brand names of the "New Berlin": For this newly developed and internationally marketable image of post-unification Berlin as "open city", "dynamic metropolis" and "fun loving capital", the Carnival of Cultures was a real asset. When it was first performed in 1996, Berlin was struggling hard to come to terms with a shrinking budget, the de-industrialization of the East, growing social polarization and a new but as yet undefined economic role. Additional pressure emerged as reports about xenophobia, racism and people attacked or even killed in rightwing attacks especially in the outskirts of Belin and the new *Bundesländer* reached the international public. In this situation, "Partner for Berlin", a public-private-partnership between the city council and about a hundred major business firms, could sell the Carnival of Cultures on high gloss paper and in multi-coloured print as "a four-day long spectacle (….) which contributes to diminishing ignorance and arrogance so often directed towards foreign worlds of thought and feeling" and which will "attract tourists and increase the turnover of Berlin's retail shops".[13] The press coverage, too, has been exceedingly positive and it is almost impossible to find any critical edge. In accordance with the much hoped for image of Berlin as a tolerant and dynamic metropolis, the Carnival is described as heady mix and site of fun. While the yellow press focuses on the exotic, the picturesque and the erotic,[14] daily newspapers from liberal to conservative praise the carnival as "platform for minorities", "colourful, varied, surprising",[15] "a stroke of luck for the City", allowing "the new capital" to "show its friendly face",[16] a proof that "living together multiculturally can be fun"[17] and that the – "integration of foreign co-citizens has been successful".[18]

As Germany rewrites its history, representing itself no longer as a mono-ethnic national state but as an open, "multi-ethnic" organisation, all prepared and ready for Europe, the Carnival of Cultures is portrayed as something profoundly "good", potent enough to counter reports about racist attacks. The cultural heritage of "ethnic" groups is symbolized as a fountain of youth, a resource that will not run dry, but relentlessly fuel the economy. "That is what the new dynamic Berlin looks like" says the caption under a huge newspaper photograph of a black man, whose face is painted with big white strokes and who wears shell necklaces and feathers, while dancing at the Carnival of Cultures. It is ironic, but also disturbing, that comparable pictures were used a century ago to advertise colonial exhibitions in Berlin (see Van der Heyden/Zeller 2002).

The official reading of the *Karneval der Kulturen* – promoted by the organizers and repeated in press reporting on the event – is not that it "constructs the other" but that it "reflects Berlin's migrant population".[19] The mirror metaphor, often used in the public representation of foreign cultures,[20] goes hand in hand with a rhetoric of "excavating" hidden treasures and of "bringing to light" cultural assets that would otherwise remain forgotten in some marginal space "deep" inside the city.[21] The organisers picture their work as a mere act of "making available" and "putting on stage" heritages, arts and traditions that always already seem to exist as bounded entities prior to their display (see Kirshenblatt-Gimblett 1998, Welz 1996). This at least is the version given in the published statements. It veils the power of the genre "multicultural carnival" to define and elicit specific forms and contents of cultural heritage performances that are only produced and created in response to this call. It relegates the contemporary instruments of display, the criteria and devices employed in the process of ultimately commodifying and reifying "heritage", backstage or even makes them completely invisible. The same can be said of the dominant discourse the Carnival team utilizes in equating ethnicity, community and cultural heritage, thereby culturalising the social position of "ethnic" minorities (Baumann 1996).

But there is yet another way in which the Carnival of Cultures actively "others": Through its alliance with a broad, pedagogically oriented form of multiculturalism, that takes it for granted that social conflicts today primarily arise out of cultural difference that could simply be solved were people more tolerant – and implies, that tolerance can be taught - it helps to create a symbolic structure, in which non-compliance with the goals and activities of the carnival is marked as a problematic, uneducated or otherwise inferior position. We have already shown how on the one hand the official discourse about the *Karneval der Kulturen* highlights purportedly "authentic traditions" and heritages, but on the other hand also actively emphasizes and encourages hybrid performances and projects that actively fuse different influences to explore new styles.²² And while the carnival organisers on the one hand use an essentialising language to describe the participating groups, they on the other hand openly reject a similar essentialism when journalists criticize the "multiethnic carnival" as fake, since many or maybe even most of its samba-drummers, vodoo-dancers and kung-fu-fighters are in fact not members of "real ethnic minorities" but "real Germans". The contradictory, but inclusive rhetoric of the organizers contributes to the public image of the carnival as very open and inviting towards all migrant groups and generally to-wards the interested public. Against this background, individuals or groups rejecting this image or refusing to participate find it hard to take up and formulate for themselves a legitimate space in the cities symbolic landscape.

The conspicuous absence of Turks in the ranks of carnival participants as well as spectators is a case in point which has itself been an issue of public debate in Berlin. Often, the staying away of Turks from the parade was explained with Turkish "values and norms" regarding shame and public appearance which supposedly had been "brought" to Germany via migration like a timeless cultural baggage. Carnival creators Anett Szabó und Brigitte Walz suggested in a published talk (*Der Tagesspiegel*, 2.6.2001) that many Turks stayed at home during the carnival because they found the festivity to be "obscene" and because "they are afraid of too much naked skin" (ibid.). This discourse left little space for the social, economic and political situation of migrants or for the possibility, that to participate in the carnival might at all be experienced as an unreasonable demand. It was also totally unsuspecting of the fact, that the carnival itself occupies a specific social place, closer to the young, to lifestyle-oriented groups, and a broad multicultural milieu than to many migrant communities. But something else is apparent here: Discourses about multiculturality are increasingly moral discourses. As such they can itself be used as a resource in social conflicts. In this perspective, the Carnival of Cultures is one of the main symbols of a morally "right" multicultural attitude that has the power to mark any unwillingness to participate as a deficiency. It is a symbolic practice wrought with power and as such part of negotiations referring to the self-definition of different social groups and to a process of exclusion and inclusion, which turns social inequalities into moral positions and cultural differences into social boundaries.

Cultural Heritage between Commodification and Social Exclusion

"Multi-cultural" or "multi-ethnic" urban festivals such as *Karneval der Kulturen* in Berlin always create a public space that is contested and contestable, a field constituted by political, social and economic forces, subject to the play of different interest groups, institutions and actors. But how exactly political, economic and social contexts play together in the creation of such events is always historically specific. Some of the shifts which have taken place in the urban contexts of European summer carnivals in recent decades become apparent when comparing the beginnings of London's Notting Hill Carnival in the early sixties with the start of the Berliner carnival 30 years later. Both carnivals share some common features. But there are also major differences with important implications for the meanings and usages of cultural heritage performance. The historical and political context in London during the 1960s was very different from the situation in which the Carnival started in Berlin. Today, however, the two festivals seem to be subject to comparable influences and as a consequence are becoming more similar in a number of respects.

The Carnival in Notting Hill started in a decade, which has been described as "settling down period" for Caribbean migrants in Great Britain, a period characterized by latent as well as open racism, full employment and the ferment of the "Swinging Sixties" (cf. Cohen 1993, Manning 1990). Notting Hill then was a poor, rather run down working class district with a growing West-Indian population. Abner Cohen has depicted the early Carnival years in Notting Hill as "successes of poly-ethnic diversity" in a working class neighbourhood, with solidarity and festivity reaching across colour lines, drawing people from Ukrainia, Cyprus, India,

Paraphernalia of Rastafarianism on sale at Notting Hill Carnival, 2002. Street vendor at Portobello Road. Photo: Michi Knecht.

the West Indies and other national and ethnic backgrounds together (Cohen 1982). Other sources emphasize the almost therapeutic role the import of Caribbean carnival arts to London – of the *mas* and steel bands of calypso and soca – played for the West Indian diaspora in the early years, building up a common identity and reconnecting people with the culture of their homelands (Melville 2002). Gradually during the seventies and early eighties the event not only grew larger, but also changed its nature. As black consciousness movements and Rastafarianism,[23] riots and anti-racist demonstrations found their way into the carnival, it became a more exclusive expression of black identity which attracted not only people from Notting Hill itself, but from greater London as well and later from all over Britain. The Carnival got political, sometimes violent, unpredictable, and a continuous source of conflict: not only over the meanings of being black in Britain, but also over police strategies, public safety and racist media reporting. "The Carnival broke all the rules" writes novelist Mike Phillips in retrospect about this period "(...) and just as we, the migrants, had been obliged, through the preceding decades, to come to terms with the industrialized patterns of urban life, so London had to begin coming to terms with a model which demanded a symbolic explosion of democracy in its public life. It was, perhaps, the first time I had a clear understanding that we actually possessed the potential to reshape the city (...)"

(Philipps 2001: 62). What – in the terminology of Cohen – had been started as a "local, polyethnic and working class event" got transformed into a "national, exclusively West-Indian and highly politicized occasion" (cf. Cohen 1982, 1993, Manning 1990). During the 80s and increasingly during the 90s the carnival got "contained" (cf. Cohen 1993: 62 ff.). Parts of it's anarchic potential were eroded by increased policing, bureaucratic regulation and growing commercialization. As in Berlin, the economic aspects got ever more important. The increasing commercialisation of the Notting Hill Carnival puts questions of profit and ownership centre stage. As notions of "legitimate possession" are closely aligned with ideas about "heritage" and always need to be historically legitimated, it is not surprising, that the history of the origins of the Carnival in Notting Hill is a sensitive issue and an unresolved dispute, centring on the question whether its original roots in London are "black", "white" or "multi-ethnic".[24] As some of the political activities of the past were being replaced through acts of consume, the changed relationship of culture, economy and politics and its impact on the way people thought about and explained their inner selves, became evident. "The vendor's stalls replace confrontation with political power as a place of important activity in the social life, while the carnival is presented as an indomitable explosion of symbols which individuals endow either with or without signification." (Arnaud 2001: 13). The transformations of the Notting Hill Carnival in the 1980s and increasingly in the 1990s also entailed a shift in what the carnival predominantly signifies: From a representation of black identity in Britain, it was converted – albeit not uncontested – into a symbol for the presentation of multiculturality (cf. Arnaud 2001). In this commutation, the carnival also "marks out Britain's multicultural evolution: an unplanned process Stuart Hall has called"multicultural drift'." (Melville 2002). This reading highlights a genuine reconstruction of "the other" as a less bounded and more hybridised identity and is attributed most often to the styles and orientations that have emerged over the years around the music of the sound systems (ibid.). But this shift also points to developments in consumer stiles and to questions of what can and will be sponsored and sold. Shortly after the 2002 carnival, Chris Mullard, the most recent chairman of the official Notting Hill Carnival Trust, declared: "I hope people will now see the carnival for what it is, a wonderful opportunity to project the multiculturalism that is metropolitan London, and I hope they will sign up to sponsor it und fund it fully" (*The Guardian* 27.8.2002). However, there is also a certain unbroken vitality, best exemplified by the fact that the carnival is still heavily and publicly contested. While some feel, it got "handed over to the authorities" who "are now defining how the culture is to evolve",[25] others are proud of and applaud the fact, that the carnival arts – the masquerades, costumes and music – have at last started to find official recognition in Britain's higher arts institutions. Criticism of the selling out of the carnival is voiced by independent music groups and new styles of music are developed that put forward images of combination and mixtures of heritage that symbolize innovation and originality. At the same time, it is especially active musicians, dancers and people from the *mas* bands and sound systems who underline the existential need for a carnival compatible with business interest and a wide sponsorship in order to keep the carnival going. From the perspective of social actors in the carnival, the ways in which the event can be used have been narrowed down – and pluralized.

These developments point to a central and fundamentally contradictory situation of late capitalist societies: on the one hand, the politically motivated demand for cultural assimilation and social integration; on the other hand, the "consumer-need" for cultural diversity and ethnic cultures. This discrepancy makes the strong political and social component of "ethnic" cultural heritage apparent. Clearly, the term "ethnic" serves primarily as a means of *social* categorization. Ethnic categorization in contemporary European political and social discours refers to culturally determined social subordination and marginality. Belonging to an ethnic group, or being classified as a member of an

Shademakers, an international active, Germany based, Carnival *Mas* Group founded by Paul McLaren, performing their 2002 theme Games Legacy att Notting Hill Carnival. Photo: Michi Knecht.

ethnic group inevitably indicates a place at the social periphery. As Edwin Wilmsen put it: „dominant groups are never ethnicities, they are in control" (Wilmsen 1996: 4). Socially dominant groups define what cultural heritage is and how cultural heritage should be represented. As a matter of principle subordinated ethnic groups have two options in this situation. On the one hand they are not forced to participate in the cultural heritage industry, they can refuse to join urban festivals, as many Turks in Berlin do. On the other hand, the cultural heritage industry offers possibilities for self-representation and for making money. But if ethnically defined people are "using" the cultural heritage industry, they have to accept its criteria and definitions as it reflects the structuring provided by the dominant groups. This intertwining is, we argue, constitutive for the social and cultural logic of the field of cultural heritage. However, it would be a mistake to think that urban ethnic groups are helpless victims of this strategy of representation. Indeed, one of the most important changes the last decades have seen is precisely that groups defined as "ethnic minorities" have learned how to manage this situation. They get engaged in the search for and the (re)-construction of their "traditional", "original" cultural heritage, their "roots", because they understand the political and social potential inherent in this practice. They recognize that their "cultural heritage" can be turned into symbolic capital – maybe the most valuable capital they can command in the social arena of late capitalist societies. This is a crucial turn in the field of cultural heritage. Cultural heritage has the ability to function as a creative arena for social and political conflicts, where ethnically defined people try to turn their cultural heritage into social practice, and – by means of this practice – try to adapt to or to resist the forces of political and social discrimination.

Notes

*   For help with the translation many thanks to Robin Cackett.
1   For an analysis of cultural heritage as part of official EU strategies aimed at fostering "Europeanisation through mass education and the rewriting of history" see Shore 2000: 56. The "construction of a common cultural heritage" focuses on three dominant symbols: "cultural continuity, moral ascendancy, and 'unity in diversity'" (Shore 2000: 28).
2   This practice of representation very much resembles what Gerd Baumann has described as the rules of the dominant discourse about urban ethnicity in London during the 90s: This discourse entails a reification of culture and cultural heritage, the construction of community on the basis of ethnicity and ultimately a very effective circular argument that equates "culture" and "cultural heritage" with "ethnicity" and "community" (Baumann 1996), thereby reducing anybody's behaviour to a symptom of this equation" (ibid.: 6).
3   With 31% so-called foreigners in its district population (according to the official census of 2000) Kreuzberg is ethnically more diverse than Berlin as a whole. But many German cities have a more mixed population than Berlin (Frankfurt being Germany's most international city with more than 30% of the urban population counted as non-German). In the year 2000, Berlins largest group of "legal" foreigners (128.700) is coming from Turkey; 66.400 from countries within the European Union; 61.200 from former Yugoslavia, 57.700 inhabitants from Asia, mostly Vietnam, 28.600 from Poland, 24.800 from Russia, 15.300 from Africa, 8.100 from Latin-America and 10.400 from the USA. (see *Der Tagesspiegel,* 17th of January 2001: 11).
4   The dominant multicultural discourse is sometimes treated with mild irony, for example by a group called the "Theatre for the Protection of the Species" performing an endangered "Swabian identity", or in the 2001 parade, when boozing punks posed as indigenous "traditional subculture", but it is never explicitly critiqued.
5   The Love Parade is a free for all street rave to techno music, which started in 1988. Today, it has grown into one of Europe's largest mass events (cf. Borneman/Senders 2000). Christopher Street Day is a parade in commemoration of the Stonewall riots in Greenvich Village/New York that evolved into the gay and lesbian liberation movements. Like the Carnival of Cultures, these parades take place annually during the summer months.
6   See their homepage under http://www.werkstatt-der-kulturen.de
7   Mas refers to "unscripted dramatic costume", "manifested and enacted" during the carnival times, most commonly in bands of up to several hundred participants. For an ethnographic case study of "playin' mas" at the Notting Hill carnival, see Alleyne-Dettmars 1998.
8   See Carnival homepage under http://www.shu.ac.uk/schools/cs/teaching/jb2/ch_sem10.htm
9   Ibid.
10 The "UK Carnival Diary 2000" under www.

carnivalnet.org.uk/events/events-main.html lists more than 80 entries for carnivals celebrated during April and September – from the Luton International Carnival ("a traditional English-style parade" which has grown "spectacularly into what the Arts Council calls "the most multicultural event in this country"" (ibid.) to Charivari Day in Folkestone, from Croydon Mela to the "Manchester International Caribbean Carnival".

11 See official Carnival-homepage http://karneval-berlin.de/html/english.html
12 Especially the districts Mitte, Prenzlauer Berg and Friedrichshain, which possessed many run down buildings from the years of rapid industrial expansion in Berlin (1890 to 1920) as well as a reputation as centers for alternative lifestyles and artistic experiments, have been the targets of inner city development (aesthetization, historization, gentrification) in the last years.
13 See: Third issue of the Journal "99/01 – Der Jahrhundertschritt", Berlin, March 2000. Ed. by "Beauftragte des Senats von Berlin für Ausstellungen und Veranstaltungen um das Jahr 2000"; supported by "Partners for Berlin".
14 "Swaying Hips, Sunburn, Sweat", BZ, 20.5.1997.
15 "Bunt, abwechslungsreich und überraschend", *Der Tagesspiegel*, 5.6.2001.
16 *Berliner Kurier*, 5.6.2001.
17 Barbara John, patroness of the event and Berlin's Commissioner for Foreigner's Affair. (Ausländerbeauftragte), quoted by the German press agency DPA, May 5th, 1998.
18 Former speaker of the Green Party and Minister of Justice in Berlin, Wolfgang Wiegand, quoted in Jungle World, 17.6.1998.
19 "Berlins international summer Carnival (…) is a reflection of the city's cultural diversity (…) [and] also a unique opportunity for ethnic communities to make their respective cultures – both traditional and modern – visible to Berliners and visitors alike." See homepage of the Carnival of Cultures, available at http://www.karneval-berlin.de/html/english.html
20 For a thorough analysis of the functions of this metaphor in the work of public folklorists in Germany and the United States of America see Welz (1996).
21 A self portrayal published as a leaflet by "Werkstatt der Kulturen", states: "Die Werkstatt der Kulturen will die verborgenen Schätze der internationalen Künstlerszene heben und den kulturellen Reichtum Berlins erlebbar machen. (…) Berlin bietet dafür ein unerschöpfliches Reservoir."
22 An example of the latter performances are the sound systems on large trucks, which often are accompanied by crowds of followers raving, jumping and dancing for hours. Sound systems are originally West-Indian discos, operated with huge amplifiers and record players by a number of DJs and "toasters", poetry artists that improvise lyrics and social critique (cf. Cohen 1993, 36–37; 99). They developed predominantly around Afro-Caribbean and other black music styles and create sounds in which improvisation, remix, dialog with the audience and social or political critique are essential. For a number of cultural analysts, sound systems are therefore important social spaces for the creation of a "genuine multiculture" (Melville 2002) and for the propagation of an identity politics that undermines dominant notions of totality and authenticity (cf. Arnaud 2001). At the Berliner carnival, sound systems are usually placed at the end of the parade, but the organizers hold them to be "very important for the credibility of the carnival" (Annett Szabó, personal communication).
23 A black political and religious movement, that got momentum during the 1930s enthronement of Ras Tafari as Haile Selassie in Ethopia and was greatly popularised, especially in the West Indian diaspora, during the 1970s by Bob Marley.
24 The conflicts about history are documented in Sherwood 1999, esp. p. 204–215, Cohen 1993: 77 ff., Melville 2002, Nunley 1988 and in city magazines and dailies.
25 Interview with Claire Holder, former chairperson of the Notting Hill Carnival Trust, 29.08.2002.

References

Alleyne-Dettmers, Patricia 1998: Ancestral Voices. Trevini – A Case Study of Meta Masking in the Notting Hill Carnival. In: *Journal of Material Culture* 3(2): 201–221.

Arnaud, Lionel 2001: "Notting like the real thing". From the politics of representation to the politics of presentation. The Notting Hill Carnival and the question of black authenticity. Paper presented for the Workshop on Identity Politics, The European Consortium for Political Research ECPR Joint Sessions, Grenoble, 6–11 April 2001.

Baumann, Gerd 1996: *Contesting Culture. Discourses of Identity in Multi-Ethnic London.* Cambridge.

Borneman, John 2001: Multikulti or Schweinerei in the Year 2001. Paper, given at the University of California, Berkeley, April 2001.

Borneman, John/Stefan Senders 2000: Politics without a head: Is the "Love Parade" a new form of political identification? In: *Cultural Anthropology* 15 (2): 294–317.

Cohen, Abner 1980: Drama and politics in the development of a London carnival. In: *MAN* 15: 65–87.

Cohen, Abner 1982: A Polyethnic London Carnival as a Contested Cultural Performance. In: *Ethic and Racial Studies* 5(1):23–41.

Cohen, Abner 1993: *Masquerade Politics. Explorations in the Structure of Urban Cultural Movements.* Oxford/Providence.

Da Matta, Roberto 1991: *Carnivals, Rogues and Heroes. An Interpretation of the Brazilian Dilemma.* London.

103

Eriksen, Thomas Hylland 1993: *Ethnicity and Nationalism*. London.

Giddens, Anthony 1991: *The Consequences of Modernity*. Cambridge.

Gluckman, Max 1963: *Order and Rebellion in Tribal Societies*. London.

Hall, Stuart 1994: *Rassismus und kulturelle Identität. Ausgewählte Schriften* 2, Hamburg.

Handelman, Don 1990: *Models and Mirrors. Towards an Anthropology of Public Events*. Cambridge.

Hannerz, Ulf 1992: *Cultural Complexity. Studies in the Social Organisation of Meaning*. New York.

Hannerz, Ulf 1993: The cultural role of world cities. In: Cohen, Anthony P. /Fukui, Katsuyoshi (eds.): *Humanising the City? Social Contexts of Urban Life at the Turn of Millennium*. Edinburgh: 69–83.

Hauschild, Thomas 1994: Kultur der Gewalt in Süditalien. In: Brednich, Rolf W./Walter Hartinger (eds.): *Gewalt in der Kultur*. Vorträge des 29. Deutschen Volkskundekongresses, Passau: 355–375.

Heelas, Paul 1996: Introduction: Detraditionalization and its Rivals. In: Heelas, Paul/Scott Lash/Paul Morris (eds.), *Detraditionalization. Critical Reflections on Authority and Identity*. Oxford: 1–20.

Herzfeld, Michael 2001: *Anthropology. Theoretical Practice in Culture and Society*. Malden, Mass. and Oxford.

Kirshenblatt-Gimblett, Barbara 1998: *Destination Culture. Tourism, Museum and Heritage*. Berkeley und Los Angeles.

Knecht, Michi 2002: "Who is carnivalizing whom?" Ethnologische Perspektiven auf neue Karnevalsformen. In: *Berliner Blätter*, 26: 7–17.

Koningsbruggen, Peter van 1997: The Spirit of Canboulay: The Socio-Cultural Autonomy of the Trinidad Carnival. In: *Focaal, Tiejdschrift voor anthropologie*, 30/31: 159–177.

Koningsbruggen, Peter van 2000: *Trinidad Carnival. A Quest for National Identity*. Warwick.

Lang, Barbara 1996: Berlin Kreuzberg. Bilder einer Vorstellung. In: Zeitschrift für Volkskunde 91 (2): 223–247.

Lang, Barbara 1998: *Mythos Kreuzberg. Ethnographie eines Stadtteils, 1961–1995*. Frankfurt a.M. und New York.

Malkki, Liisa, 1997: National Geographic: The Rooting of Peoples and the Territorialization of National Identity among Scholars and Refugees. In: Gupta, Akhil/James Ferguson (eds.): *Culture, Power, Place. Explorations in Critical Anthropology*. Durham: 52–74.

Manning, Frank 1990: Overseas Caribbean Carnivals: The Arts and Politics of a Transnational Celebration. In: John A. Lent (ed.): *Caribbean Popular Culture*. Bowling Green: 20–36.

Mason, Peter 1999: *Bacchanal: The Carnival Culture of Trinidad*. New York.

Melville, Caspar 2002: A Carnival History. In: *Open Democracy*, 4.9.2002 (on line).

Miller, Daniel 1994: *Modernity. An Ethnographic Approach. Dualism and Mass Consumption in Trinidad*. Oxford/Providence.

Moser, Dietz-Rüdiger 1986: *Fastnacht-Fasching-Karneval*. München.

Murray, David 2000: Re-Mapping Carnival: Gender, Sexuality and Power in a Martinican Festival. In: *Social Analysis*, 44: 103–112.

Niedermüller, Peter 1998: Stadt, Kultur(en) und Macht. Zu einigen Aspekten „spätmoderner" Stadtethnologie, In: *Österreichische Zeitschrift für Volkskunde*, 101: 279–301.

Nunley, John W. 1988: Festival Diffusion into the Metropole. In: John Nunley/Judith Bettleheim (eds): *Caribbean Festival Arts*. Seattle.

Nurse, Keith 1999: Globalization and Trinidad Carnival: Diaspora, Hybridity and Identity in Global Culture. In: *Cultural Studies*, 13: 661–690.

Phillips, Mike 2001: *London Crossings. A Biography of Black Britain*. London.

Schindler, Norbert 1984: Karneval, Kirche und die verkehrte Welt. Zur Funktion der Lachkultur im 16. Jahrhundert. In: *Jahrbuch für Volkskunde*, 1: 9–57.

Scott, Allen J. 2000: *The Cultural Economy of Cities*. London.

Sherwood, Marika 1999: *Claudia Jones. A Life in Exile*. London.

Shore, Chris 2000: *Building Europe. The Cultural Politics of European Integration*. London.

Smith, Michael Peter 1992: Postmodernism, urban ethnography, and the new social space of ethnic identity. In: *Theory and Society*, 21:493–531.

Turner, Victor 1988: Carnival in Rio: Dionysian Drama in Industrializing Society. In: *The Anthropology of Performance*. New York: 123–138.

Van der Heyden, Ulrich/Joachim Zeller (eds.) 2002: *Kolonialmetropole Berlin. Eine Spurensuche*. Berlin.

Welford, Megan 1998: Carnival! A Study of the Relationship between Carnival and Society. In: *Cultural Studies from Birmingham*, 2 (online).

Welz, Gisela 1992: Das Gallus. Deindustrialisierung und Tertiarisierung eines Frankfurter Stadtteils. In: *Multikultur Journal – Weltstadt Frankfurt am Main?* Tübingen: 81–87.

Welz, Gisela 1994: Der Tod des Lokalen als Ekstase des Lokalismus. Am Beispiel des Frankfurter Gallus-Viertels. In: Noller, Peter/Prigge, Walter/ Ronneberger, Klaus (Hg.): *Stadt-Welt. Über die Globalisierung städtischer Milieus*. Frankfurt a.M./ New York: 218–225.

Welz, Gisela 1996: *Inszenierungen kultureller Vielfalt*. Berlin.

Wilmsen, Edwin N. 1996: Introduction: Premises of Power in Ethnic Politics. In: Wilmsen, Edwin/ Patrick McAllister (eds.): *The Politics of Difference. Ethnic Premises in a World of Power*. Chicago: 1–24.

Wieviroka, Michael 1998: Kritik des Multikulturalismus. In: Heitmeyer, Wilhelm/Rainer Dollase/ Otto Backes (Hg.): *Die Krise der Städte. Analysen zu den Folgen desintegrativer Stadtentwicklung für das ethnisch-kulturelle Zusammenleben*. Frankfurt a.M.: 97–142.

Zukin, Sharon 1995: *The Cultures of Cities*. Oxford.

History as a Cultural Playground

Kirsti Mathiesen Hjemdahl

> Hjemdahl, Kirsti Mathiesen 2002: History as a Cultural Playground. – Ethnologia Europaea 32: 2: 105–124.
>
> There is growing belief within the discipline of cultural studies that heritage no longer relates to our historical past, but attempts to recreate a mythological past. We are witnessing a progressive process in which the Land of the Past is changing into the Land of the Different, a world which may well be charged with moral messages; an arena designed to create random continuity and cultural identities, a past designed to provide experiences and identities. A past intended to convince through its credibility rather than its genuineness, to be experienced rather than understood.
>
> In order to discuss what happens in this "muddled past", in the transition between history and heritage, this article focus on the specific praxis that makes the Lands of the Past materialise. Detailed, first-hand descriptions and interpretations of how school children encounter, perceive, and invest two Norwegian historical parks with significance, play with traditions, consume and practice heritage, and make the past happen. To establish further knowledge regarding the cultural processes associated with modernity's relationship with the past, comparative analysis of the traditional museums is also taken into the discussions.
>
> *Kirsti Mathiesen Hjemdahl, Ph.D., Dept. of Cultural Studies and Art History, Ethnology Section, University of Bergen, Nygårdsgaten 6, N-5015 Bergen.*
> *E-mail: Kirsti.Hjemdahl@ikk.uib.no*

The Land of the Past Extends Its Frontiers

In the autumn of 1995, the Norwegian Broadcasting Corporation transmitted a documentary from the Bronze Age Settlement (Bronseplassen), one of the new historical theme parks in Norway. People's curiosity was raised by the opening sequence and they let their channel hopping fingers rest: first focusing on the rustling leaves at the top of an oak tree, the camera then glides slowly down the trunk, until it finds a creature with a little peaked hat made of tawny leather and edged with white fur. His long beard is in a plait that curls over his white woolly jumper and down his grey woolly coat. The man is clearly concentrating, standing with closed eyes and hands touching the trunk. After a couple of seconds he turns round, looks straight into the camera, and says:

"This is how it all started, ten years ago. I suddenly discovered that there is a force within the trees. I believe that all living things have a force within, and that we, people, are able to experience this force if we're willing to open up and tune in to the frequency of everything that surrounds us. Trees are exciting, they take in whatever you might tell them. And you can use the force actively as well. So I would recommend that people go out and find their own tree."

In the woodland surrounding their own home, Helge Grønli and his wife, Eli Solgård, have built a bronze age settlement, complete with longhouse, maze, hunters trail, sacrificial site, burial mound, herb garden and tree-trunk boats. Their programme offers everything from storytelling round the bonfire for families on a Sunday outing to longhouse and tent accommodation for holiday breaks, corporate schemes for alternative business excursions, and a Viking market which gathers Vikings from all over Europe for courses in marshall arts and traditional crafts. In addition to all this, the Bronze Age Settlement offers customised courses for primary school classes who want to learn about the Bronze Age in a different way. The hosts themselves dress up in wool and leather, appropriately for the times, and change their names to Gorm and Urd as they enter the past. This time-change takes place as you pass under the elk scull, which adorns the gate that takes you through to the Bronze Age Settlement. This is a journey in time which offers not only an experience of the past, but which serves as an important comment on the present as well. This is how it is phrased in their leaflet:

"The Bronze Age Settlement is an attempt to show that our forefathers lived in a close and direct relationship with nature. Their everyday life had a totality, which we have lost. On the threshold of a new millennium we are about to kill Mother Nature, she who gives life to us all. The Bronze Age Settlement raises the question of which people are the primitive ones."

There is growing belief within the discipline of cultural studies that heritage no longer relates to our historical past, but attempts to recreate a mythological past. We are witnessing a progressive process in which the Land of the Past is changing into the Land of the Different, a world which may well be charged with moral messages; an arena designed to create random continuity and cultural identities, a past designed to provide experiences and identities, a past intended to convince through its credibility rather than its genuineness, to be experienced rather than understood. This process has been described as a shift from *general history* to *individual heritage* by geographer David Lowenthal (1986), from a *genealogic* to an *organic* perception of history by social anthropologist Odd Are Berkaak (1992), and from *history* to *memory* by social anthropologist George Marcus (1992).

The fact that museums, curators and other representatives of antiquity-protecting authorities no longer hold the indisputable right to interpret and present the past, "muddles up the landscape of times past", says historian Svante Beckman (1993). Approximately ten years ago Beckman forewarned that once the spontaneous heritage enthusiasts, amateurs, prophets and directors start building "Lands of Yesteryear" for the voracious experience market, the antiquarian professors will be left holding their authentic, representative, high-quality baby. Was he right?

There is a deep conflict of interests between the new flourish of popular demand for pasttime experiences and the institutions that are set to administer our traditions. While the specialists are delighted to see a healthy increase in the general interest in history, they are clearly concerned with the apparent shortfall of expertise. The long, extensive series of strict and scientific requirements that govern the selection, storage and exhibition of artefacts, is allowed to give way to the ideal that history should be made to come alive in a straightforward way. This disneyfication of the past obviously challenges the authorised definitions and the existing perceptions held at museums and within other value hierarchies.

There is reason to assume that the existence of these historical theme parks will have a major if somewhat unpredictable impact on our cultural heritage and on people's cultural identity. But rather than joining the general choir of ideological voices in a heavy-handed intellectual condemnation, and rather than considering this rush to the Land of the Past as compensation for the disorientation that people experience in modern society, I will seek to understand this change by focusing on *what happens* rather than what the change *represents*. "Things have always spoken, but people have not always paid the same attention. Today we listen", says ethnologist Jonas Frykman (this volume), wondering whether this is why the past and our cultural heritage have escaped from the prisons that museums and historians have put them in. How does the past take place in historical theme parks, and how does it acquire its materiality? Who are listening, apart from the children? Is anyone being forced to listen? What are the consequences of such shifts in our understanding of and approaches to history, for individuals, and for heavy traditional institutions such as the education authorities and the museum council?

Even if this analysis is based on particular, specific parks and museums in Norway, there is no reason to believe that the Lands of the Past flourish in a national context only. The same trend can be found throughout Europe, with Terra Mitica in Spain as the most monumental and innovative example. What might be the historical theme parks' significance and impact in terms of how we come to understand European history and identity?

Fieldwork and Phenomenology

There is every reason to take the Bronze Age Settlement seriously. The same applies for the Viking Farm, which is another Norwegian historical theme park. The Viking Farm is a far cry from a small site built up round someone's home; it is owned by NorgesParken, a limited company which also runs one of the largest amusement parks in the country: Tusenfryd. The Viking Farm used to be a whole Viking Land with an entire Viking Age community, including an earl's court, storage house, burial mound, shipbuilding yard, tar mill, law-court, smithy, pier where Viking ships were moored, market, sacrificial site, silver smithy etc. But the Viking Age is also brought to life by means of modern high-tech equipment: "3–4 times an hour you can experience a hazardous voyage with Leiv Eiriksson at the helm, facing severe attacks from other ships and mythology. This is a highly realistic performance, created by means of modern technology and special effects", the leaflet promises. Animals have now replaced some of the Vikings, and some of the market square has been turned into a farmyard, to make the place commercially viable. But even if family tourism introduced a need for renewal after a couple of years of Vikings, the education service at the Viking Farm is as robust as ever.

One of the most interesting aspects of these historical theme parks is precisely their impact on schools. Despite the fact that they impose even heavier burdens on tight school budgets, an ever-increasing number of primary schools opt away the traditional museum visits for the benefit of day trips or overnight excursions to the more entertainment-oriented historical theme parks. We have even found that these new past-times-experiences inspire changes in the curriculum. For example, the offer of a 24-hour excursion to Viking Land triggered a change in the way history was taught to 4th form pupils at a primary school outside Oslo. Replacing their previous approach of teaching a little about a number of historical eras, they now opt to concentrate their efforts on a single historical era throughout the school year. And rather than learning about Vikings in history class only, the children are now exposed to the Viking Age in a variety of ways through subjects such as music, Norwegian, home economics, and physical education. The idea is clearly that if you receive varied and thorough input about one period of history, this will have significant transitional value once you need to acquire knowledge and understanding about other periods.

In order to find out what happens in the "muddled past", I believe we need to look into specifics. We know a good deal about the structural processes that go on in the transition between history and heritage, but have less knowledge about the specific praxis that makes the Lands of the Past materialise. Detailed, first-hand descriptions and interpretations of how children encounter, perceive, and invest these places with significance, play with traditions, and consume and practice heritage, provide an opportunity for us to establish further knowledge regarding the cultural processes associated with modernity's relationship with the past – i.e. a phenomenological approach. This is how anthropologist Michael Jackson expresses it:

"Phenomenology is the scientific study of experience. It is an attempt to describe human consciousness in its lived immediacy, before it is subject to theoretical elaboration or conceptual systematizing ... Rather than examine the epistemological status of beliefs it is more important to explore their existential uses and consequences. Our emphasis is thus shifted from what beliefs "mean" *intrinsically* to what they are made to mean, and what they accomplish for those who invoke and use them" (Jackson, 1996:2–6).

It follows from this understanding that fieldwork is essential, or as anthropologist Keith H. Basso (1996:84) expresses it: "Everything, or almost everything, hinges on the particular, and because it does, ethnography is essential".

This is why I chose to join two primary school classes on their respective excursions to the Bronze Age Settlement and Viking Land. I met up with the pupils at school, before the day of the excursion, and then joined one of them for a daytrip to the Bronze Age Settlement and the other on an overnight excursion to Viking Land. Following these past-time-experiences I returned to the respective schools as I wanted to listen to the children's discussions and reflections concerning the excursions, and to take part in the movements, social conventions and rhythms they used for preparing, undertaking and rounding off their journey back to "the Land of the Past" – in line with the practical mimetic research ideal of "thinking with one's feet" (Jackson, 1996:28f.). "By using one's body in the same way as others in the same environment, one finds oneself informed by an understanding which may then be interpreted according to one's own custom, or bent, yet which remains grounded in a field of practical activity and thereby remains consonant with the experience of those among whom one has lived", as expressed by Michael Jackson (1996:340f.).

However, my fieldwork did not confine itself to the 10–11-year-olds whose journey back in time I was allowed to join. While it is essential to find out what happens in the Lands of the Past, it is (almost) equally important to investigate why the museums fail to trigger as much action, and so I decided to follow the trail which is now becoming disused: I paid a visit to the museums which have lost out on visits from primary schools.

The Boring Museum and the Enjoyable Theme Park

Text displays and guided tours make up the usual exhibition format at the traditional historical museum, and this is probably the format most of us remember from our own

This is part of the Bronze Age exhibition that has lost at least one of its visiting school classes. The pupils are now travelling to the Bronze Age Settlement instead, as a supplement to their history classes!

school visits. At indoor museums you walk from one display case to the next while the guide interprets the significance of the carefully selected objects; or rather the *fragments* of original objects, which is most often the case when we are dealing with a past as distant as the Bronze Age. A knowledgeable guide tells you what you are looking at, where it comes from, what is typical of the times etc. "This is where you learn to think", as ethnologist Billy Ehn (1986) says in his book *Museendet*.

The outdoor museum variety offers a similar format. You walk from module to module; first the stave church, then the Setesdal farmyard, or first the urban setting, then the rural setting. You receive general information while standing in farmyards or courtyards, and more specific information as you get seated round the fireplace or the long table indoors. Once the questions and answers session starts, an indoor setting is preferable. For most of us are probably familiar with the situation in which the five people closest to the guide are conducting a lively discussion while the fifteen visitors trailing behind struggle to hear anything at all – gradually giving up as they start to lose their concentration and get talking amongst themselves.

There are clear expectations regarding the length of the guided walk. "Three quarters of an hour is considered the maximum for a guided tour", says the manager of Oslo Folk Museum's education department, because "people are generally able to take in only three different things in the course of a single 45-minute lesson. And I always wonder what three things will stick with people after the tour".

Museums are undoubtedly perceived as boring. "Some times it seems as if they come to life only when they pass a mirror", one of the Folk Museum guides sighed. Hopefully, things are not quite as bad as that, but the attitude is sufficiently well established for the Oslo Museum Council to dedicate the first page of their leaflet "Class visits to museums 1996" to this problem:

"Use the museum! Museums are **NOT** dusty collections of boring objects neatly placed in line upon line in gloomy, cold halls. Museums are full of **colours, questions, experiences, tasks, activities and news**".

There is a clear difference when you compare this experience with the school excursions to

What is so enjoyable about stacking wood in the Viking Age?

the Land of the Past – in terms of hours spent as well the degree of involvement. "Great fun, really exciting and informative. And exhausting, but we didn't notice that until we got home" the pupils summarized the excursion to the Vikingland. Some of the children had slept for 24 hours after their return.

Throughout the time we were enacting Vikings, the children's degree of involvement was also very different from what you would normally expect from a 45-minute guided tour. The Vikings were divided into four different groups; two of them would be cooking, one would be sentinels, while the last group was assigned the task of carrying and stacking wood. Because some of the tasks were considered to be more enjoyable than others, and to make sure that the pupils would gain a varied range of experiences, a changeover system was introduced. In the end, everyone would have had a go at everything. But this is not what happened. The wood-stackers were so keen to find the most effective system for transporting the wood from the untidy heap at the centre of the yard to the neat pile adjacent to the storehouse, that they succeeded in doing just that. At the time of the first group changeover, there was not a single log left to move, and for a moment there was hectic activity in order to find a set of replacement tasks!

The same tendency – involvement, curiosity and keenness – was evident in the children who visited the Bronze Age Settlement. As we walked the round from the dance maze to the burial ground, the beaver lodge, the wishing tree, the sacrificial site, the ancient oak tree and the clearing water, I soon found that there was no point in trying to get to the front of the crowd. The children were rushing from one module to the next, and you had to be careful not to be run off the path. When the tasks for making vegetable soup were being distributed, the children were fighting for chores such as picking stinging nestles, peeling carrots, cutting onion and fetching water. Were they all highly experienced kitchen assistants, or would some of their parents have been equally surprised to see how easily they were recruited for kitchen service? Why is it so much more fun to be peeling carrots in the Bronze Age, or to be stacking wood in the Viking Age?

Why does a whole school day at the Bronze Age Settlement, or 24 hours in Viking Land, feel as if it's not enough? And why do they want to repeat the experience as soon as possible? In his work jotter, one of the pupils ended his report from the Bronze Age Settlement in a similar fashion to the class summary from the trip to Viking Land: "it was time to leave, and although we didn't really want to go, we had to, and we left after having spent a wonderful day in the Bronze Age."

Making the Past Come Alive

There are probably a number of reasons why traditional museums and historical theme parks generate different levels of involvement and perseverance. One of them is their degree of accessibility. There is no doubt that museum visitors who have already acquired a degree of expertise, or people who enjoy surreal museum ambles, can pick up a world of knowledge, associations and appreciation from a Bronze Age pot in a display case, accompanied by this text: "Grave find from the Roman Era (0–400 A.C.) from Risholt, estate no. 11, site no. 3, Øyestad. Upper part of bronze pot, found in a grave mound in 1845, filled with ash. Gifted by Tellef Jonsen Risholt". However, for all of those who have neither a special eye nor special expertise, like a bunch of 10-year-olds, it would be considerably easier to understand the past if they were allowed to use the pot the way we think it may have been used. The very act of reconstruction gives a completely different dimension to the experience for all those who have yet to be initiated. The past is thus made much more accessible; it feels as if it is readily at hand and alive.

Understanding the past on the basis of tiny bits of flint and shards of pottery displayed side by side according to registration number and geographic location, is obviously far more difficult than if you make the pottery yourself after having dug out the clay from the soil and mixed it with the correct amounts of sand and water. It takes a completely different level of attention to understand what life was like with an open fireplace in the centre of your house if you are not actually experiencing the burning

The past becomes much more accessible if you are allowed to take part in the reconstruction process.

eyes yourself, which soon teaches you how to move with care not to aggravate the smoke development. And similarly, you need to be far more concentrated in order to grasp what life was like in the Viking Age by looking at a Viking garment on a hanger rather than by wearing the outfit yourself for 24 hours.

The museums are aware of the problem. "We have been too arrogant, because we've never needed to change our ways. We have simply assumed that people would come". This was the response from the Head of Education at the University Museum of Antiquities when she was told about the class that opted them away in favour of Viking Land. For their Viking exhibition, the Museum of Antiquities has introduced interpretive panels of different length and format. There are brief texts that give a general idea as to how to approach the object, such as "everyone was not the same" next to the royal costume on display, or "some believed in other gods" next to the presentation of different religious communities. Other display cases are accompanied by poetic elaborations, and all of them offer additional in-depth information – up to as many as four A4 sheets. Obviously, a personal guide is also available. Nevertheless, even if the public are given a number of options, they are primarily asked to take in information through their usual senses: their eyes and ears.

In order to alleviate the interpretive problems, the Folk Museum follows strict rules when employing their guides. Ethnologists are preferred; they know the difference between grindstones and whetstones, between staves and logs, between ridging ploughs and normal ploughs, between southern and northern building traditions.

However, one may ask whether this focus on textuality and verbal communication is what is required for the past to become more accessible. Is it not rather the case that the theme parks' anchorage in action-based communication of historical knowledge is what makes the past come alive in their Lands of the Past, and so enjoyable that even peeling carrots is fun. At least for as long as you are in the past.

True, many traditional museums have attempted to bring history to life in a number of ways. At the Folk Museum, the fireplaces are

Folk costume at the Folk Museum.

tended by griddle cake makers, at the general store you can buy sugar candy and other Past Times sweets, and on the benches round the courtyards, girls dressed in historically correct attire are sitting knitting while they answer questions, let people feel the material of their costumes and study the seams. However, it all seems rather tame compared with the magnificent re-enactments found in the historical theme parks.

While the children at the Bronze Age Settlement were welcomed by Gorm and Urd, the buildings and environments in Viking Land are equally appropriate for the times, yet far more crowded with craftsmen, singers, actors, children, earls, slaves, Vikings, ticket inspectors and guides. People are shown how swords were made in the smithy, how woodcarvers used to shape their wood, they listen to stories about the lives of earls and slaves, farmers and warriors, feel the taste of real Viking fare, see and take part in Viking games and learn how to carve runes in stone. The communication of information relies on frequent performances of rehearsed plays, mixed with improvised interaction with the school children. For while the ethnologists at the Folk Museum are there to ensure historical accuracy and correct detail, Viking Land is dominated by actors, drama teachers, directors and musicians. Their job instruction is to play with the children, sing and dance to create the atmosphere of the times among the public. Every now and again their exuberant energy seems almost provoking – how can they bear being this funny, lively, playful all day?

In the course of the 24 hours that the children from Oslo spent in Viking Land, they never listened to a single summary or talk about the Viking era. When I asked the Vikingwoman Gudfrid why she never gathered the class around her to give them a few general points about the period, she responded by returning the question:

"Do you think I should?" Gudfrid felt it was important for the children to access the Viking Age through that which is non-verbal and non-narrative; they were experiencing and doing – while she was there, prepared to explain, answer questions, sing songs, tell stories, assist, initiate. The pupils would also walk round with their

Orm Viking in Viking Land.

workbooks and have their questions answered by talking to the various Vikings they encountered.

The visit to the Bronze Age Settlement was different in this respect, as action was not the be-all and end-all, even if there were lots to do here as well. The alternative school day started with a gathering in the dim, smoky, rather cold longhouse, where Gorm gave a talk about the Bronze Age. On the ensuing walk round the site, to the maze, the sacrificial site, the burial mound, etc., everyone was given a joint introduction to each module, before the children were allowed to have a go themselves, climbing, listening or touching. Nevertheless, a tour of the Bronze Age Settlement is completely different from what we are used to at museums, because the information is communicated in another voice, with a different motivation. Helge Grønli sees his role as a Bronze Age intermediary almost in contrast to all things strict and scientific.

"We have worked in close partnership with the archaeological museum in Stavanger, and if they're not good enough... Well. What I'm doing is to put some meat on the bare bones, and that's what the museums dislike. They dislike the fact that I'm bringing the past to life for the public. But what the hell should I be doing then? Just sit there like a mummy and tell them that "this and that and then the other"? You see, when I tell them that the walls are made from clay, sand and cowpats, I also tell them the story of the bloke who helped us make the wall and who swallowed some of this mix and thought he was going to die. I suppose I'm that commercial that I know you need to crack a joke every five minutes or so to make your audiences choke with laughter. And then you'll be able to take them with you all the way."

Of course, to Helge Grønli strict historical accuracy is not the most important point; his primary objective is to make people become involved. He is an idealist, and "slightly demented", as he puts it himself, which is undoubtedly a prerequisite if you make your own home into a public access Bronze Age settlement which receives an increasing number of people every day, and if you are to cope with showing round school children all day, entertain corporate visitors in the evening, organise weekend trips, and constantly be prepared to talk to curious people who really only want to check out what this visitor attraction is about. What is his job description? What drives him? Why is he telling stories?

"I've got a message, and the Bronze Age settlement has a religious foundation. An animistic foundation, and that's important. That's what I want to convey. And for that I don't mind a little historical prostitution. That's all right by me. 'Cause people need things to be edible, and they're great suckers for chocolate topping. And the museums don't like that. But people do. And that's what I'm concerned with. I've never had a positive potter in the workshop, but then that's not who I'm selling to."

The two theme parks may have adopted slightly different communication practices, yet they both seek to make the past come alive by appealing to all senses. The encounter with the past is not achieved through eyesight and hearing only; verbal interaction is important too, talking and touching, testing, tasting and smelling, and not least: *doing* is imperative. For the visitors themselves are the most important travel agents on their journey back to the past.

Becoming a Citizen of the Past!

"Gorm, is it all right if I change my name?" An 11-year-old comes running up to us from behind, and I look with interest to the man in front of me.

"Of course you can", Gorm answers. "What would you like to be called?"

"I'd like to be called Sol rather than Gaupe, and Line would like to change her name as well. From Binna to Vår. Is that all right, for her as well?" the girl asks excitedly.

"Of course she's allowed as well", chuckles Gorm in his good-natured way.

In the Land of the Past, the children themselves are key resources in the process of making the past come alive, and at the Bronze Age Settlement, the name-change ritual is an important part of entering into the Bronze Age. Inside the maze, a ritual reminiscent of an initiation ceremony was performed with great formality. Gorm gave the instructions:

"This is like a picture of the earth; when you enter these corridors, you enter the earth as if you're entering a cave. When you get to the centre, you may even get to meet Mother Nature herself. That's when anything may happen. But you're going to use this maze to change your names into a real Bronze Age name. And then you'll need to remember that name for the rest of the day. To get to the centre, you'll need to walk 300 yards. And you'll need to move with care; make sure you don't kick any of the stones. For the galiator lives under one of the stones, and he's a tiny green creature with sharp teeth that will bite your toes if you kick any of the stones. OK? Walk as if you were ballet dancers all the way. And then, when you get to the centre, and this is important, you'll need to remember the

When you get to the centre, you might meet Mother Nature. That's when anything might happen.

name you've been given, and then you'll have to shout that name out as load as you can to make sure you can hear an echo from both sides. Listen to what I'm doing; then I hit that stone and shout: GOOORRRM. Did you hear that? And then you skip over the stone."

Gorm squatted down by the maze entrance and the children whispered their favoured name into his ear. The first Bronze Age people chose names like Raffiki, Timon, Pumba and Baloo – Walt Disney appears to be a source of inspiration in most contexts. The children who were unable to think up a proper Bronze Age name themselves, were assisted by Gorm: Falk, Binna, Gaupe, Ørn, Bjørn and similar names with an old-fashioned Norse ring to them. It would probably be too much to expect a 3 000 year-old man to be entirely up-to-date in terms of name trends. And this is why the girls requested a name-change; after a good 30 minutes they had found something better themselves. Names they were comfortable with, and which they were happy to live with for the remainder of their day in the Bronze Age.

They were also given garments that were appropriate for the times, made from hemp, sacking, wool or leather. In Viking Land, daytrip Vikings are dressed in simple sacking, whereas 24-hour Vikings are given coloured shirts and grand robes to protect against the night chill; and of course, everyone who suffers from allergy are given garments in a non-allergenic material. The hemp rope to be tied round your waist is the device that makes sure your knife is always easily accessible. Once you are inside the park you can complement the outfit by making additional accessories yourself, such as headgear made from carded wool and hand-dyed yarn.

You learn to speak a different language as well: in the past you never say "hi", but "greetings", a mate becomes a companion, the earth is female and is called Mother Nature, to bury is to inearth; you never ask "What are you up to?" but "What is your errand", and when you part, you say "walk in peace" rather than "bye". In Viking Land, the children found it particularly easy to integrate the new language in their vocabulary. This may have something to do with the fact that they had recently been rehearsing a specially commissioned Viking play at school. The play is written by Torild Svarstad Haugland, who has published a number of historical novels from the Viking Age, particularly aimed at teenagers. The play forms part of the educational material prepared by Viking Land. Of course, the school children's delight peaked when they were given the opportunity to stage their play in the Viking Land amphitheatre, yet they benefited from being acquainted with the characters, language and plot of the play throughout their 24 hours in the Viking Age as they experienced encounters of a more random nature.

Last, but not least, you work your way into the past: you pick stinging nestles, peel carrots and rip cabbage to make vegetable soup; you grind your cereal with a stone to make flour for bread; you light a fire to cook the soup or bake the bread – under constant supervision; you carry and stack wood so that there's fuel for the fire; and you take your turn as a sentinel, to avoid being surprised by robbers or anyone else with a hostile attitude.

It is through these tasks that the children gain experiences that make them become more and more of a Viking, or Bronze Age man, as the hours pass. By sitting round the fire making bark bread or pancakes, they get sooty, dirty and red-eyed and their throats get sore. By eating pancakes with honey the way they used to do before knives and forks were introduced, their hands get so sticky that everything they touch gets stuck. The butter for the pancakes or bread becomes less yellow and blacker as the stir or dough is taking shape. Teeth are gnashing with grit from the home-ground flour. Brushing their teeth is out of the question, morning or night – as there were obviously no toothbrushes in the Land of the Really Old Days. But apples are good for cleaning out the grit between your teeth. Their bodies are tired after all the work and a night spent without springs in their mattresses. Their body odour becomes more distinct, their hair more knotty, and their nails accumulate black lines of dirt and grime after only a couple of hours in the past. Imagine how they must have smelt back then, when they had a bath perhaps only once a month. Or worse still, once a year. Imagine how hard they had to work just to make a single meal. Imagine how frightened they must have felt at the very real prospect of being attacked by robbers. Imagine how worn their teeth must have been from eating all that grit with their food. Imagine.

Creative Imagination

"At the Bronze Age Settlement we were welcomed by Helge and his wife Eli. We followed Helge to a gate. When we entered, it said: simboli-bambili bom-tom-rom-bom, and suddenly we were in 1800 B.C., where Helge turned into Gorm and Eli turned into Urd."

This is how one of the pupils described her journey back to the Bronze Age in her workbook after the trip. However, travelling back to the past does tend to take more than the waving of a magic wand. Even if substantial efforts are put into making the past come alive, the demands on the participants' willpower and creative abilities are high. In many ways, historical theme parks are places where creative imagination is being cultivated; it is the magic of make-believe that drives the time back and makes things happen.

It's all about dreaming with care rather than looking too closely, says philosopher Gaston Bachelard (1992:23). He is concerned with creative imagination rather than reproductive imagination, and thinks that the indistinct is at least as productive as the distinct. If anything becomes too clear and obvious, this will block the imagination, says Bachelard (2000:159).

He is concerned with the thoughts and dreams triggered by the objects rather than the objects per se. He has written appreciatively about artists of virtually no artistic merit, yet whose works have prompted dreams and thoughts in him. Similarly, dirty butter, logs, bonfires and pancakes with honey are completely uninteresting in terms of objects of the past – yet the grime, toil, smoke and stickiness nevertheless give rise to dreams and thoughts about life in another era.

Consequently, Bachelard's reasoning about dreams relates to the way in which things material – the artefact, the place, the exhibit – can no longer be ascribed significance as an object, but as a subject: how they work on us and how we discover new aspects of ourselves by dreaming about them. This explains how the focus that historical theme parks' put on using rather than watching, on action rather than reflectivity, works as an effective introduction to a spirited dream about the past for the school children. For as Frykman (this volume) points out, presenting the impact of material customs on cultural heritage, is not about materiality in a historically materialistic sense. Rather, the material culture needs to be displayed as something more than relics and objective evidence in order to become part of a present-day dialogue with the past.

"For places to be able to answer questions about identity", says Frykman – and we might add: to make the past happen – "they have to be equipped with a biography, a life story, a proposition which is constantly open to new interpretations and surprising insights. We thus see how something local is once again populated, filled with revived narratives and mysteries that suit our own times. It is not the history of the place we seek, but its ambience, its soul, and its ability to accumulate memories and dreams" (Frykman, this volume).

The way that things operate as subjects and are filled with mysteries that suit our own times is probably clearest seen at the Bronze Age Settlement, where nature is vested with powers and is able to talk to those who listen. Gorm points to two trees in particular. The Tree of Good Fortune is a wish-fulfilling birch. Visitors sit down on a small seat-like branch a metre up the trunk; they lean back, close their eyes, and make a wish. No-one needs to know what you have wished for, as that's a private secret, ensures Gorm. However, certain restrictions apply. "You're not allowed to wish that you'll win the Lottery", says Gorm, looking strict and serious at the children. The other tree is an oak, which will talk to you if you are tuned to its frequency. "I heard the tree rustling", said one of the children convincingly when I joined their group. According to Gorm, 95% of the children will hear something if they are urged to listen to the trees.

In many ways, the lands of the past are founded on the magic of make-believe. Even if

At the Bronze Age Settlement the trees have special powers and talk to those who listen.

much effort is put into creating a setting which makes the past come alive as you pass through the time gates, the journey back in time clearly fails to take you all the way: "We're using a modern lid for the pot, even if that's not really right for the Bronze Age. That's to make sure we won't get too much ash in the soup. There's no need to adopt all the Bronze Age practices", admits Urd once the ingredients for the real Bronze Age vegetable soup are ready to go on the fire. "Eli, no, I mean Urd", says Gorm, constantly slipping up, but pleading for understanding as it is clearly difficult to be moving back and forth three thousand years at the time.

For of course, it is impossible to experience the past as it used to be. We prefer to stay put in the present as we take in the past; we can but interpret, play, imagine, dream our way into history. However, we have a number of atmosphere-enhancing props that will make it easier for us to dip into the past.

The children are highly concerned with what fits in and what does not, what is right in relation to the fact that they are now in the Land of the Past – not based on a historical assessment, but based on what is credible in relation to the make-believe magic which is required for them to act their part as a Viking or take on their new Bronze Age identity. Consequently, none of them have brought their watches, pocket money or chewing gum. And they are vigilant enforcers of time-appropriate-ness as well, albeit with a twinkle in the eye:

"I saw you, so there," one of the boys exclaimed triumphantly as he climbed the stairs up to the horse-mounting platform. "You're eating chocolate! You're not allowed 'cause they didn't have chocolate in the Viking Age. I saw you, you've got a chocolate wrapper in your hand as well". The horse minder tries to deny the accusation, but he's unsuccessful. For it is not particularly easy to speak with half a chocolate bar in your mouth, hurriedly shoved in as you realise you are about to be found out. "I won't tell your boss if you give me some", is the ultimatum he is given by the boy, who cunningly seizes his chance to exploit the situation.

Perhaps the creative imagination, the magic of make-believe, actually helps develop the eye? It triggers thoughts about what is seen to be correct, albeit on the basis of what is felt to be authentic rather than historical correctness. And their curiosity is raised. The toilets in Viking Land are a good example of the difference between authenticity and correctness. Of course, there were no toilets in the Viking Age, so historically speaking they should not be there at all. When for obvious reasons the toilets are nevertheless a must in a present-day Viking village, they have been built the way you would imagine toilets would look like if they had in fact existed back then, in apparently old and uneven timbers, with a turf roof, and crude outlines of a Viking man and woman on the two doors. And when the children are seated there, on the incorrect toilet seats, they are encouraged to think for themselves. There is a poster on the bathroom wall, designed by one of the park's sponsors:

"What did the Vikings do? They had no water closets, no two-ply toilet paper, and no cream soap. Did they use moss? Or a sprig of spruce? Perhaps wet new snow worked well? We're only asking."

The posters, framed in 10-centimetre grey strips of leather, are signed "SABA-Mölnlycke, suppliers of sanitary products to Viking Land". And undoubtedly, their message makes you think as you sit there, enjoying the luxury of SABA-Mölnlycke's soft, high-quality toilet paper. Imagine how cold it would be if you had to use snow. Or a prickly sprig of spruce. Moss sounds best, but it would probably get itchy afterwards, and on and on.

However, not even the magic of make-believe is surrounded by "authentiquarian" considerations. In certain contexts, the children appeared not to care the least about obvious credibility flaws. In the morning, as we were having our breakfast after a long Viking night, the quiet was shattered, the bird song and the children's voices interrupted, by an outrageously inappropriate intrusion in our past-time bliss: a tractor came driving up the gravel track, with a load of firewood in its grab. What an incredible double-blunder, I thought. First, the tractor is obviously not part of the Viking Age, and second, four of these children had been working their guts out the day before to make the yard tidy by transforming the heap of wood at the centre into a neat pile at the side. And now this highly modern tractor is bringing more logs, all of which are deposited in a heap at the middle of the yard. As the tractor made not only one trip,

but three and four as the morning passed, I started getting really annoyed. Was it really impossible to get some peace and quite during breakfast? The children responded differently. At first they seemed not even to notice. But suddenly some clever souls realised they could make use of the empty grab on the return trip, to get a ride on the tractor. And thus the morning's entertainment was secured, even for yesterday's wood-stackers who seemed not to be the least bothered that their work had been obliterated in a single tractor trip.

When the past happens in a historical theme park, the happening reaches beyond history. Children who travel to the make-believe land of times past, all bring one glaringly inappropriate object: a camera. This is a happening of sufficient note to be worth photographing, and which deserves a space in the album. This is something they want to show their friends, and which earns them attention. Also, it is an experience that will take its place among other childhood memories, to be included in the autobiographical production.

What about the Museums and the Magic of Authenticity?

It is easy to criticise the historical theme parks for their unorthodox accounts of history and lack of antiquarian accuracy. Of course there were no toilets in the Viking Age, and it is clearly annoyingly easy for anyone with expert historical knowledge to spot incorrect building solutions. It is even more appropriate to ask scientifically founded questions about talking trees, or wish-fulfilling trees, particularly when they reject material wishes such as lottery wins. Helge Grønli has in fact received death threats based on his preaching of what some consider being idolatry. Nevertheless, most of the criticism is directed against commercialisation and popularisation. Many feel that the imagination is given too loose a rein in historical theme parks.

"What's so sad about Viking Land", said one of the researchers at the Folk Museum, "is that it's so superficial, the exhibits become worthless, it's all hip-hop." "Fun and games and amusement parkish", is the immediate negative characteri-

A historically correct souvenir from the past? This authentic rose-painted T-shirt is for sale at the Folk Museum in Oslo.

sation given by the Head of Education at the Folk Museum when I ask her to describe Viking Land. The Head of Education at the University Museum of Antiquities gives a fuller, but quite similar assessment:

"All the staff at the museum of antiquities visited Viking Land last week. Some of them think it's really ghastly, deplorable, but personally I don't think we should reject it all. The educational programme seemed very good; that part about *doing* things. The education staff appeared to be genuinely concerned with this, they're not just thinking about earning money. That's probably the management's line, rather. More ale and fewer stories, that's my impression. But I fail to understand why they're not more thorough and correct in terms of their buildings, as that would have given them much greater legitimacy."

Or in the words of the Museum Director at Vest-Agder Regional Museum speaking about the Bronze Age Settlement: "What we have here are originals, while they've only got replicas. Yes, they're not even replicas. They're assumptions, replicated assumptions".

Admittedly, Bachelard wishes to focus on artefacts as subjects rather than as objects because he finds the dreams generated by the artefacts to be of interest rather than the artefacts per se. Does this mean that the artefacts, as objects, are completely uninteresting? Such as the original artefacts on display in museums? The artefacts that *are* the past? The Museum Director points out that:

"The fact that we have, say, the Oseberg ship, and are able to say that this ship looked precisely like this more than 2 000 years ago – it's the original – then that's different from making a replica of it. Making a replica of the actual Oseberg ship, which would look similar to this, that's another experience than looking at the original object knowing that this is in fact the original.

Do you think that's the case for everyone?

I don't know. I think it applies to an awful lot of people, at any rate. Otherwise people would never travel to where they can see the actual originals. Otherwise they might as well have travelled to see the replica. Which is never as interesting. I do believe that for an awful lot of people it really means something to be looking at original objects. That's what I imagine, anyway. If that were not the case, there would be no point at all in the whole museum idea in terms of the public. Not in terms of research, you'd need them for research whatever. If original objects have no effect on people, I'd have to say that museums like this would be rather pointless."

Of course artefacts have a value as objects, and the original, dating from the past, has a special value relative to the copies. "The difference in value between the original and the copy can only be understood in this way: that the hand of the Master has touched the former but not the latter. This certainty gives a sense that the Master is virtually present in his work, as a part of our past", says media expert Anders Johansen (1996:124f.), referring to what Walter Benjamin called the aura of the original artefact. This reflects the ability of old original items to feign the elimination of time and history. Whatever its aesthetical qualities, the work is suddenly considered to have no value at all once it becomes clear that it is not genuine.

But even if the originals *are* the past, and have their own aura, they do not necessarily make the past come alive, at least not if the artefacts are left to speak for themselves, as is often the case in Norwegian museums. Certainly, the originals convey information, provide experiences and make the past come alive for those with sufficient knowledge to retrieve the aura of originality, even from shards of pottery on neat display – but there are few 10 and 11-year-olds among them. For pre-teenagers, three quarters of an hour is the upper limit for a visit to a historical past, and their first aura-experience comes when they pass a mirror!

We may wonder why it is that while original artefacts represent the museums' greatest pulling power, they can also be considered their greatest drawback as well, particularly in relation to children. For even if the museum educationalists are skillful, you can sense that they are working against the odds in face of the awkwardness caused by original items: "don't touch the things on the tables, they're so old they'll disintegrate"; "you can't have anything to drink in here"; "no, you can't go down to the basement, up to the attic, in the cowshed, in the barn, sorry". During the tours of the Folk Museum this was the constantly repeated refrain. And of course you have to be careful; original artefacts are valuable objects.

This is why they are placed in display cases, or behind a rope. And how much magic is left when the children are barred from touching the tankard, or from entering the house, because it is cordoned off at the door. In the more visitor-friendly variety, the artefacts are allowed to remain on display, although they are secured by various means, such as filling pots with steel pellets to make sure any attempt to remove it will be easily heard. However, how much of an atmosphere is it possible to soak up by being inside a blackhouse, how much past are you able to dream when you have to concentrate on not ruining or touching anything that you're not allowed to touch?

The overall objective for most museums is to be faithful to their authentic artefacts. However, the authentic artefacts are no longer in their authentic setting, or are no longer used for their intended purpose, and so their authenticity is diminished. The curatorial dilemma that museums are regularly faced with is well exemplified by the story of this tour of the Folk Museum during which a group of nursery school children were meant to be given an experience of "an old-fashioned cowshed".

In order to get into the cowshed, the children needed assistance, and any adults would need to be supple. For the door was tiny, and half-way up the wall. "How do you think the cows got in," the guide asked the children, but had to answer her own question in the end: "The level of the ground outside used to be much higher, so that the door was in fact at ground level, like normal doors. And the cows were smaller, too". The remainder of the tour was a continuous explanation of what things were really like in this authentic cowshed when it was actually being used for its intended purpose.

When the children wondered why there were no pens in the shed, they were told that: "Well, there used to be pens. The reason why there's none now, is that the old ones are ruined. And it would be a bit daft to make new ones, which wouldn't really fit in and might not be quite right". At the centre of the cowshed floor a huge, strange-looking wooden structure was looming. The children obviously wondered what it might be. "Well, that thing really shouldn't be here. So it's a secret. Just pretend it's invisible," was the guide's answer.

It *is* quite difficult to be faithful to the original in new contexts. It *is* difficult to stop the past. It is actually impossible. Because the original artefacts from the Really-Old-Days are as old as they are, there is obviously not that much left of them, as is the case, for instance, for shards of pottery from the Bronze Age. They are quite inaccessible to most people. To ensure that the exhibited artefacts are comprehensible and meaningful representatives of a past, the originals are often augmented, even at the museums.

Should we be better at stating that these are replicas?

Director at Vest Agder Regional Museum admits that not everything is as it should be, not even in their antiquity exhibition:

"For example, from prehistoric times we have virtually nothing wooden. You know. And then we put wooden shafts on original arrowheads or knives or whatever, in order to illustrate what they may have looked like. And we're doing that as well. And it's obviously debatable to what degree we should be better at saying that these are replicas, and that these are attempts to show what it may have looked like, instead of simply exhibiting it. There's clearly a whole lot of this thing going on, here as well as at a lot of other museums, so we're far from consistent. This is an awfully difficult issue, and there are no easy answers. It would be difficult to sit down and document every little tiny object for the public; that would simply make it boring."

It is easy to reject or disapprove of the museums' criticism of the historical theme parks, or to direct the very same arguments back to the traditional conveyers of history. "It's a bit like opening the door of a toilet that's taken. You surprise the museums with their pants down", says Billy Ehn (1986) about discovering underhand practices. In some ways you could say that it is worse for museums to sail under false colours by exhibiting replicas as originals without saying so, because their prime claim to fame is precisely the fact that they are in possession of the historical originals. For as Anders Johansen pointed out: whatever the aesthetic quality, the object or work is suddenly considered to have no value at all once it becomes clear that it is not genuine.

An Era with No Sense of History?

It appears that everyone agrees about one thing, whether they come from the commercially or religiously based lands of the past, or from the traditional museums with a more antiquarian profile: we live in an era with no sense of history. The Bronze Age Settlement constantly presents examples of our lacking sense of history: people have forgotten about love and care, we no longer know our natural environment and consequently we no longer know how to manage the earth's resources, we fail to exploit our own potentials. The reason why we must fight not to lose our sense of history is that the past provides the answer to the problem. Helge explains:

"The way ahead goes back. There is no way we can continue the current trend. The only thing that'll happen then is that we'll get to the top of a cliff and make a nosedive, pulling with us every other living creature. We're not allowed to do that. If we do that, we will have elevated ourselves not only to god, but to the devil as well. We need to go back to the past, and we need to use the best of what we've had through the times. We mustn't loose our sense of history. If we loose our sense of history, we'll loose the chance to hang on to the good things only, cause then we'll have to go through it all again, good *and* bad. And to me, it often seems as if we're only hanging on to all the worst features."

The Head of Education at the University Museum of Antiquities in Oslo also talks about loosing the sense of history, but in very different terms: "It's not that the children don't learn enough about history and the past. Sometimes they know so much it's quite impressive. But at one point, as they're growing up, it all becomes uninteresting. And today's adults are so void of knowledge that we can but admit to having failed in our task. We have failed."

The paradox is obvious: while there is a deep conviction that we are loosing our sense of history, there is unsurpassed interest in the past! It is clearly because people are in fact interested in the past that the present-day Viking Lands and Bronze Age villages keep cropping up. Should this not indicate that we are anything but loosing our sense of history? "An era with no sense of history" can probably take on two different meanings: that we don't care about history, or that we go about it in the wrong way. Could we perhaps compare museum-style history accounts with an exam: they require a type of knowledge that needs to be revised and learnt by heart for the sake of a day's performance, only to be forgotten once the exam is over? And this is perhaps why we are warranted in saying that both the knowledge and the interest disappear with age? Perhaps the intensely personal and physically anchored past-times-experiences from Viking Land and the Bronze Age Settlement make history take a deeper hold? On the other hand, is it at all possible to point to these tree-trunk-embracing men, talking trees, or chocolate-munching actor Vikings and call it history?

When people begin to imagine that it is possible to make direct contact with the past through the place, the land, and things, it can give them a dangerous certainty about their own excellence. Things are so palpable, they do not argue, and they can therefore be used as evidence that we really have something genuine of our own, in contrast to the complexity of the surrounding world, says Frykman (this volume), pointing to a key element in relation to all perception of history.

To school teachers this is so obvious that they will never even consider taking their pupils to a historical theme park for a history lesson without supplementing the park experience with further input. On the contrary, we have already seen how the trip to Viking Land has been context-ualised through a series of different subjects in class. The preparations leading up to the trip to the Bronze Age Settlement, and all the class-work afterwards, show precisely the same: "Tomorrow we'll try to live as much as possible as they did in the Bronze Age. And so we have to leave our watches, radios and sweets behind at home", says the teacher to his class the day before the big day. "Do we have to take off our ear-rings as well?" wonders one of the girls. "Well, what do you think? Did they wear ear-rings in the Bronze Age?" asks the teacher in return. Following a quick discussion, they decide that they should be able to bring their ear-rings only if they were made from flint or bronze.

When the pupils' accounts of their trip are read aloud in class after their return from the Bronze Age, it is clear that they all tend to emphasise the talking and wish-fulfilling trees, the clearing water and the maze that can be used for naming ceremonies. However, the teacher turns this into an opportunity to problematise the relationship between the present and the past: "Some things we know for certain about the past; for example, we know that there were mazes for they have found some in their excavations. But then there are lots of things we can only fantasise about. Like what the mazes were used for. These things about the trees and water are also good examples of things we need to imagine and that we'll never know for certain."

Rather than being presented simplistic historical knowledge through experiencing and dreaming their way back in time, we might find that the perception of history they are in the process of developing, is in fact quite sophisticated, in that problematisation and contextualisation are considered natural and essential parts of all historical information. In this respect, we might say that the historical theme parks' louder and perhaps even speculative depiction of a historical era has introduced a vital input for understanding the past. For problematisation and contextualisation are just as essential to our encounters with traditional museums and their antiquarian correctness.

At What Age do You Become a European?

Was Svante Beckman right when he forewarned 10 years ago that the antiquarian professors would be left holding the authentic, representative and high-quality baby? Yes and no.

They find it difficult to compete with the historical theme parks in terms of making the past come alive. Not only does their academic background complicate the animation process; publicly funded museums have access to a much smaller purse than the privately run historical theme parks, which tend to be backed by multinational sponsors. However, there is no need to be left holding the baby for this reason. There are many who would take no pleasure at all in dressing up and enacting Vikings or Bronze Age men, cutting up vegetables or stacking wood, or embracing talking trees. Many would probably consider these activities to be totally unrelated to the past. They would however find it exciting and informative to visit a traditional museum and walk from one display cage to the next, from one original artefact to the next, while letting themselves be surprised and entertained, or while reflecting on the museum's layout of the past. These are people who would love to attend seminars organised by the museum, and who take great joy in and feel reassured by the fact that our past is preserved by sound, reliable institutions whose job it is to record, document, restore, exhibit and research the original artefacts of history. In fact, the museums have every opportunity to specialise in the areas where they already excel.

However, this group of people will hardly be inundated with pre-teenage children. And it is with respect to these pre-teenagers that I believe Svante Beckman's predictions were right. Perhaps the children will come to the museums as they grow older, but while they are still in their pre-teens I do believe that they will spend an increasing amount of time on the playgrounds of historical theme parks. And if this is correct, what does it imply?

Theme parks like Viking Land and the Bronze Age Settlement are often considered to be some of the most important sources of de-localisation of cultural phenomena (as are airports, hotel chains, television, and similar modern installations). In the words of cultural researcher Alexander Wilson (1992): "It's at once every place and no place; it is on the land but not of it." Yet this may be the very reason why they also have this incredible ability to provide substance and life to imaginary worlds, to people and cultural identities.

For example, if we look at Benedict Anderson's (1983) familiar concept of the imagined community of a national identity, we could easily say that theme parks like Viking Land and the Bronze Age Settlement are very much linked to the narrative and feelings of a national community. Ethnologist Orvar Löfgren (1993) discusses how the magic charge of the national territory arises from different forms of symbolic earthing of national themes. "Much the same way as maps change colours to simplify and clarify the nations, the emergence of national landscapes and scenarios means that the nation is taking *place*; these arenas have a wide variety of changing moods, memories and myths assigned to them, thus generating a cultural condensation of the national", says Löfgren (1993:90). These locations become sacred places, places of pilgrimage, which is what the museums have traditionally been. In many ways, the Folk

Museum in Oslo displays and performs national identity; it is a Norway in miniature. In my opinion, this is what the historical theme parks are in the process of becoming.

It is interesting to reflect on the age perspective in relation to the feeling of belonging and citizenship. According to Orvar Löfgren (2000), the kindergartens' virtually insatiable need for cultural props and their use of material culture constituted the principal contributing factor to the homogenisation of customs in the various Nordic countries. The kindergartens filled rituals and festival celebrations with new vigour and colonised worlds that sidelined traditions and the peasant community. "The rituals of childhood help define citizenship, or the sense of belonging to a system", says Frykman (1999), maintaining that "the solution to the problem of how to reach the citizen, appears to go via the land of childhood".

At what age does a person become a citizen of Europe? How old do you need to be to become a European? Construction européenne is clearly aimed at the traditional channels, where national belonging is based on a set of narratives about a perceived community, whether you believe in the significance of the printed word, like Anderson (1983), or in education, like Gellner (1983). However, these modes of expression are rarely important to the smallest children, so is this perhaps a community which appeals to those approaching the end of their teenage years? Anna Burstedt (this volume) refers to a different line of thought in relation to the belonging of identities as she discusses the slow food movement. She points to the ways in which food on a plate represents the embodiment and anchorage of a place, and she sees this as an example of the new regionalism which is thus in line with EU's device *In Uno Plures* – Unity in diversity. However, the slow food tables are certainly not crowded with children. They want fast food. Is Europe considered to be important and significant, something of which one wants to be a part, only after the playful years of childhood have past? Is it too boring for kids to be European citizens? Will EU have to change their way of thinking if they wish to unite the European cultures, and start going via the playgrounds of childhood to recruit citizens among the very youngest Europeans?

References

Anderson, Benedict 1983: *Imagined communities. Reflections on the Origin and Spread of Nationalism.* London: Verso.

Bachelard, Gaston 1992: *Jorden och viljans drömmerier.* Lund: Skarabé.

Bachelard, Gaston 2000: *Rummets poesi.* Lund: Skarabé.

Basso, Keith H. 1996: Wisdom Sits in Places: Notes on a western Apache Landscape. In: Feld, Steven and Keith H. Basso (eds.): *Senses of Place*, pp. 53–90 Förlag??

Beckman, Svante 1993: Oreda i fornsvängen. In: Jonas Anshelm(ed.): *Modernisering och Kulturarv Essäer och uppsatser*, pp. 25–57. Stockholm/Stehag: Brutus Östlings Bokförlag.

Berkaak, Odd Are 1992: *Ressursbruk, bevaringsideologier og antikvarisk praksis i fartøyvernet.* Kolsås: Norsk forening for fartøyvern.

Ehn, Billy 1986: *Museendet. Den museala verkligheten.* Stockholm: Carlssons.

Frykman, Jonas 1999: Festen i barndomslandet Om ritualernas återkomst och kulturens infantilisering. In: Palmenfelt, Ulf (ed.): *Barndomens kulturalisering*, pp. 51–66. Åbo: Nordisk nätverk för folkloristik.

Gellner, Ernest 1983: *Nations and Nationalism.* Oxford: Blackwell.

Jackson, Michael 1983: Knowledge of the body. In: *Man (N.S) 18*, pp. 327–345.

Jackson, Michael 1996: Introduction: Phenomenology, Radical Empiricism, and Anthropological Critique. In: Michael Jackson (ed.): *Things as they are. New Directions in Phenomenological Anthropology.* Bloomington and Indianapolis: Indiana University Press.

Johansen, Anders 1996: *Gratie og andre forsøk på å finne seg til rette i det moderne.* Oslo: Tiden Norsk Forlag.

Lowenthal, David 1986: *The past is a foreign country.* Cambridge: Cambridge University Press.

Löfgren, Orvar 1993: Nationella arenor. In: Ehn, Bill, Jonas Frykman & Orvar Löfgren (eds.): *Försvenskningen av Sverige. Det nationellas förvandlingar.* Stockholm: Natur och Kultur.

Löfgren, Orvar 2000: The Disappearance and Return of the National: the Swedish Experience 1950–2000. In: Pertti Anttonen et al. (eds.): *Folklore, Heritage Politics, and Ethnic Diversity: A Festscrift to Barbro Klein.* Botkyrka: Multicultural centre.

Marcus, George 1992: Past, Present and Emerging Identities. In: Lash, Scott and Jonathan Friedman (eds.): *Modernity and Identity.* London: Blackwell.

Wilson, Alexander 1992: *The Culture of Nature. North American Landscape from Disney to the Exxon Valdez.* Cambridge MA & Oxford UK: Blackwell.

The E-economy and the Culinary Heritage

Karin Salomonsson

Salomonsson, Karin 2002: The E-economy and the Culinary Heritage. – Ethnologia Europaea 32: 2: 125–144.

This paper shows how the rhetoric of food can be used as a tool in the construction of European identities. Meals, shopping, cooking, manufacture and marketing are used as a mean to achieve the goal of a distinctive European character – particularly through the encouragement of culinary diversity. By talking of identities in the plural, I want to demonstrate that, parallel to the intention of strengthening a pan-European community, food can be used to highlight many contrastive identities. The labelling of food with texts and pictures offers a symbolic field that is redolent with meaning, where questions of distinction and categorization, belonging and anchorage in a changeable world are both raised and answered.

Karin Salomonsson, Ph.D., Department of European Ethnology, University of Lund, Finngatan 8, SE-223 62 Lund. E-mail: Karin.Salomonsson@etn.lu.se

"This year's great fad for offal and extremities of various kinds is a sign of how well Swedish restaurant culture has been integrated in the European food community [...] At present no single national cuisine – whether from Europe or from other parts of the world – is celebrating any great triumphs on the plate. After having travelled round the Mediterranean and made some stops in the Middle East and North Africa, more and more food creators are now back in France" (*Gourmet* 1/99).

"Euro-fusion" or Euro-cooking is the very latest fashion that the trend spotters of the food magazine *Gourmet* can distinguish in the diversity of restaurants in Sweden. Safe cards like duck liver and sweetbread have to give way to fried ox cheek and *brandade* (a purée of dried cod). A robust and somewhat rural food tradition refined with the classical French culinary art, truffled with the rebellious 1990s fondness for crossovers and bold combinations of taste. The editors interpret this renewed contact with the hegemonic French cuisine as a sign of the strong gastronomic self-confidence thriving in other European countries. It is certainly not by chance that the prefix *Euro-* is put to use. It has been launched – above all by the EU – as a synonym of culture and breeding, authenticity and quality, history and tradition. An express goal of today's EU policy is "to increase the sense of belonging to the same community" and to enhance "the cultural area common to Europeans"[1] (cf. Shore 1999, 2000). One way to realize this vision of European strength and integration has proved to go via the mouth and the food that we in today's society eat and also increasingly talk about.

My intention is to shed light on two different but interacting cultural processes. Firstly I want to show how, above all, the rhetoric of food can be used as a tool in the construction of European identities. Food and meals, shopping and cooking, manufacture and marketing can have both an inclusive and an exclusive effect, depending on the discursive context in which they occur. Food is used as a means to achieve the goal of a distinctive European character – particularly through the encouragement of culinary diversity. By talking of identities in the plural, I want to demonstrate that, parallel to the intention of strengthening a pan-European community, food can be used to highlight many contrastive identities. As examples of this I describe the ambition of the Swedish food market to be perceived as concerned with consumers, production, and animal ethics.

Secondly, I want to show how Europe and "the European" are terms frequently used to sell more food on the increasingly important food market. During the 1990s a whiff of Europe functioned almost as a trade mark which guaranteed the consumer *added cultural value*, a lease on a certain lifestyle associated with certain ideals (cf. Östberg 1999). This "Europeanization" is obvious in the marketing, packaging, and labelling of foodstuffs. To be able to launch a new product as an outstanding choice, it literally has to stand out so that it can be selected in preference to other items. The consumer wants to be able to associate the commodity with a specific origin, documented manufacture, and declared contents.

I want to use the possibilities of interpretation offered by the labelling of food. What can we read about global flows and local networks, about European policies, about the nation-state and transnational regions, about social differentiation and social identification, and about the distribution of responsibility between state and individual? The labelling of food with texts and pictures offers a symbolic field that is redolent with meaning, where questions of distinction and categorization, belonging and anchorage in a changeable world are both raised and answered.

The Guises in Which Food Appears

There is an obvious link between food, mouth, and speech. It is with the aid of the mouth that we consume food. The mouth also functions as a border guard by verbally formulating what is edible and inedible. In this respect cultural representations are as decisive as physical perceptions of what is considered palatable (Fischler 1988; Falk 1994; Kayser Nielsen 1997:8). Declarations of contents, symbols, hints, and recipes, along with pictures of the commodity, shape a cultural pre-understanding of what we may put in our mouths. Different genres for the description of food, its fashion-bound narrativity and poetics, indicate the changing relationship between humans and food in different periods and different social spaces (Mennell 1985; Caplan 1997:2ff.). Since food and eating play such a crucial part in people's lives, these fields function as seismographs, sensitive to change. They capture and highlight every cultural shift of meaning, helping to shape new fields. For a cultural researcher, the plain fact *that* we eat is overshadowed by questions such as *what* and *where*, *when* and *how*, *why* and *together with whom*.[2] As we know, food is infinitely "more than food" (A. Salomonsson 1987).[3]

The rhetorical dimension of food and eating today seems to be as important as – if not more important than – the actual intake of food (cf. Bell & Valentine 1997). "Foodies" – people who passionately love to look at, read, write, and talk about food – are an ever-growing group.[4] A special genre for describing food experiences has emerged. Consider this opening of an article about raw food, which could be read in *Gourmet* (6/98):

"On the plate, wafer-thin, light-beige slices of pilgrim scallop are spread out over a layer of warm, greyish-green lentils which have been turned in the fat from duck liver. The scallop slices are raw and almost melt on the tongue. The tender consistency contrasts with the roughness of the lentils, which is in turn softened by the duck fat. The generous, slightly sweet taste of the scallops meets the mineral, salty flavour of the lentils. The strange aroma of duck hits my nostrils as I swallow. The place is Brussels, the two-star restaurant L'Ecailler du Palais Royal."

Another characteristic feature of the guise in which food appears today is its intertextuality. Olive oil may be taken here as an example of a key symbol in a field of discoursing voices. *Compatible* is the heading of a text under a beautifully shimmering picture of a little bottle of balsamic vinegar and a large bottle of olive oil.[5] – "Like tomato and basil. Pasta and parmesan. Pizza and oregano. Garlic and lamb. Like a horse and carriage, they go together; the tasty, fruity, genuine virgin olive oil ..." the text continues in the minimalist language of advertising. Definitely compatible with the first message is the next advertising text, which is propaganda for the EU quality labelling of food:

"Legend has it that the gods once wanted to give mortals a gift. They therefore created an area that was ideal for growing olives, that is, with plenty of sun and high above sea level. In this way they brought together the two factors that give olive oil its unique aroma and taste, and which still today adds a hint of sun to all the dishes of which it is part."[6]

The idea of associating the golden liquid with the sun is a wise move on the part of the adverti-sers. For many people the taste of sun is syno-nymous with the taste of holidays. Memories of a special time and a special way of life are materialized back in the everyday cooking situation when the cap is screwed off the bottle. The same imaginative escape can easily be achieved by flicking through a Mediterranean cookery book or a travel account with gastro-nomic details. Olive oil also takes on a special shimmer in the EU Commission's em-phasis of its importance for "the cultural heritage of the Mediterranean region". Its special position is comprehensible when it is presented as one of the proofs that cultural aspects are also taken into consideration in agricultural policy. Moreover, writers about food confirm the image of the nutritional superiority of olive oil, and the spread of olive oil to other countries has become a subject of scholarly study (see e.g. Skjelbred 1998). Descriptions of Mediterranean food capture readers with the aid of the same key words in tourist brochures, food magazines, and menus as in health recommendations and the EU's regional policy (cf. Bell & Valentine 1997:156). Together they form representation regimes, convincing and persuasive descriptions with specific purposes: to see, reform, influence, or seduce.

There is covariation between the materiality of food – as raw ingredients or refined into dish-es, as cookery books and culinary journalism, as large-scale industry and export commodities – and the *processes* of which it is an example: movements and anchorage in social and geographical spaces, the production of similarity and difference, demarcation and solidarity. In the last few decades food has proved to be excellent fuel for flows – whether global or local – of cultural and economic capital, not infrequently intertwined with each other (cf. Zukin 1991, 1995). In this way, talk about food is also dependent on the inter*con*textuality that exists between, for example, the world of finance, the development of technology, media coverage, and the "ethnification" of food (cf. Appadurai 1997:187).

For food, as for other consumer goods, there are two main lines in the discussion of its role in cultural processes (Crang 1996:47). The first stresses the global homogenization of patterns of consumption, marketing, and the range of goods on offer, the process of Coca-Colafication or MacDonaldization (Hughes 1995). The second modifies the homogenization by drawing attention to the local practices that recharge global messages and commodities (cf. Miller 1987), resulting in "glocalism" (Featherstone 1995:9).[7]

Food production today shows a high degree of what we could call *displacement*, a reduction of the significance of physical space, in the direction of freedom of movement but also homelessness. Production no longer automatically takes place near the consumer; imports and exports criss-cross the globe. In multinational capitalism with rapid communication technology, "globali-zation", with all its social relations and mean-ings, is intensified, redirected, and speeded up (Massey 1994). One result of this can be "a new order of uncertainty" (Appadurai 1998:228). Many researchers have responded to this uncertainty by reappraising and dissolving established concepts, such as culture and identity. A contrary way to handle this feeling is to consolidate and define words like culture and identity, often in terms of regional, local, ethnic, or original, and use them as tools in the ongoing organization and conceptualization of everyday life. Many consumers ask questions about traceability and production methods. They receive important answers in words that associate goods with certain places like "the region", "the locality", "the home". Similarly, words like "genuine" and "traditional" insist on an explanation that includes determining origin and history. This genealogical interpretation (cf. Frykman 1999; Salomonsson 1999) of food calls for concepts which can problematize a specific understanding of time, space, and place.

In the following text Europe will be treated as a conflict-ridden field of meaning-bearing practices and identity formation, a figure of thought under constant (re)construction (cf. Delanty 1995), rather than a defined place. Yet the narrative of "the European", as so often, starts from "the national" (cf. Johler 1999a). In this case the nationality of the country is Swedish.

We Sell only Meat from Swedish Farmers

Conditions in Swedish chicken cages, pigsties, and cowsheds have become a national concern. Not just because Sweden has one of the world's strictest laws on the prevention of cruelty to animals, but because animal welfare has become a crucial sales argument and a way to compete on the European market, where animal protection, food manufacture, and the labelling of food in Sweden are portrayed as *different*. Swedish pigs are more fortunate than their European counterparts. This is emphasized by the producers and displayed in full-colour signs and bold slogans in food stores: "We sell only meat from Swedish farmers" hung for a long time over the refrigerated counters of the Hemköp chain.

"In between the cheese shelves and the meat counter I hear a familiar voice. Well-articulated tones, accustomed to appearing in the media, in the secure and convincing dialect of Dalarna. What on earth is Gunde Swan doing at Hemköp in Ystad? Then I hear the voice of an older man from Skåne answering him, and I turn round. There I see the skiing hero striding over a beautifully flowering meadow together with a farmer in blue overalls. Their dialogue is enacted on a small, graphite-grey television monitor. The video is an advertising campaign for Hemköp's own all-Swedish pigs. Gunde is visiting Annelöv in Skåne and talking about antibiotics.

'You know, it's just like in our day-care centres. If there's too many children in one place, they get sick,' says the farmer, scratching a perky piglet behind the ears. I can clearly see the straw in which the pigs are allowed to root around, and I am then assured that his pigs – just like our children – are not given antibiotics except when they are sick. The door of the pigsty opens toward the meadows and the light pours in." (Extract from field notes.)

The short film is skilfully built up around certain powerful symbols, each of which suggests a dark opposite. The farmer in his overalls, with the flowery meadow in the background, is a distinct contrast to the "pig factories" where the animals live a degrading and anonymous life. The assurance that there are not too many animals in this pigsty (which would cause sickness), leads our thoughts to overcrowding and neglect. The door stands open to the sunlight. In non-Swedish agribusiness there is no transparency or control; it is difficult to know what goes on in the darkness. Antibiotics and straw are two key concepts in today's debate about food and cruelty to animals. Unlike many countries today, Sweden has a restrictive attitude to the use of antibiotics and growth hormones. The straw, which makes it possible for the pigs to root around, if not outdoors then at least indoors, has been made into a symbol of ethical livestock rearing. The pig in the logotype for Scan's "Piggham" pork now stands on a stylized bed of straw, "which leads many consumers' thoughts to animal welfare".[8]

The subtext to which the marketing alludes consists of dead animal carcasses ground down to make fodder, cooped-up beef calves and pigs with mortal dread in their eyes as they go to slaughter. But these images do not originate in Sweden. They come from somewhere else: France, Germany, England, and even Denmark. And although the EU constantly has these issues on its agenda, it does not seem to have had an impact on all of Europe's farmers. The media frequently show films about animal transports and terrible slaughtering methods, and the Swedish minister of agriculture, Margareta Winberg, once again gets the opportunity to state Sweden's stance on the matter. The ghastly images that haunt us when we look at Italian or German sausages in the supermarket are here to stay, having become a virtually constant element in today's society (cf. Gordon 1997:7) – possibly because Sweden is now also a member of a European market without borders.

In 1995 the government appointed a commission "to analyse the market situation of the Swedish food industry after Sweden's entry into the EU" (SOU 1997:25, p. 9). The report was entitled "Swedish Food – on EU Plates". The title is a good reflection of the wishes shared by the Swedish government, farmers, and food producers: the food served on plates in Europe should be Swedish. The background to the inquiry was of course the anxiety that it would be European food on Swedish plates after the borders with the continent were opened. Would the domestic food industry be knocked out by cheaper, more sought-after European goods? The debate in the last decade about Swedish food and the food producers' endeavours to provide "clean and safe food" were further heightened. Inquiries and forecasts about the future of Swedish agriculture and the food industry's chances of survival, about market niches and sales arguments, were written from a special – European – perspective (cf. Jansson 1998). Sweden's relation to Europe in general and the EU in particular set its stamp on the conclusions and recommendations, depending on whether the continent was regarded as a threat or an opportunity, as an impediment or a source of inspiration.

Even before this, different segments of Swedish food manufacture had been investigated to find new niche markets, specific export destinations which would fit the Swedish profile (Hanf & Böckenhoft 1993; SOU 1997:102). At the same time, television and newspapers were filled with scare stories from Europe about mad cows with BSE, salmonella, and methods of keeping livestock that were beneath criticism from the Swedish point of view. The first reaction was fear that infection and hazardous foods would pour in over the borders, but gradually the chaotic situation in Europe was turned into an advantage for Swedish exports. Salmonella checks, the prohibition of growth hormones and antibiotics in fodder, plus far-reaching legislation to protect animals now became sales arguments to present to frightened European consumers. The Federation of Swedish Farmers, for example, coordinated a project called "Swedish Farm Assurance", which involved the sale of dairy produce, cured meats, and vegetables on the British market. Trust in the goods is created by the general image of ecological and ethical production which the Swedish Trade Council and the organization Food from Sweden have sought to give all Swedish food manufacture, partly through the possibility of tracing every milk carton and piece of cheese by means of a photograph and the name of the producer. The British consumers would even be able to come and visit the farmer or grower in Sweden.[9]

When formal borders are crossed and erased, uncertainty can result in new kinds of obstacles: when restrictions on the import of foreign food disappeared with Sweden's entry into the EU, ideas about infection, unclean food, and unethical treatment of animals set up new borders (cf. Jansson 1999). Like other "fears", those about food are culture-specific and tied to a particular time. What makes buyers define Sweden as a producer of desirable goods? How does one build up the image of a place which cares about animals, humans, and the environment?

Happy Shit and Swedish Country Food

It is becoming increasingly difficult to go into a food store to buy something for dinner without being afflicted at least once by a guilty conscience for not choosing the more expensive but environment-friendly egg box, milk carton, or detergent refill bag. Despite this, only 10–15% of the consumers in a survey in 1998 chose these products, mainly because of the high price (*SDS* 1 February 1999). The food stores have realized what a good sales argument an ecologically labelled product has become and have therefore launched their own quality trade marks or, like Hemköp, have selected their own pig breeders and egg suppliers who do not keep their hens in cages.[10] A discussion on quality and ethics has also been going on for some time in the production stage, among both management and unions, and in the Federation of Swedish Farmers, under the motto "Sweden's Farmers on the way towards the world's cleanest agriculture". An important role was played in this debate by KRAV; the full name of this organization is now *Kontrollföreningen för*

The expression "happy shit" (for which an English equivalent might be "cheerful bugger") comes from a poster showing the rear end of a happy, dirty pig with a curly tail. Photo: KRAV.

ekologisk odling (Association for the Control of Organic Cultivation), but the older acronym also gives the Swedish word *krav*, meaning "demand". The expression "happy shit" (for which an English equivalent might be "cheerful bugger") comes from one of their posters showing the rear end of a happy, dirty pig with a curly tail. Through time, however, KRAV has become much more than politically correct pigs.[11] At their website (www.krav.se), for example, you can order a book of "Delicious Recipes with Modest Demands", in which Anders Olsson, chef at the KRAV-certified restaurant in the Swedish Parliament, "leads us into the realm of tastes and aromas", serving dishes such as "barbecued steak with tomato and zucchini ragout", with all the ingredients apart from salt and water being KRAV-labelled.

In 1985, the year when KRAV started its operations, the meat-producing companies in the Scan group (owned by Swedish farmers) started their programme "Care in Animal Husbandry" to counter the consumers' criticism of "stressed pigs". This criticism culminated in December 1985, when it was revealed that the carcases of dead animals were used as fodder, that substandard cured meat products were sold, and that distasteful slaughtering methods were used to produce food. And this time the criticism concerned conditions in Sweden (Jansson 1998). The business has been cleaned up since then, and Swedish agriculture has acquired a good reputation by European standards. Yet this does not mean that there is no resistance. The actions carried out by Swedish animal rights activists, for example in Umeå, show that there is still criticism of Swedish food production (Abnersson 1998).

It has been found, however, that the consumers in the long run want something more than just to feel safe. In a debate book about food and Europe written in 1993, Marit Paulsen said "competing on a free market is not just a matter of being clean underneath, as Swedish honesty demands, but of being both clean underneath and attractive on the surface" (Paulsen & Andersson 1993:61). The same idea colours the ambition to give "added value" to customers who choose Scan, a familiar and dependable but rather boring and respectable trade mark. Through product development and different packaging, Scan Foods want to inspire the joy of food, to generate experiences, warmth, and appreciation, as we read in an article in *Nytt från Skanek* (1999/2:8).

Another marketing attempt is "Swedish Country Food",[12] an association for local small-scale production, with farm shops bearing names like Gloria's Apple Farm, Knorrevången (Curly Tail Field) Pork, Nicoll's Snail Breeding, and Agneta's Flowers and Bees. In brochures, one for each province, we are urged to "Discover the pleasures of country life and search out the different shops." Small symbols indicate whether there is a café or restaurant, parking for tourist coaches, and handicap-friendly premises. These little signs reveal the intention of making a visit to the shop into a special experience (cf. Berger & Kindblom 1996). Munkebäck Farm, for example, entices visitors to its shop with the words "Buy your food in peace and calm, while the children pat the small animals on the farm, feel the idyll of the farm and the rural smells…"[13]

The counterpart published by KRAV is called "Guide to Farm Shops". The greatest advantage of these special places is that the customer can buy directly from the farmer'– and of course buy organic produce. "Imagine finding a shop where they sell new-laid eggs, tender early vegetables, freshly baked bread, sun-warm tomatoes, sweet-sour strawberries. […] Then imagine that you have a shop like that just round the corner. It's not a dream, it's reality."[14]

KRAV labelling, programmes for ethical treatment of animals, picking your own strawberries can all be interpreted as attempts to restore confidence and give people a sense of increased control (cf. Beardsworth & Keil 1997:168; Ljungberg 2001). It is striking how often the past is used in the argumentation, partly to evoke a "more natural" kind of agri-culture, partly as a source from which to draw original and unadulterated food. The food is usually described in comparative terms: safer, more natural, more secure, guaranteed genuine in relation to an anonymous production chain in our deceptive modern times.

"Do you want to create a better future for you and your children? Then you should join forces with the "backward" people here at Hemköp. For we are indeed backward. We are endeavouring to get back to a world that was simpler, more clearly coherent. We want to recreate a society that puts the environment, health, and the future first. A society where our food comes from close by, where we know how the crops are grown and how the animals are reared. Then, and only then, can we assume responsibility for the environment, for ethics and quality" (From Hemköp's environmental information).[15]

If it had only been as simple a matter as taking a step backwards and suddenly finding oneself in a bygone time like the one evoked above. But instead of finding unambiguous signs in the study of what things were like in the past, we see ambiguity and contradictions. Of course there were no synthetic additives, but the food was not always fresh. Of course it was reassuring to know that it was your own pig you were putting on the table, but it was far from certain that the same pig had lived in particularly happy circumstances in its draughty, dark, tumbledown sty. "Recreate" may not be the right word to use if we want a society where environmental concern and the health of animals and humans are always put first.

New contexts are now being created, which are neither a copy of the old ones nor a continuation of modern ones. Today the idea is that the consumer should be combining pre-packed salad mixtures (oak-leaf, rossi, frisée) from Italy, ecologically bred chickens from the farm shop, bake-up ciabatta from the ICA chain, and blueberry soup with health-promoting bacteria from ProViva. Specially imported quality is crossed with sure ecology, fresh-as-it-could-be with functional food, local tradition with hi-tech. A representative of one of Europe's biggest marketing companies, the Gira group, pointed out in a forecast that the fragmented identities and differing social tastes of the twenty-first century will make it easier for exclusive niche markets to become established.

The EU and Traceability

The strong feelings of anxiety and indignation, powerlessness and anger that are often expressed in the debate about the quality and safety of food are materialized in the discussions about labelling. Labelling is used to give information about the designation, composition, price, volume or weight, uses, qualities, durability, and origin of a commodity, or to attract people to buy it.[16] The demand for facts and transparency must be balanced against comprehensibility and clarity. "Water, salt, flavour enhancers (E 621, E 631, E 627), veal stock, sugar, aroma, vegetable oil, thickener (E 415), acidity regulator (E 262 citric acid), red wine, preservative (E 202), lactose." From this declaration the consumer who wants to buy a 125 ml bottle of veal fond has to work out whether there are substances that may be hazardous to health, ethically indefensible, or politically unacceptable.

Labels, stamps, and certificates have become important cultural symbols at the interface between the consumers' anxiety and ambivalence about modern food production, and the producers' attempts to convince people and improve their tarnished reputation in the wake of BSE, salmonella, synthetic additives, and genetically modified vegetables. The EU regulations for "new foodstuffs" underline the safety assessment, possible risks for the consumer, misleading marketing claims about, for example, health benefits, and how much the new food differs nutritionally from the food that it is intended to replace.[17] The regulations include the foodstuffs made with GMO (genetically modified organisms). The opposition shown by Swedish consumers to genetic modification does not seem to be due to fear or a sense of ignorance, but more than anything else to rejection on ethical grounds (cf. *Genvägar till ny mat* 1998; Wibeck 1998; Fredriksson 2000).

The need to legitimate and control, to classify and label, is found in consumer organizations and ecological associations, as well as among EU officials and food producers. As a result, the EU's Consumer Protection Directorate-General has examined the matter in depth, and at the end of 1997 the Swedish government appointed a person to inquire into consumer information about food (cf. SOU 1999:7). The labelling of food has to cover increasingly larger fields of information: health aspects, allergenic substances, and religious, ethical, and political considerations. For many people, labelling has become a symbolic issue which is a matter of democracy and citizen's rights (cf. *Om märkning av gentekniskt modifierade livsmedel* 1996, *Märkning och marknadsföring av livsmedel* 1998).

The locally produced food that is sold at markets and in farm shops rarely has any declaration of contents. On bread that is baked right in the grocery store, no one demands a list of ingredients (cf. SOU 1999:7, p. 79). We trust in the quality and genuineness of the product, since the transparency and presence act as a guarantee (cf. Berger & Kindblom 1996). It is more difficult to convince the customer of this guarantee when the food is produced in a distant factory. Here quality guarantees and environmental certificates replace transparency and direct contact.

"From Stable to Table" is the umbrella term for the EU's attempt to integrate agriculture, producers, retailers, and consumers in the assessment of safety and risk in food manufacture. A new approach was presented at the end of 1997, the basic idea of which is based on "the commitment to full transparency".[18] Scientific committees, risk analyses, and inspections guarantee this.[19]

In the EU there is a fundamental difference in views on consumer guidance. The side represented by Sweden and other countries advocate control and labelling of goods before they reach the supermarket shelves. Whatever product the buyer chooses, certain fundamental safety requirements and properties must be satisfied. Other countries, however, think that it is the responsibility of the consumer to examine the product and decide whether or not to buy, say, a children's bicycle without brakes. This difference is also exemplified by the campaign for food safety that was mounted at the end of 1998 in all the EU countries. France's aim in this venture was to make consumers aware of their own responsibility for what they choose to buy. The title of the campaign, "Food safety is a shared responsibility: the responsible consumer is informed and active", reflects a compromise between different outlooks.

A Swedish publication entitled "A Foreign Assignment in the Service of the Consumers" (1996) describes how European consumer guidance can be perceived from a Swedish point of view. Concerning the fact that producers and lobbyists in Europe get indignant about Swedish consumer laws and the "know-all" attitude they reflect, the Swedish representative of the National Board for Consumer policies writes:

"That is when you bring out the European in you. The people out there should not have worse conditions than we have! This is an example of how to make a virtue of necessity – thinking in terms of Europe instead of Sweden ... the only strategy for retaining what we already have. [...] That is how we Scandinavians can become Europeans. And we Swedish consumer representatives will become increasingly better strategists – on behalf of Europe's consumer" (1996:20).

The task of controlling how producers comply with legislation on food safety is the duty of each member state, but the EU is supposed to monitor how this responsibility is handled. This point has proved controversial. In the group of representatives from different consumer organizations which has an advisory function to the EU Commission, it is emphasized that EU legislation on food must permit the member countries to adopt laws of their own when they feel that the EU laws give insufficient protection to the consumer. The group also says that the harmonized regulations must permit regional differences and the local character of food.

The question of self-determination has been highlighted in Sweden in the debate about the "monster bull", the Belgian Blue. Swedish authorities wanted to prohibit the breeding and import of this bull but were overruled by the EU. Now chefs, restaurateurs, and food writers are being urged to boycott the meat, which is said to taste worse in both a physiological and a moral sense.

An important aspect of labelling that is rarely in focus in consumer organizations, but frequently among producers, is the labelling that makes the consumer choose one particular product rather than another: for example, ecological rather than industrial, Italian rather than German, vegetarian rather than animal, and – European rather than American.

Protecting European Distinctiveness

"In the fourteenth century, in a mountainous little part of Europe, the farmer who leased grazing land was obliged to pay rent to the owner in proportion to the amount of milk that was produced. When the owner came to visit, the crafty farmer did not milk his cows fully, waiting instead until the owner had gone before he finished the milking. Not only was the milk from the second milking illegal – it was also different from the first. The farmer made a cheese that was not like any other. It was homogeneous, soft, and lightly salted. A forbidden but alluringly delicious cheese. After four centuries in secrecy, and as soon as payment in milk was replaced by jangling coins, our cheese could finally take its place on every table."

The tale of the farmer milking in stealth can be read in an advertisement (*Allt om mat* 1997/14) financed by the European Community. The text is flanked by a full-page portrait of a rosy, shorthaired young woman dressed in a blue checked blouse and a white apron; a modern-style dairymaid with a lovely round cheese in her arms. The advertisement is not really trying to sell cheese, but to publicize the EU's quality-promoting measures for "products with a history". To protect this history, producers can apply to have a product certified with stamps such as Protected Designation of Origin (PDO), Protected Geographical Indication (PGI), and Traditional Specialty Guaranteed (TSG). Registration of the first two designations began in the summer of 1996, soon filling several pages to which names are constantly being added, such as Sobrasada de Mallorca (Spanish ham), Caciotta d'Urbino (Italian cheese), and Katlenburger Burgbergquelle (German mineral water). Only two Swedish products are registered, Svecia cheese and the pyramid cake that is a specialty of Skåne.

The Traditional Speciality Guaranteed has not enjoyed the same success. Only a few products have been registered, most of them being brands of Belgian beer. Mozzarella will be registered, while applications for a Spanish ice cream and a Spanish ham are being considered. Another Spanish product, roughly "special milk from a quality-assured farm", was turned down after protests from Northern European countries, which claimed that all their milk is produced in the same way as the Spanish milk. These protests indicate that the labelling process is not just a curiosity or a matter of playing to the gallery, but can have consequences for the sales success of a product.

The justifications for the three EU designations may be read on the website of the Sixth Directorate-General, which deals with agricultural policy, and where quality issues have an icon of their own. The visitor is greeted by eleven smiling people, one of whom is the dairymaid in the advertisement. They are either wearing aprons of different kinds, overalls and boots, or equipped with special attributes like the beekeeper. They are all holding out a selected product: olive oil, Parma ham, oysters, a baby lamb, and so on. The text says "Specific products catch the eye", and the aim of the designations is to specify certain products above others and to protect their manufacturing processes against copies and forgeries. To label a product with the words Protected Designation of Origin, it must have a certain quality or certain characteristics which are the result of unique geographical and human factors, such as the farmer being forced to milk his cows in stealth and therefore keeping the best milk. Certain ecological conditions lead to specific ways of preserving food, for example, by drying, while other climatic conditions give rise to specific products, such as Alpine cheese. Production must take place in the defined *type* of geographical area. It must therefore be possible to associate the geographical designation of origin with one particular place on the map, for example, Parma, which is famous for its air-dried ham.

Until November 1998 the actual marking of foodstuffs was extremely discreet. On the plastic-wrapped Danablu cheese from Denmark I have to look for a long time before I see the small combination of letters that stand for the designation. It is clear that the labelling was not intended as a sales argument in the shops, with the aim of attracting customers. Gradually, however, all three designations have been given their own logotype – "a logo guaranteeing authenticity". The blue and yellow emblem is a graphic representation of furrows in a newly ploughed field, placed in a sun of twelve stars indicating the member states of the European Union.

The quality drive for certain products has a symbolic meaning for EU policy (cf. Johler 1999b). Firstly, it is a way to counter criticism of a common Europe that is said to advocate uniformity and the levelling out of all that is local and specific. Emphasizing geographical differences and underlining "traditional" methods of production is a way to display the EU's regional policy and simultaneously a proof of solidarity with socially vulnerable areas within the community. Perhaps the two new logotypes will function as a clearer, more obvious testimony that the regions will be allowed to play a crucial role in the future Europe. Secondly, the drive is an important part of the common agricultural policy which seeks to make surplus farmers find niches, to produce things that cannot be replaced by any other product. Thirdly, these three designations can also be interpreted as a response to the consumers' criticism of non-transparent manufacturing processes and questions of origin.

In the construction of the regional, certain places are formulated and articulated. Districts and provinces, towns and villages are pinpointed and become particularly "regional". The representations that emerge – regions with distinctive regional features – are used to include and exclude, to demarcate and define what is in and out. The EU's different designations to guarantee a geographical origin are helpful in this process. In the justification for the designations and in advertisements for the certified products, we find an emphasis on the importance of "belonging" somewhere, and how crucial local characteristics are. It is a matter of creating order by placing products on a certain point on the map and protecting this unique position against the threat of pirate copies. At the same time, the result of a "guarantee of geographical designation" is a paradoxical lack of place. The actual geographic place of production is of no interest; the decisive thing is the *ideal type* of an Alpine environment, a coastal climate, or specific social conditions. This form of *displacement* makes it easier for products and producers to move between different markets and still be perceived as "genuine". This is a time when the particular has great chances of becoming universal. The recipe for the authentic and unique regional cuisine can be found in Skåne, in Slovenia, in Galicia, and in many other places where people have realized how useful the region is for strengthening – or weakening – identities.

Regional Pragmatism

The EU is anxious to present the aura of a long historical tradition, cultural heritage, and genuineness associated with "regional" food as a *European* characteristic. On the home front, however, the regions are primarily local entities, which would prefer to assert uniqueness rather than community. The talk of food and the talk of the region have interacted for a few decades to reinforce each other's position, for example, in the struggle to attract tourists (Köstlin 1998) or in local cultural life (cf. A. Salomonsson 1987, 1994). In recent years this cooperation has been extended; from having primarily involved museums, local history societies, and study associations it now engages local business, municipal and county councils. The purpose is not so much, as it used to be, to search out forgotten dishes, the older and more original the better. The president of the Skåneland Gastronomic Academy, Sven-Olle R. Olsson, writes in the preface to the book *Skånsk mat och kultur* ("Scanian Food and Culture", 1998:7): "Our Scanian cuisine should not stagnate and become an antiquated museum piece; it must be constantly developed with Scanian ingredients and according to the principles of Scanian food culture." Problems of where to draw boundaries may arise, as for example when a company like the Bästekille Tomatoes, which is part of the "Regional Culinary Heritage" project, in its brochure "Recipes & Hints! Genuine Food from Österlen" launches Bästekille chutney: "Delicious with meat, in stews, with tacos, when you wok." The Academy's definition of "Scanian food" as something "which has been made for several generations in Skåne [...] from Scanian ingredients" (p. 7) is difficult to satisfy when it comes to either tomatoes or chutney. But I do not believe that any of the involved parties is interested in taking the definitions to extremes. In practice, regional food culture seems to be an inclusive rather than an exclusive concept.

"Region" is often used as a word with an automatic, natural meaning of belonging and local pride, besides genuineness and tradition (cf. Hughes 1995). This use of the word, which is so often described in research as being essentialist (cf. e.g. Idvall & Salomonsson 1996), also has a pragmatic aspect. It is these cultural meanings that reinforce the sales value of the region and the regional products. The word is supposed to function as a tool for creating a local *economic* identity, in the sense that it will be possible for people to make a living within the region. That is why "region" often becomes synonymous with production and networks of economic connections (cf. Törnqvist 1998).

Despite the pragmatic elasticity of "regional food culture", it is interesting to ask oneself when "regional" or "genuine" food ceases to be regional or genuine. *The New Soul Food Cook Book*[20] presents healthier variants of traditional favourites. Soul food need no longer be "off-limits because of excess fat, cholesterol, sugar, and salt". The book claims to offer a new view of Afro-American cuisine, the food being made with "leaner meats, egg whites, less (or no) oil, nonfat dairy products, less sodium, and fewer calories".[21] In the days of seasonal self-sufficiency, the now shunned butter, cream, and eggs were sought-after ingredients, which also manifested prosperity and good taste. Fat is no longer a wholly positive element in the food that is presented as rustic, solid, rural, and natural. Today old dishes and ingredients are being reinstated in low-calorie variants (cf. *Skånsk mat och kultur*). The changed symbolic charge shows the difficulty of holding up certain phenomena as referents to a shared past (Massey 1994). For some people, for example, the Scanian culinary culture signals natural ingredients and tied and tested recipes, while for others it means fatty, unappetizing food.

A Culinary Heritage

For anyone interested in food, the region is an appropriate scene for tourism. Distances are short enough to allow a morning excursion, afternoon coffee, and Sunday dinner. Above all, regions are perceived as pure and secure. The consumer can feel safe in eating and drinking things that are produced locally, in a way that both business and tourist interest claim is more natural, genuine, and traditional. Maybe it also tastes better because of "the flavour of knowing" what you are putting in your mouth. Eating locally or regionally is simultaneously an act of showing solidarity with the district, perhaps in opposition to national or supranational power.

This longing for purity recurs in other ways of articulating and practising the regional. The growing cultural heritage industry may be seen as "a nostalgic attempt to revivify pure and indigenous regional cultures against what are perceived as threatening forms of cultural hybridity" (Morley & Robins 1995:8). A harmless but economically significant threat is the global fast food industry, which is singled out as an enemy that is best combated with the aid of lively regional cuisines. A "food without identity" will be conquered with "the flavours and savours of regional cooking and banish the degrading effects of Fast Food", as we read in the manifesto of the Slow Food Movement.

The tourist brochure "Regional Food Culture in South-East Skåne" never mentions the food experiences that are much more common than eel feasts and goose dinners, namely, the Friday pizza, the Saturday kebab, or the family hamburger. Although these are statistically a "part of the region's natural food and culture", they are not in the list of restaurants that boast the blue-and-white enamel sign with the chef's cap and the words "Regional Culinary Heritage". These include restaurants like Snogeholm Castle, Måns Byckare, Karlaby Kro, Vitemölle Badhotell, and Värdshuset Österlen. The *regional* is interpreted and translated into different symbolic languages, which vary from solid traditionalism to bold innovation:

"Brösarps Gästgifveri:
Pink-roasted Haväng lamb
with tomato crème, young spring vegetables
and sage gravy
Price: 190 kronor
Lamb from Haväng. Tomatoes from
Bästekille.
Root vegetables from Löderup. Herbs from
Rörum.
Situated at the door to Österlen is this romantic Inn going back to 1684. Inside its warm red brick walls you will experience the genuine traditional of Scanian inn-keeping. [...] Every meal is a feast. Enjoy tasty, well-cooked Scanian food in a pleasant, cosy atmosphere in rustic style. The food comes from our neighbours, that is to say, the growers and breeders in the district. It could not be fresher or more wholesome.

Brummers Krog:
Stolen herring
Raskarum chicken with tasty root vegetables
Home-made cake
195 kronor
[all of the above in untranslatable local
dialect]

Just a few tables, the first roses of summer, a friendly reception. Monsieur at the pots and pans, Madame in the dining room. A handwritten menu that requires a great deal of verbal explanation and numerous gestures [...] In the dining room a distinctive buzz of human voices and laughs. We are all musicians in the same orchestra – the only real restaurant music. Hunger and expectations. [...] That particular page in the photo album smells of laughter, roses, and tarragon."

The "Regional Culinary Heritage" project was started in 1995 in southeastern Skåne in collaboration with the nearby Danish island of Bornholm. It is a part of the "Four Corners" project, partially financed by the EU Commission as part of their "network for rural development", which also includes Rügen in Germany and Swinoujscie in Poland. The aim is "to offer tourists and consumers regional food in an easy way" by supporting restaurants, food producers, farmers, and fishermen "who have a distinct regional connection". It is also considered important to create a distinct image for the region's whole culinary culture,[22] and one way to do this is to hold fairs, seminars, and conferences with delegates from regional authorities, business, and research.

In 1997 the project was entrusted by the EU's Tenth Directorate-General with the task of conducting a pilot study to see how a similar concept could be built up elsewhere in Europe. One of the main aims was to strengthen and highlight cultural and specific characteristics of the different regional identities in a united Europe.[23] Regions, which are interested in participating in the network, apply for membership and are for a time candidate regions. They have to observe certain criteria to become full members, and to ensure that everyone understands the criteria; a two-day information course is held for two representatives of the region. When this has been accomplished and co-operation between different local parties with an interest in food has been established, the region can apply to become an approved region, after which it can use the logotype with the white chef's cap with the name of the region under it. Restaurants and shops can also display the same sign to attract customers. The region is also presented on the network's website.

These presentations differ depending on whether the text has been written especially for this purpose or the content comes from a general tourist brochure about the region. De Peel in Holland, Lüneburger Heide in Germany, and Öland in Sweden are those which are most sparsely described, and with the emphasis on the geographical justification for being regarded as a distinct region. Demarcated by the River Maas as a natural boundary between two provinces, De Peel is described as "an area with many possibilities to serve as a natural heart of a big region".[24] Østfold in Norway invokes more traditional rhetoric in tourist contexts: "Here in the footsteps of the Vikings, among exciting cultural ruins, you can enjoy fishing, canoeing, golf and cycling, and of course traditional food based upon the raw materials of the seasons and deliciously served." The presentation concludes by welcoming people to visit "a land of adventure and daydreams".

Galicia, La Rioja, Levante, Castilla y León in Spain and Central Macedonia in Greece have all placed greater emphasis on distinctive culinary features. They plant clues about the reasons for the strong position of the Mediterranean cuisine at present, emphasizing the fresh, natural products that are said to give infinite sensations of colour, flavour, and smell. The wealth of variation tends to be exemplified with lists of different kinds of fish, shellfish, meat, vegetables, cheeses, and more specific delicacies such as "the dried meat from León, the ham from Guijuelo, the morucha's flesh, the

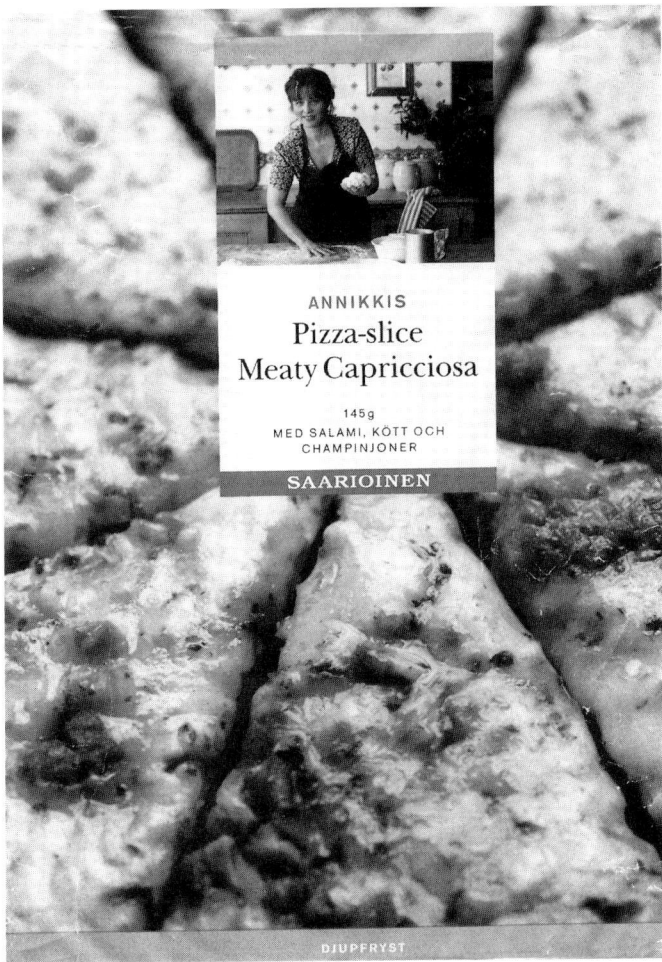

You can feel quite safe when you know it is homemade! A telling example of marketing strategies built on intimacy and a personal relationship.

Zamora's cheese, the kidney bean from Barco de Avila, the lentil from Armuña..."

"Regional food" is not just any food. It has an established origin and a documented history and therefore is not anonymous or insignificant. Products that cannot invoke a specific place of manufacture, "a geographical lore", must create other sales arguments to inspire confidence, such as "a cultural biography" (Crang 1996:53). An example of how geography is "culturalized" is "pesto-flavoured diced bacon" (which moreover contains chicken extract!), a product that could hardly be sold in Italy, but which is associated here in Sweden with "Mediterranean food" (cf. Hodgson & Bruhn 1993; Askegaard & Ger n.d.).

When Food is Given a Face

A woman leans forward invitingly, smiling at the package. She is wearing an apron and has flour on her fingers. Annikki is baking pizza slices in a rather well to do Mediterranean kitchen. Behind her on the sideboard is a pot with twigs of olive, lemon, and bay. White tiles with a Mediterranean pattern in blue make up the backdrop. Yet it says on the package that the company that makes the product is not in Italy but in Finland. Annikki is probably not in Italy either, unless she has gone there and taken with her the first-class ingredients from Finland's pure nature, that is, Finnish pork and Finnish salami.

The packaging concept – Mediterranean romanticism on the front and Finnish security on the back – is successful and proven today. There is a brief, almost self-ironic comment on the promise of Annikki's "genuine pizza tradition". The advertisers have chosen not to translate the words *Tosi hyvää* ("Really good"); instead the buyer is urged to "taste so you will understand what she says". The Mediterranean charm is mixed with the exoticism of the Finland's primeval forests. It really makes no difference whether the pizza is of Finnish or Italian origin, if it is national at all. The crucial point is that there *is* an origin to tell people about.

Different aspirations are exemplified in this type of marketing. One is to regain the lost confidence of the consumer in food produced on a large scale. The manufacture is given the illusion of having been moved from the factory back to the home. This type of marketing is a guarantee that nothing "unnatural" occurs in the production process, which is intrinsically natural and genuine. New products are launched with the aid of personalization and intimacy. Mamma Scan, Mother Anna's gherkins, pictures of genuine farming couples stuck on the chicken wrapper, rosy women at the baking table, wine growers in berets screwing up their eyes, ancient Asians on packages of frozen dumplings. The faces that meet us on various goods today come from two different categories: those who have actually made the things we buy, and those who have been selected to represent a product with a picture taken in a completely different context.

The first group includes the rule of the KRAV organization, which states that none of their products may be sold anonymously (although there are not always pictures), and the campaign for Swedish food on the British market, where all goods were traceable to a specific maker. It is often "unsafe" food, such as chicken, meatballs, or pork that is sold in this way. Yet even in the launching of a new brand of soured milk, Öresundsfil, by the dairy Skånemejerier, traceability was held up as an important benefit for the customer. On the dairy's website, under the heading "Trace the origin of Öresundsfil", you can click your way to the soured milk, which is "produced by and for people in the Öresund region". Under the name of each farm there is a description of where the farm is located, who owns it, who farms it, what type of agriculture is pursued, and the business philosophy of the farm. "The owners Yvonne and Arne Nilsson own equal shares of the property, and together they have four daughters, Monica, Malin, Maria, and Marlene, who help out when there is a lot of work to be done." The text is accompanied by a picture of the family having a coffee break in the grass together with the cows. Several suppliers of milk are presented, together with a presentation of the company responsible for the dairy transports. Yet here the traceability comes to an end. The personalization lets us know the names of the children, but does not really tell us very much about the production process. What does the certification of the milk mean? What happens inside the factory where the soured milk is finally produced? The transparency and

Njut en stund av Medelhavet.

Instead of actually going to Italy you can enjoy the Mediterranean atmosphere just by serving a ready-made, frozen pasta-dish, the company of Findus tries to convince us of.

wealth of detail risk becoming deceptive instead of convincing.

Perhaps that is why the second category of representations is all the more important for convincing the customer. Above all this concerns "lifestyle food", for which the advertisers want to establish a mimetic relation with the buyer. Here the photographer has shifted the focus from the supposed producer to a metaphorical image. On the pasta dish there is a fat Italian restaurateur shaking a tablecloth at his trattoria; on the Mexican beans we see a bent woman with a child in colourful clothes; the Swedish meatballs are accompanied by a sturdy, healthy-looking young blond woman in wellington boots. The calm, uncomplicated, sincere life radiating from these pictures can be shared by anyone who eats the same food. This way of marketing and labelling a commodity may be called mimetic because it seeks to resemble a particular lifestyle and particular values by material transmission, that is, by eating (cf. Taussig 1992, ch. 8). Sitting down to an inviting Mediterranean meal with home-produced wine among friends and family hour after hour is enticing for those who have a round-the-clock career in one place, a family in another place, and friends in a third. Time is an important component in these picture-based narratives. Calm, harmony, a relaxed tempo or timelessness are in stark contrast to one of the product's strongest sales arguments: that it takes only three minutes to cook in the microwave oven.

The market's stylization and iconization of certain ideals and ways of life is one way to answer the consumers' questions, similar to what the EU is attempting with its quality labelling. Origin, history, and local character are captured in pictures and snappy sentences. According to a venerable catering company named Maison Pierre, this is a sign that "the emotion society is replacing the IT society. The consumer of the future wants to buy something more than just food, preferably something that tells a story, or food with a home-made character that you recognize" (*Gourmet* 1998/6:18).

Yet there are certain representations that would be impossible in marketing. It is difficult to imagine pictures of Danish chicken breeders, or geneticists in the laboratory, busy modifying soya beans or tomato plants. There are some things the consumer does not want to be reminded of.[25]

The Added Cultural Value of the E-economy

European food, as we have seen, has for many people become associated with an imagined "Mediterranean cuisine", where refined tastes are conjured out of healthy ingredients in a relatively simple and comprehensible form of culinary art. This is a model, a pleasurable ideal, for people who lack the time and opportunity to cook the food in the way a Tuscan farmer's wife can. They resort to pesto-flavoured diced bacon and pasta sauce in powder form. Moreover, the Swedish flag on the bacon is perceived as a guarantee that the pigs have not been transported and slaughtered in painful forms. For however enticingly the European cuisine is presented, it has been surrounded by suspicion and criticism after a series of food scandals. The EU has tried to intervene with the aid of white books, scientific committees, and increased controls. Yet it seems as if the most useful tool for resolving this paradox of boundless admiration and profound suspicion has been the talk of the region and the campaign for regional food.

Regions right now are extremely effective political instruments (cf. Idvall 2000; Berg et al. 2000). As entities they are easy to grasp, of a manageable size for rapid mobilization. They do not bear the same historical ballast of power, and they do not have the same problem with democracy that afflicts supranational associations. They seem natural, self-evident, organic formations and have therefore acquired an almost unquestioned right to exist.

There seems to be a vigorous notion that regions are good examples of cultural variation and diversity, of the unusual and the unique. The way they are described nevertheless shows many similar features. Similar advantages as regards landscape and climate, history and cultural heritage, traditions and customs are emphasized. Being European, which is often formulated in terms of history and culture, is an important epithet, for example, in descriptions of the regions belonging to the Regional Culinary Heritage project. This highlights the profound historical heritage through four thousand years of Greek civilization or through prehistoric remains. The emphasis on Europe's fine culture is exemplified in the monasteries, places of pilgrimage, and cities approved by Unesco as World Heritage Sites.

The European Community today, according to the English journalist Neal Ascherson, "will travel from the western Europe of nation-states via the Brussels superstate to the Europe of Heimats" (cited in Morley & Robins 1995:89). The alleged security and sense of belonging of the Heimat is often portrayed as regional in the EU's efforts to reduce the significance of the nation-state. The *regional* has been allowed to symbolize the failures of the nation-state.

Above all, regions are *local*, and in the ontology of the local we find today one of the most powerful tools in the rhetoric about European food. The poetry of local foodstuffs (cf. Taussig 1992:4), that is, the narrative and visual portrayal in marketing and labelling, typically promises small-scale production and traceab-ility. The region has become the EU's space for staging the desire for European solidarity, a European cultural heritage, and European quality. In many ways, the local breeder or food producer embodies the promise of authenticity and naturalness, tradition and history, which the EU wants to emphasize as a counter to the scandal-ridden food industry or the American market.

By buying a product that has been categorized as a part of the culinary heritage, one also becomes part of the new "e-economy". This time the "e" does not stand for electronic trade on the net, but – according to the trend-conscious magazine *Elle Interiör* – says something much more. "The real e-economy is beginning to grow among all those who understand that ethics, esthetics, ecology, and empathy are more important issues." A company in keeping with the times has a clear identity, genuineness, honesty, and nearness, and its operations must be based on trustworthiness and inner values (*Elle Interiör* 3/2000, p. 64).

E-trade could also mean European trade, in which European goods are given the same aura of culture and historical legitimacy that the EU fondly stresses in its descriptions of what constitutes a common European identity. One of the goals set up for twenty-first-century European cultural policy is increased mutual knowledge of the European peoples' culture and history by exhibiting inherited culture of European significance.[26] By making people conscious of "shared cultural values and roots" it will be possible to achieve the express goal of increasing "the sense of belonging to the same community", while also maintaining respect for national and regional differences.[27]

Perhaps the EU, by launching "European" food that is certified and traceable and with designated origin, is "a company in keeping with the times", which has understood the importance of a trade mark that gives added cultural value. A trademark must communicate a clear feeling and image, but this image also needs a spatial anchorage. Here the region comes into its own.

Notes

1. From the European Community's First European Community framework programme in support of culture (2000–2004).
2. At the same time, some scholars stress that the specific thing about the analysis of food and eating is the dual nature: the element of cultural construction is balanced by the fact that the object of study is one of "the areas of our lives that is close to biology, to which we must all relate, making up the constants in our lives: the intake of food, sexual maturity, love, ageing, etc." (Kayser Nielsen 1998:4). However, I do not find this reason enough to become part of the "post-constructivist cultural analysis" advocated for food studies by the Danish researcher Niels Kayser Nielsen (1997:19). This is not to say that the sensual and bodily dimensions of eating are not interesting – on the contrary, but as cultural variables rather than constants.
3. Swedish ethnological food research has sought to place dishes, ingredients, cooking, and eating in a social and historical context in order to draw attention to cultural meanings in a broader context (cf. Valeri 1977; Bringéus 1988; Nordström 1988).
4. Cf. Anna Burstedt's discussion of the cookery book as a form of experience (1999).
5. From *Allt om Mat* 16, 1997, advertisement for Zeta olive oil.
6. From *Allt om Mat* 16, 1997.
7. The idea that globalization in terms of flows, movements, and increased cultural contacts is a late modern phenomenon is criticized by, among others, the anthropologist Jonathan Friedman, who argues that "globalization" as a flow of power, goods, money, and information has existed ever since the first commercial civilizations traded with each other (Friedman 1997:269; cf. Appadurai 1997 and Hall 1991 for a discussion of "new" and "old" globalization).
8. From *Nytt från Skanek* 1999/2, p. 9.
9. Article in *Sydsvenska Dagbladet (SDS)*, 17 June 1998, and conversation with one of the certified milk suppliers. Compare also the launch of the soured milk Öresundsfil by Skånemejerier, discussed below.
10. The Hemköp chain claims that it tired of politicians not being able to implement a ban on poultry cages in 1998 as they had promised, so it simply signed contracts with its own egg suppliers. This initiative was rewarded with an invitation to Astrid Lindgren, the author who has combated cruelty to animals, and a diploma from the Swedish Society Against Painful Experiments on Animals (http://www.hemkop.se, as of 9 November 1998).
11. Today there are over 2,000 approved products, compared with roughly a hundred in 1985, when the association was started on the initiative of four ecological organizations. The aim was to achieve a credible labelling system for ecological food, by compiling rules for ecological production and by supervising compliance with these rules.
12. See further the brochure from Svensk Lantmat, Handla Din mat direkt från gården!, "Buy Your Food Direct from the Farm", 1998.
13. From the brochure God och nyttig mat odlad på ett naturligare sätt, "Tasty and Wholesome Food Grown in a More Natural Way", Munkebäcks Gård.
14. From Gårdsbutiksguiden Smultronställen, published by KRAV in 1997.
15. www.hemkop.se, as of 9 November 1998.
16. An inquiry into the labelling of foodstuffs has recently been conducted; see the report Märk väl!, SOU 1999:7.
17. Foodstuffs or ingredients are reckoned as "new" when they have been changed at molecular level, when they are made from animals and plants not previously used for food production in the EU, or when made by production methods not normally used; the definition also includes new types of bacteria, fungi, and algae manufactured with genetically modified organisms (GMO).
18. www.europa.eu, as of 8 November 1998.
19. The scientific committees set up by the European committee with the task of assessing and pronouncing judgement on risks concerning, for example, plants, foodstuffs, or animal fodder, were reformed at the end of 1997 to attain a more independent position. The eight members of the Scientific Steering Committee appointed the members after more than a thousand scientists

had expressed an interest. These committees deal with matters such as hormones in animal fodder, genetically modified plants, and of course the consequences of BSE. The neutral position that these scientists are expected to maintain is to serve as a guarantee against accusations of protectionism, for example, when the EU wants to ban the import of hormone-treated meat from the USA. When stating reasons for such a decision, it is important to be able to cite a reliable assessment of the risks involved. That is why the Consumer Protection Directorate-General has set up a special "risk analysis group" to carry out "transparent risk analysis" by integrating risk assessment, risk management, and risk communication. The group is also to serve as an interface between research and society.

20. See Regional Cookbooks in the United States, www.foodbooks.com/regional, 23 October 1998.
21. It is also significant that the interest in non-European tastes and habits leads to goods being marketed as unspoiled and genuine, but in restaurant kitchens and on supermarket counters here they actually do not look the same as they do in Thailand, Bombay, or Mexico (cf. Burstedt 1999).
22. From the Carrefour Sydsverige newsletter of May 1998, no. 1, www.culinary-heritage.com
23. See the application for EU project funding for a pilot study, 29 May 1997, www.culinary-heritage.com
24. All quotations from the regions' self-presentation come from www.culinary-heritage.com.html, 23 October 1998.
25. It is not certain that the pictures always find the right tone, that they succeed in evoking the desired associations. A great deal of this marketing concept is based on a romantic view of the original and natural, the genuine and unaffected. An ambiguous combination of picture and text appeared on the shelves of the Swedish state alcohol monopoly, Systembolaget, in the autumn of 1998. In the series Bengt Frithiofsson Collection a wine called Primitivo was launched, after the grape with the same name. "Our Primitivo comes from 60–90-year-old vines in Pulia with roots going back to classical antiquity. From the Latin 'Primitivus', the first of its kind, original. " To launch this collection, every wine was labelled with the portrait of a person working in some way with wine. The label for Primitivo showed a man with a bull-like neck, multiple chins, and tousled white hair, wearing a sleeveless vest and apron, working hard at a barrel. We read on the back label that he is a cooper. Yet for a consumer who sees the picture in combination with the big letters spelling out Primitivo, he looks like a primitive, uncivilized savage, with a touch of the Mafia. Working with cultural representations of the Other can be a tricky balancing act between seduction and alienation.
26. From the Commission's proposal for the European Community's framework programme in support of culture (2000–2004).
27. It is precisely this form of European community that has been criticized for ignoring all the people of non-European origin who are now living and working on the continent (Morley & Robins 1995; cf. Nilsson 2000). In the EU's endeavour to achieve a shared identity they search for an inner European characteristic and deny the crucial links with the surrounding world, both historical and present-day. If relations with others are recognized as identity forming, it is by negations: "non-Muslim", "non-American", etc.
* This paper has earlier been published in *Fönster mot Europa*, Studentlitteratur, Lund 2001.

References

Abnersson, Veronica 1998: "I stormens öga. Veganrörelsen och motståndets metafor." *Kulturella Perspektiv* 3.

Allt om Mat nos. 14, 16, 1997.

Appadurai, Arjun 1997: *Modernity at Large. Cultural Dimensions of Globalization*. Delhi: Oxford University Press.

Appadurai, Arjun 1998: "Dead Certainty. Ethnic Violence in the Era of Globalization." *Public Culture* 25.

Askegaard, Søren & Ger, Güliz n.d.: "Product-Country Images as Stereotypes: A Comparative Study of Danish Food Products in Germany and Turkey." Mimeo.

Beardsworth, Alan & Keil, Teresa 1997: *Sociology on the Menu*. London: Routledge.

Bell, David & Valentine, Gill 1997: *Consuming Geographies. We Are Where We Eat*. London: Routledge.

Berg, Per Olof, Linde-Laursen, Anders, & Löfgren, Orvar (eds.) 2000: *Invoking a Transnational Metropolis. The Making of the Öresund Region*. Lund: Studentlitteratur.

Berger, Monica & Kindblom, Inga 1996: *En säck potatis och ett flak ägg. Om gårdsbutiker i Kristianstads län*. Länsmuseet i Kristianstad.

Bringéus, Nils-Arvid 1988: *Mat och måltid*. Stockholm: Carlssons.

Burstedt, Anna 1999: "Besök i främmande kök." In: O'Dell, Tom (ed.): *Nonstop! Turist i upplevelseindustrialismen*. Lund: Historiska Media.

Caplan, Pat 1997: *Food, Health and Identity*. London: Routledge.

Crang, Philip 1996: "Displacement, Consumption and Identity." In *Environment and Planning A* 28.

Delanty, Gerard 1995: *Europa, idé, identitet, verklighet*. Göteborg: Daidalos.

Elle Interiör 3, 2000.

Falk, Pasi 1994: *The Consuming Body*. London: Sage Publications.

Featherstone, Michael 1995: *Undoing culture: Globalization, Postmodernism, and Identity*. London: Sage.

Fischler, Claude 1988: "Food, self and identity." *Social Science Information*, vol. 27, no. 2.
Fredriksson, Cecilia 2000: "Den designade potatisen." In: Lundin, Susanne & Åkesson, Lynn (eds.): *Arvets kultur. Essäer om genetik och samhälle.* Lund: Nordic Academic Press.
Friedman, Jonathan 1997: "Simplifying complexity: assimilating the global in a small paradise." In: Fog Olwig, Karen & Hastrup, Kirsten (eds.): *Siting Culture – The Shifting Anthropological Object*. London: Routledge.
Frykman, Jonas 1999: "Hem till Europa. Platser för identitet och handling." *Rig* 2, 1999.
Genvägar till ny mat? Forskare kommenterar genförändrade livsmedel. /källa/51, 1998 Forskningsrådsnämnden.
God och nyttig mat odlad på ett naturligare sätt. Munkebäcks Gård, 1998.
Gordon, Avery F. 1997: *Ghostly Matters. Haunting and the Sociological Imagination*. Minneapolis/ London: University of Minnesota Press.
Gourmet no. 6, 1998; nos. 1, 6, 1999.
Gårdsbutiksguiden Smultronställen. KRAV, 1997.
Hall, Stuart 1991: "The local and the global: Globalization and Ethnicity." In: Anthony, K. D. (ed.): *Culture, Globalization and the World-system*. New York: Macmillan and Binghamton: SUNY.
Handla din mat direkt från gården. Svensk Lantmat, 1998.
Hanf, Claus-Henning & Böckenhoff, Gerd 1993: *Food Industries in the Transition from Domestic Predominance to International Competition – the Case of the Swedish Pork Industry*. Occasional Paper: SNS 50.
Hodgson, A & Bruhn, C 1993: "Consumer Attitudes toward the Use of Geographical Product Descriptors as a Marketing Technique for Locally Grown or Manufactured Foods." *Journal of Food Quality* 16.
Hughes, George 1995: "Authenticity in Tourism." *Annals of Tourism Research* 22.
Idvall, Markus 2000: *Kartors kraft. Regionen som samhällsvision i Öresundsbrons tid*. Lund: Nordic Academic Press.
Idvall, Markus & Salomonsson, Anders (eds.) 1996: *Att skapa en region – om identitet och territorium*. NordREFO 1996:1. Stockholm: Nordiska institutet för regionalpolitisk forskning.
Jansson, Sören 1998: "Galna kor i moderna landskap. Frågor om mat och tillit i det nya Europa." *Kulturella Perspektiv* 3.
Jansson, Sören 1999: "Mental Borders on the European Open Market? A Case Study of Swedes and their Notions of Swedish and Imported Foods." In: Daun, Åke & Jansson, Sören (eds.): *Europeans. Essays on Culture and Identity*. Lund: Nordic Academic Press.
Johler, Reinhard 1999a: "Telling a National Story with Europe." *Ethnologia Europaea* 29:2.
Johler, Reinhard 1999b: "Food in Europe: Some Actual Trends and Some Ethnological Observations". Paper presented at Summer School, Department of European Ethnology, University of Lund.

Kayser Nielsen, Niels 1997: "Madens kulturelle verdener – mellem opbrud og permanens." *Dansk Sociologi* 4/8.
Kayser Nielsen, Niels 1998: "Madkultur mellem det lokale, det nationale og det globale". Arbejdspapir Kultur og formidling. Center for kulturstudier, Odense universitet.
Köstlin, Konrad 1998: "Tourism, Ethnic Food and Symbolic Values." In: Lysaght, Patricia (ed.): *Food and the Traveller*. Cyprus: Intercollege Press.
Ljungberg, Charlotta 2001: *Bra mat och dåliga varor. Om förtroendefulla relationer och oroliga reaktioner på livsmedelsmarknaden*. Lund Dissertation in Sociology 39. Lund: Sociologiska institutionen.
Massey, Doreen 1994: *Space, place and gender*. Cambridge: Polity Press.
Mennell, Stephen 1985: *All Manners of Food: Eating and Taste in England and France from the Middle Ages to the Present*. Oxford: Blackwell.
Miller, Daniel 1987: *Material Culture and Mass Consumption*. Oxford: Blackwell.
Morley, Davis & Robins, Kevin 1995: "No Place like Heimat: Images of Home(land)." In: Morley, Davis & Robins, Kevin (eds.): *Spaces of Identity. Global Media, Electronic Landscapes and Cultural Boundaries*. London: Routledge.
Märkning och marknadsföring av livsmedel. Rapport från nordisk workshop. TemaNord 1998:516. Nordiska ministerrådet.
Nilsson, Fredrik 2000: "Insiders and Outsiders." In: Berg, Per Olof et al. (eds.): *Invoking a Transnational Metropolis*. Lund: Studentlitteratur.
Nordström, Ingrid 1988: *Till bords. Vardagsmoral och festprestige i det sydsvenska bondesamhället*. Stockholm: Carlssons.
Nytt från Skanek 2, 1999.
Om märkning av gentekniskt modifierade livsmedel 1996.
Paulsen, Marit & Andersson, Sture 1993: *Europa och djuren. Om Sverige, EG och maten*. Hedemora: Gidlunds.
På utrikes uppdrag i konsumenternas tjänst. Konsumentverkets Årsbok 1996. Konsumentverket.
Recept & Tips! Genuint från Österlen. Bästekille.
Regional matkultur i Sydöstra Skåne.
Salomonsson, Anders (ed.) 1987: *Mera än Mat*. Stockholm: Carlssons.
Salomonsson, Anders 1994: "Pitepalt, värmlandskorv och äggakaka. Om mat, regioner och regional mat." In: Blomberg, Barbro & Lindquist, Sven-Olof (eds.): *Den regionala särarten*. Lund: Studentlitteratur.
Salomonsson, Karin 1999: *Utmärkt mat. Kulturella förtöjningar i europeiska flöden*. Rapport 1/99 i projektet Europeiska mellanrum. Lund: Etnologiska institutionen. Mimeo
Shore, Cris 1999: "Inventing Homo Europaeus." *Ethnologia Europaea* 29:2.
Shore, Cris 2000: *Building Europe. The Cultural Politics of European Integration*. London: Routledge.
Skjelbred, Ann Helene Bolstad 1998: "The Foreign in

the Domestic: Garlic and Olive Oil between Taste and Health." In: Lysaght, Patricia (ed.): *Food and the Traveller*. Cyprus: Intercollege Press.

Skånsk mat & kultur. Arena, GörmanGruppen, 1998.

SOU 1997:25. *Svensk mat – på EU-fat*. Betänkande av Utredningen om en ny konkurrenssituation för livsmedelsindustrin. Stockholm.

SOU 1997:102. *Mat och Miljö. Svensk strategi för EU:s jordbruk i framtiden*. Betänkande av Komi CAP – Kommittén om reformering av EU:s gemensamma jordbrukspolitik. Stockholm.

SOU 1999:7 *Märk väl!* Stockholm.

Svensson, Birgitta 1997: "Vardagsmiljöer och söndagskulisser. Landskapets naturliga förflutenhet och kulturella samtid." In: Saltzman, Katarina & Svensson, Birgitta (eds.): *Moderna Landskap*. Stockholm: Natur och Kultur.

Sydsvenska Dagbladet (SDS), 17 June 1998, 1 February 1999.

Taussig, Michael 1992: *The Nervous System*. New York/London: Routledge.

Törnqvist, Gunnar 1998: *Renässans för regioner – om tekniken och den sociala kommunikationens villkor*. Stockholm: SNS Förlag.

Valeri, Renée 1977: *Le confit et son rôle dans l'alimentation traditionnelle du Sud-Ouest de la France*. Lund: Liber.

Wibeck, Victoria 1998: *Föreställningar om genmodifierade livsmedel*. Delrapport 1. Linköping: Arbetsrapporter från Tema Kommunikation.

Zukin, Sharon 1991: *Landscapes of Power: From Detroit to Disneyworld*. Berkeley: University of California Press.

Zukin, Sharon 1995: *The Cultures of Cities*. Cambridge, Mass.: Blackwell.

Östberg, Jacob 1999: *Consumer Perceptions of Novel Food Products*. Research Proposal, School of Economics and Management, Lund.

The Place on the Plate!

Anna Burstedt

> Burstedt, Anna 2002: The Place on the Plate! – Ethnologia Europaea 32: 145–158.
>
> This article proposes reflections about how food and restaurants can be a comment on territorial issues. Empirically it mainly departs from two different eating experiences in Istrian restaurants in Croatia. It illustrates different understandings of what Europe can represent and how our understanding about food cultures reflect our interpretation and reflection about concepts such as cultural heterogenisation / homogenisation, national identity and globalisation.
>
> *Anna Burstedt, Ph.D. candidate, Department of European Ethnology, Finngatan 8, SE-223 62 Lund. E-mail: Anna.Burstedt@etn.lu.se*

Cultural Standardisation or Diversity?

Cucumbers, strawberries, and the percentage of cocoa in chocolate – not many issues on the E.U. agenda capture the interest of the Swedish general public as strongly as those relating to food. In a recent newspaper article (*Sydsvenska Dagbladet*, 24 Feb. 2000), the question of sugar in jam was raised. How much sugar can jam contain and still be called jam? Will the Swedish standard requirements for jam have to be adapted to those of other E.U. member countries? Presented in this way, the whole issue may appear insignificant, but the fact remains that many people are concerned about it. The Swedish jam producers concentrate on their right to preserve the traditions of their trade and its distinctive character. From the European Union's perspective, their main concern is to vouchsafe the consumer's right to know that what is sold as jam is the same product whether bought and consumed in Sweden or in Spain.

This jam debate reflects two contemporary phenomena. Firstly, the sugar content in the jam will only be a problem in a context where people and foods are increasingly mobile across borders. This in itself can be seen as a result of modern society's efficient logistic technology and increased tourism. Secondly, there is a connection between this debate and the effects of increasing mobility and a tendency towards open borders, and the ways in which these effects are reflected within the European integration politics. Will today's mobility and current politics result in a conservation or a standardisation of cultural and national distinctive features? What follows is an excerpt from a book of recipes, *Culinaria – Europeiska specialiteter* (2000), intended to further develop the subject.

"Europe is a fascinating mosaic of landscape, climate, peoples and cultures, passions and lifestyles. But regardless of whether you find yourself in countries as diverse as Norway or Greece, Ireland or Hungary or in any other country in this multifaceted continent, there is one common theme which we never tire of discussing, it is so varied and exciting: food and drink. Every country and culture has its own distinctive character expressed in culinary specialities, dishes and drinks. Fortunately, most European countries have reached a rapprochement and borders once closed no longer exist. [- - -] Naturally, the culinary horizon has also widened and with it the offering of fruit, vegetables, cheese, cured meats, wine and spirits. Whilst we are eating and indulging ourselves, however, whether at home or whilst visiting other countries, there is a risk that products will increasingly begin to resemble each other, resulting either in an international or uniform taste. For that reason, this comprehensive book seeks to emphasise the distinctive gastronomic character of every country" (*Culinaria – Europeiska specialiteter* 2000:9).

An opposition is described in this quotation between words such as mosaic, multifaceted, variation, distinctive character and standardisation, implicitly emphasising the need to safeguard the distinctive culinary characters of Europe. In the text, increased mobility and integration are presented as threats against Europe's gastronomic diversity. The cookery book quotation as well as the jam debate demonstrates that food, together with the conceptions and feelings, which come with geographical origin, sometimes go hand in hand. The purpose of this article is to show how food is linked to geographical origin and how this place-bound affiliation[1] and food are also linked together and become a food-cultural identity.

There is a debate going on in food media[2] that focuses on the development of food cultures in today's society. At the heart of the debate a fear of cultural uniformity and homogenisation can be discerned which seem to be the result of a tendency towards globalisation and supranational politics. The jam debate illustrates how a political body can impact our culinary traditions, whilst the cookery book shows the existence of a reaction against this streamlined development (James 1996:89). To demonstrate the interaction between these two tendencies I will illustrate how different culinary expressions can relate to a regional affiliation and will discuss how this affiliation and origin is/can be linked to a more theoretical discussion about the existence and meaning of Europe as a concept. The text will move between a general discussion of the connection between food and geography and empirical examples from Istria/Croatia where I carried out fieldwork in the autumn of 1998 and 1999.

The Territories of Food

The perception of different food cultures has been increasingly intertwined with the notion of the national state. Food is associated with specific geographical areas through the defining of various "cuisines". Although *Culinaria* stresses tolerance and the dissolving of borders and boundaries, the distinction between different national cuisines forms the basic structure of the book. Thus *Culinaria* affirms these boundaries rather than dissolving them. In fact, the materialisation of "the national" through food is one of the most obvious nationalisation projects of the late 20th century (Bell & Valentine 1997:167ff, James 1996: 78, Murcotte 1996:69).[3]

The jam debate and *Culinaria*'s emphasis on European diversity also points to the presence of a specific, non-national context: Europe. How, then, does one approach the concept of Europe in food culture on a local level? Is it possible to find ways of relating to the various administrative, political and geographical entities that form Europe through every day practices? All across Europe, cooking and food products are used as a way of expressing geographical affiliation. The local culinary every day customs and expressions have become a means of defining affiliation in relation to a larger, abstract geographical context (cf. Frykman 1999). At the same time, tourist food and local products become a way to provide consumers with a local, geographically specific experience.

What then do we mean by "local"? Today, as Ulf Hannerz points out, what is local can no longer be limited to a particular geographical area. Since the cultural and social circles have broadened considerably, even the national can now be regarded as the local in some contexts (Hannerz 1990). The national states that are described in *Culinaria* can be seen as local entities relating to global ones, in this case to Europe as a large geographical context. This renders the study of "the local" anything but obvious. The cookery book represents food cultures existing in places, which are separated from the reader, i.e. various areas across Europe, whilst simultaneously connecting the recipes to local practices, although with national overtones.

Europe as a geographical entity and a bureaucratic system, and perhaps above all, E.U. politics in the examples mentioned above – symbolise the threat of cultural streamlining and a dissolving of differences. The historian Niels

Kayser Nielsen (1997, 1998), who discussed the tension between homogenisation and heterogenisation in relation to food in particular, claims that today's widespread fear of food culture dissolving is exaggerated, since culinary traditions possess an inherent cultural inertia. Kayser Nielsen points out that change and resistance can be viewed as contemporary tendencies in relation to culinary novelties on the one hand and the preservation of local culinary traditions on the other hand. An important question in connection with this is whether the geographical belonging of particular foods has become more significant, and if this is the case, how that development is expressed. Is the emphasis on food traditions and the revitalisation of food products "merely" a reaction against an increasingly internationalised society where food becomes a compensatory excuse offering familiarity and safety? When the food business focuses on geographical defined products with the place of origin clearly marked, do economic interests control the process, or is the emphasis on the place as a local arena, which provides opportunities for transactions? In order to discuss these questions, I will refer to different theories about the interaction between global and local processes as well as the ways in which food is used to create belonging in a larger context.

In this text, Europe is seen as a conceptual territory that various food cultures relate to. The term E.U. is often used to denote an administrative reality, whilst the term Europe indicates a concept. In this article, however, E.U. and Europe are used more or less synonymously. Both terms represent a territory consisting of national states, where the number varies according to the context.[4] It could be said that its geographical map works better as a concept than in reality (Delanty 1996:21, Persson & Lindström 1999:19, Shore 1999:53f).

The problem of the Swedish jam standard in relation to other European countries highlights one of the E.U.'s political dilemmas: How can a federation like the E.U. foster co-operation between such different countries? The mosaic of states and the culturally multifaceted continent present both assets and problems (Shore 1999). How will the increased mobility and shorter distances of our time affect the way people experience and create geographical affiliation?

The economic geographer Gunnar Törnqvist (1999) paints three different possible future scenarios for Europe, three possible developments which may coexist, but which all make the presupposition that geographical origin plays an increasingly important role in today's society, since "placelessness" has become a possibility. The first, Törnqvist explains, is an increased division into regional units, which are smaller than the earlier national states. The second would result in a stronger integration within the E.U. and the third would see a reassertion of power by European national states over their respective territories (a.a.: 89).

In the light of these possible scenarios, the question of the role of food cultures in this development arises. How do general assumptions about national states and regions coexist with opinions about and expressions of the origins of foods? In a time when food seems to become less bound to a particular place and more mobile, it has become more important to connect food products with geographical belonging (Salomonsson, K. 1999). In agreement with Törnqvist and Kayser Nielsen, I believe that these two coexist. The questions are where, how and when does the geographical affiliation of food becomes important, and how can it be used to relate to and create pictures of contemporary geography.

The Locations of Food

One of the most visible examples of food as an expression of national belonging is in today's urban variety of restaurants. Occidental cities display a diversity of Chinese, Italian, Russian, Greek, Indian, Thai and Mexican restaurants. This contradicts the claim that globalisation and supranational politics will lead to a neutralisation of variations in food culture. When the national or regional origin of a particular dish is highlighted, the food, or the recipe, appears as an alternative, something different. The near-at-hand, local (or, in this case, even national) aspect is stressed as opposed to more stand-ardised restaurant concepts, which appear more or less without geographical affiliation. Foods which could be said to be without geographical affiliation are for example the foods that exist everywhere, at all times, which don't belong anywhere and which materialise in the shape of various fast food concepts and products (cf. Ritzer 1993).

My point, however, is that there is no such thing as food without geographical belonging. Even the fast food concepts have their arenas. All food is bound to a specific location, whether it is territorial, regional or national, or whether it is related to a rural setting or a royal dinner. There is no dish, which does not belong anywhere. All food fits into specific contexts. Even our Swedish every day food, like sausages and macaroni, belongs to weekday meals in the family kitchen, and perhaps to nowhere else. In the same way a regional dish, like *black soup* (a soup based on pig's blood originating in the region of Skåne in southern Sweden) belongs within a context where the regional feast of *Mårten Gås* is celebrated, or where a regional affiliation to Skåne is to be highlighted. Longtime best-selling Swedish cookery books like *Rutiga kokboken* and *Vår kokbok* may appear to lack such an affiliation as compared with cookery books that refer to other countries and exotic places, but these books do have a specific identity and they do belong within a specific context. It's just that this belonging is so much taken for granted in Swedish kitchens that it goes without saying. In this respect, the term *place* is synonymous with *context*, i.e. the social and cultural context to which the food belongs.

Food culture is a more or less a generally applicable and an all-embracing concept often used in food media, that is to say in cookery books, restaurants and texts relating to tourism. The term denotes an entity representing the distinctive culinary qualities of a territory – regional or national. Nationally or regionally defined food cultures serve to connect the consumer with the soil, with traditions and cultural heritage. The food embodies territorial belonging. Used in the definite form, the term *the food culture* gives the food a geographical identity, which incorporates notions and knowledge about other cultural expressions of that location, including history, tradition and origin (cf. Eriksson *et al.* 1999:44). When an Italian restaurant is described as "Italian", a connection is made between place, in this case a national territory, and a cultural expression, in this case food products and traditions. The food is a materialisation expressing a concentration in space. When this connection is taken for granted the cause for and origin of food cultures are presented in a manner that renders them essential and natural. Underlying this process of connecting food culture and origin in place, it is possible to find the deterministic assumption that nature generates a predetermination of what the food culture will contain. It is important to point out that such an understanding of the concept of food cultures as more or less static entities may serve to strengthen dichotomies and categories of cultural differences between "here", i.e. within a national border, and "there", beyond the border. As a consequence, notions of cultural differences between "us" and "them" are reinforced (Abnersson & Burstedt 2000).

Geographers Ian Cook and Michael Crang point out how the connection between a territory and the various expressions of its food culture originates not only in ecological conditions but also in the process where places are constructed symbolically, which in the long run affects the ways in which the symbolic representation of the food culture is shaped.

"[...] food does not simply come from places, organically growing out of them, but also makes places as symbolic constructs, being deployed in the discursive construction of various imaginative geographies" (Cook and Crang 1996:140).

As this quotation points out, food cultures rarely, if ever, follow strict national or regional borders (Bell & Valentine 1997:169, Bringéus 1994:20). Our ideas of different "cuisines" are social and cultural constructions, which have emerged from complex historical events and patterns (cf. Goody 1982:32).[5]

When food cultures are defined and geographically labelled they are also elevated to where they become accessible to the general public. The act of describing a dish or a food product using its geographical origin legitimises its position in relation to other food cultures; at the same time, the food culture is incorporated into a context where the differences define the shape of other entities pertaining to food culture. Thus it could be said that food cultures have created their own cartographic system (Burstedt 1997; 1999:175f).

How Come Restaurants are so Good at Taking up Space?

The connection between food, culture and space contains several levels in this text, and restaurant settings are empirical arenas where other places and spaces are articulated and shaped.

Firstly, restaurants are arenas where food culture takes place, i.e. happens. They are places where people can eat, talk, smell, taste, hear, socialise, drink, chop and fry food, hang around, etc. The restaurant as a place contains all the things that can be done on the premises. There, national and regional belonging can find practical expression. They can materialise in dishes and interior decoration interacting with staff as well as with guests (Beardsworth & Kiel 1997:120). Even if most people don't visit a restaurant every day, the possibility is there. At the same time, the restaurant is a workplace where many people come every day to earn their living. Restaurants are places where the concept of food is shaped and expressed on several levels: the day-to-day practice of its preparation, the intentions of the producers, the finished product, the encounter with the consumers, the reception of the product.

The other level where place is important to food is when dishes and ingredients are linked to a place, i.e. when the origin of the food is defined through words or objects. As I have shown above, this is often done within the field of food in terms of defining food cultures, where food, territory and origin are all connected to each other. The concept of place is to a certain extent concrete, which is reflected in how local ecology and climate shape the food culture. At the same time, the connection between food, place and culture indicates that food culture is also a result of human action, with its conceptions and relationships revolving around a location and thereby playing a part in the shaping of food cultures. If we find ourselves in a restaurant serving national or regional food, this restaurant represents a food culture, a geographical affiliation, a geography, and this location of food culture has been shaped by the environmental conditions of the area as well as by people's notions about this place. This articulation of locations deals with something that is "here", close and tangible in the form of a particular expression of food culture in the restaurant, but also with something which is "there", something distant, an abstraction, an idea or a notion.

When a geographical origin is expressed through a restaurant, the "here but at the same time there" is expressed. When a food culture is shaped in a restaurant setting it is moved from one food cultural context to another, from one place to another. The notion of the food's place of origin creates a conceptual space. This space is culturally constituted, and the food in the restaurant materialises the notion of the food's place of origin. At the same time, it must be pointed out that at the root of the notion of the food's origin there are experiences that were made "on location". Before food cultures are moved, even if it is just from a home kitchen to a restaurant where they are shaped as symbolic representatives of a culture and a location, they have been experienced somewhere, in a specific context.

Twice I went to Kastav

Autumn 1998. Croatia. In the far northeast corner of the region of Istria (some people would claim that this area is not even in Istria, since it is on the wrong side of the mountain Ucka). The weather is warm, although we are in autumn. We, four Swedish ethnologists, get on the local bus, which meanders its way up the hill, higher and higher. The closer we get to our goal, the more the road is lined with pedestrians and parked cars. We are all heading the same way, towards the annual street market at the village of Kastav at the top of the hill. The situation reminds me of similar events in Italy, and the phenomenon never ceases to fascinate me. Everybody knows where he or she is going and how best to get there. No ads in the local paper, no posters on the walls. Everybody knows that there is a market in Kastav; everybody

Kastav, autumn 1998. Photo: Anna Burstedt.

knows that there is no point in bringing the car all the way up. You just park your car in the first available spot and walk the rest of the way. You join in the crowd and the caravan of people going up the hill becomes an extended part of the market itself. There are no complaints, no reflections on how the whole thing is organised. For me as a Scandinavian, the scene is like something taken out of the Middle Ages. Constant noise, people everywhere, and the smell of the roasted whole pigs sweeps past us in the hot air. All around us business is made: trinkets, gadgets, market stuff, the things that you always find in a market but couldn't sell anywhere else. A million kinds of wooden kitchen tools, pictures drawn or painted by ten-year-old local children, personal horoscopes, handmade jewellery, wicker baskets in all sizes etc. And perhaps most important of all, in every other street corner you can sample this year's wine harvest. Not yet fully fermented, of course, but the old hands give their predictions about the finished products. We work our way up through the village along the narrow streets. It is the Middle Ages, winding, cramped alleys, which keep leading us to the next wine sampling, the next market booth. The whole village seems to be made for the purpose of hosting a market. At any rate, it's not designed for cars.

Every ten yards or so, we walk past a temporary restaurant. Some have even been given names to mark the occasion, and I suspect that several of them keep reappearing on an annual basis. Their barbecues and frying plates all display more or less the same food: fat-dripping, homemade sausages, *cevapçiçi*, spare ribs, whole roasted pigs, sauerkraut and bread. The whole range is often served up on a single plate. Plastic plates are precariously balanced and carried past over-populated wooden tables and wobbly white plastic chairs. The situation calls for a Mediterranean linguistic and public social competence that we lack, timid Northerners that we are. This must be the most poignant illustration of tourist restaurants' adaptation to tourists that we have ever seen. Driven by an increasing hunger we continue along the village high road. A square appears behind the crowd in front of us, and at the far end we see an open-air restaurant under a canvas roof. This seems to be more of a permanent restaurant, and so we direct our path there hoping to find more a formal, organised taking up of orders. At long last we find seats at the terrace under the tent roof, by an old, rickety table surrounded by plastic chairs in different colours. We are not quite sure what is expected of us, if we should order at the counter or if a waiter will appear at our table. After a while, a smiling, elderly man turns up. Luckily, he speaks Italian, and I ask to see the menu. He laughs a little and starts numbering names of dishes I can't understand. Then he shows me into the kitchen at the back, an ordinary home kitchen equipped with a few more cookers, but not really adapted to professional use. The furnishing is worn down after many years of hard use, and many of the tiles are broken. The man shows me the various pots and pans and lifts off the lids as he repeats the names of the dishes. I point my finger to a large pot of sauerkraut, then to some small, fried sausages and an enormous frying pan filled with *cevapçiçi*. All this is very exotic to me compared to our visits to more formal restaurants during the earlier part of this trip. As we sat there on the rugged cement terrace

Kastav, autumn 1998. Photo: Eva Persson.

with our gigantic portions of, as far as we could tell, authentic Croatian everyday fare, absorbing the merry market atmosphere, the crowd passing by just a few yards from our table, we agreed that this was one of the most memorable moments of the entire journey.

Autumn 1999. Croatia. In the far northeast corner of the region of Istria (some people would claim that this area is not even in Istria, since it is on the wrong side of the mountain Ucka). The weather is chilly, although it's a sunny autumn day. We are going up the winding hillside road that leads to the village of Kastav. When we last visited the village, one year earlier, it was at the time of the big market. On this autumn day, however, there was no crowd of people and not many cars around. We drove all the way up to the village and parked in a gravelled yard. At the edge of the yard I saw trees planted along a low stone wall. On the other side of the wall was the slope of the hill and from there we could see the valley beneath. I remembered the scene from the previous year, with several large barbecues and white plastic chairs scattered around, and the whole yard packed with hordes of marketgoers munching on pieces of fried meat dipped in *ajvar*. Now the place was quiet and deserted. The reason for our visit this year was not the market, but a restaurant someone had told us about. We walked up the narrow road to the main square, and there it was, at the far end of the square – *Restoran Kukuriku*. We noted with surprise that it was situated in the same building as the establishment we had visited one year earlier. As we approached, however, we realised that some changes had been made. The terrace had been refurbished, and the canvas roof was new. Inside the restaurant, the whole interior was replaced, and I was at pains to remember the rough state of the place at our last visit. The stained wallpaper, the broken tiles and the old tables were all gone. Instead, the walls were whitewashed and decorated with art in subdued colours. We seated ourselves at a side table with a bright yellow linen tablecloth underneath a white one, both immaculately clean and apparently newly starched. Although the hour was getting late for lunch, the premises were more than half full. A man in plain clothes came up to our table and explained that the restaurant's policy was to serve the season's local dishes as they themselves deemed appropriate. Thus, there was no menu to order from. Instead, small dishes, beautifully and carefully presented, kept arriving at our table until we explained that we had had enough to eat. The meal consisted of a number of small dishes, most of them based on mushrooms since it was the season for this. The way the dishes were presented on the plates reminded us of the sober aesthetics of the late 1990s, and the flavours came from either the natural taste of the ingredients or from various herbs.

The Direction of a *Cevapçiçi*

What had happened here in the space of one year? What had actually changed? The place was exactly the same, and yet it wasn't – the restaurant was completely transformed. What was different? On the way back from *Restoran Kukuriku* and Kastav I thought to myself that I would probably never use the interview I had made there. The restaurant was different from the ones I usually looked for and studied, i.e. restaurants that emphasise their regional and national belonging through their choice of dishes on the menu and their interior decoration. At the same time, I felt that my two visits to Kastav had conveyed an increased sense of understanding for the connection between a place and its food.

Although *Kukuriku* is not aimed at tourists, and the owners don't market their restaurant as a representative of the local food culture, the restaurant is still dependant on its local connection for produce and recipes. During the interview, Nenad explained *Kukuriku*'s restaurant concept as part of the *Slow Food movement*. This is an organisation that was founded in Italy in 1986 as a reaction against a general trend in society. The name is the opposite of fast food, and the goals of the movement are: enjoyment, knowledge, development of taste, slow tourism, quality of life, preservation of culinary traditions, ecological cultivation, biological diversity, cultivation of the art of living, etc. This movement would probably look favourably upon the struggle to let Swedish jam keep its content in accordance with "old" cooking traditions. Slow Food is a stance against culturally bland compelling processes. Just like *Culinaria*'s and the restaurant business' division of food cultures into national cuisines, *Kukuriku* can be seen as a cultural critical comment on globalisation in general and E.U. politics in particular. It is not without interest to see *how* this profile is created, although in the case of *Kukuriku* it is also a question of making a name for themselves and raising their profile in a line of business where competition is fierce.

Through its menu, *Kukuriku* expresses a geographical affiliation that is more than a result of its roots in the Slow Food movement. Istria is a region where the local cuisine is well defined and highly profiled. I noticed no marketing relating to this during either of my two visits to Kastav. Yet through the food, which is served the owners, express a connection with the culinary and geographical conceptions around the Istrian food culture. Istrian cuisine is a result of the complex history of this region. Influences from Italian, Balkan and Central European cuisines can be traced in what is today labelled Istrian food culture. In spite of the foreign influence and the culinary mix, restaurant staffs agree with the locals in this area that this is a food culture with an identity of its own, in many ways distinct from those of its territorial neighbours (cf. Burstedt 1997).

The anthropologist Daniel Miller (1998) shows how "material matters" for people, and how things are used, not only as symbols and identity markers on a semiotic level, but also because things involve people on an individual level. Not just to express identity but also in order to *experience* belonging, and because things offer people the possibility to express affiliation, to actively participate in the process of positioning themselves on the world map. When restaurants serve French, Danish, British, Istrian food, i.e. territorially limited food cultures, they celebrate the small-scale, every day, slow and resistant aspects as opposed to an international and global flow of goods, services and information. Restaurant food, which is mobilised to express belonging, functions as a material used in every day life to deal with the surrounding world. When people feel belonging through food, they simultaneously define the food towards which they feel no affiliation. The materiality of the food grants the power to express a cultural position in relation to others. Food offers the possibility to assign a place to belonging and identity. "Eating is one of the ways that the spatiality of our bodies is brought into being" (Valentine 1999:49). Eating is a way to connect something very intimate and physical to processes and products from far away places (Bell & Valentine 1997, Mintz 1985:4).

In order to show how *Kukuriku* keeps an eye on a European context at the same time as it resists a geographical dissolution, we return to the visit to Kastav in 1998. At the market, what were on offer were typical market foods: all kinds of meat. In Sweden, the quintessential market food is hot dogs, in Greece, *shish kebabs*, and in Kastav, spare ribs, fried sausages and grilled *cevapçiçi*. During the interview with Nenad, I told him about my visit to Kastav the year before, and how I had, strangely enough, had my meal at exactly the same place. We both commented on the restaurant's refurbishment, and Nenad explained that there was no comparison between the food that had been served last year and what was offered now. What, then, was the difference between the two visits? What was served was still Istrian food, wasn't it? After several field studies and discussions on Istrian food a clearer picture emerges of what belongs within its confines and what does not. The oblong meatball called *cevapçiçi* is a product that is usually found in a border zone, depending on whom one is talking to in Istria. To Nenad, serving this dish at his restaurant was completely out of the question. It was not until I put our conversation into the perspective of the visit one year earlier that the role of the *cevapçiçi* became obvious. The market at Kastav is a popular event where the food plays a simple but crucial role. Serving *cevapçiçi* during the market was not a problem – everybody in the area is familiar with the dish and it forms part of most people's every day menu. At *Kukuriku*, on the other hand, the preparation and serving of *cevapçiçi* would be making too strong a connection to Balkan cuisine, since the "new" restaurant turns northwards, to Europe, for inspiration. Here, "Europe" represents something positive, an idea of "The Modern". In *Culinaria*, similarly, Europe represents something positive, an asset, consisting of local food cultures with respect for local produce and local traditions.

In a way, the Slow Food movement is a European creation, a cultured project formed by people having the time and money to spend on the preservation of food culture. The fact that *Kukuriku*, in accordance with its Slow Food agenda, gets its impulses from the north, means that it turns towards civilisation, towards the future, and, paradoxically, towards the modern. A European belonging is emphasised in this way by means of the restaurant menu. The simple *cevapçiçi* embodies a geographical conception of the Balkans as a primitive, regressive and uncivilised region compared to the rest of Europe. The belonging and the compass needle of the *cevapçiçi* are directed southwards, not the other way. True, one could claim that the Balkans in itself personifies the ideals of the Slow Food movement, but the "slow" and "local" aspects of the Balkans are of the "wrong kind". *Kukuriku* depends on its local connection, but at the same time the selection of dishes on the menu is connected with a modern, cultured celebration of the place.

Michael Herzfeld (1998) has shown how the celebration and invocation of what is national often encompasses the traditional, local and "slow" aspects. Paradoxically, this feeling of nationality, steeped in tradition, is often diametrically opposed to the development strategies of the national state. There is no room for this kind of nationalism within the modern national projects where society is to be shaped. National food cultures are often associated with a nostalgic "then", and people's attention is turned to a place and a time long ago as if they possessed an inherent power. Nenad acts in the same manner when he highlights his restaurant's local roots and ties. Instead of adopting the contemporary, increasingly industrialised and internationalised trend of food fabrication, he chooses to slow down, by means of the food, and return to the produce offered by the area. By means of the food, cultural heritage and geographical and ethnic belonging is mobilised. This materialisation and expression of the origin of the food functions as a selling concept in local restaurants as well as in *Culinaria*, where European diversity is exemplified by local cheese production, traditional production methods and local produce. While Europe functions as the antipode here, marked by its freedom from boundaries, the food represents what is local and bound in place. To Nenad, however, Europe also contains a tempting modernity, which is in opposition to the image of the Balkans as a regressive region.

Thus, the conception of Europe and the E.U. varies according to the context. In *Culinaria* and within the restaurant business, Europe is represented as a many-faceted culinary attraction. In the example concerning the Swedish jam debate, the E.U. comes across as a threatening supranational power. The conception of Europe both as a threat of excessive standardisation and as a promise of an appealing modernity appears in the example from *Kukuriku*, where the manifesto of the Slow Food movement coexists with a wish to approach a European belonging.

Places and Geographical Imagination[6]

When food alludes to a geographical origin the meaning of the notion of "place" is brought to the fore, since it synthesises the territorial and cultural identities of food. Edward Casey speaks of the importance of place for cultural expression in the following way:

"Given that culture manifestly exists, it must exist somewhere, and it exists more concretely and completely in places than in minds or signs" (Casey 1996:33).

Here, Casey affirms the place as the concrete location where we sit, stand and walk, i.e. the reality in which we live, and he contrasts this with an abstract world of ideas, constructed by symbols and conceptions. As an antithesis to the concept of *place*, he establishes the abstract concept of *space*. Space is less of a concrete noun and refers to a spherical, abstract domain (Harvey 1996:24, Massey 1994:1). In a place, people can perform actively, whereas in a space, we are on a conceptual level.

Edward Casey describes place as the basis for everything; place is where temporal and spatial aspects take shape, and it is also the object for the repercussions of time and space (Casey 1996:19).[7] Above all, this choice of perspective is a methodological stance in order to approach culinary experiences where they actually happen, where their flavours are actually tasted, but also in order to show how place is the arena where culinary discourses have their practice.[8] Place becomes the arena for concrete action while space defines spatial conceptions, notions and concepts. Instead of using *space* in order to explain how a food culture is shaped when transferred, the term *geographical conception is* used here.

When a local affiliation is expressed in a restaurant, cultural heritage and culinary traditions are evoked and together they create the desired food culture on a conceptual level. There is no need for restaurants to be situated in the place that they choose to materialise; they can stage other places than those within the actual spatial confines of the restaurant, imagined places beyond the physical place. While restaurants can be seen as an actual place its content is rather more of an idea about a particular place, which is made concrete, materialised, in whatever way the restaurant expresses this *place beyond the place*. Restaurants in themselves are arenas where the territorial connection of the food is expressed. The content of this concentration depends to a large extent on what is focused in the restaurant.

In order to analyse how place is expressed in restaurants one has to consider how the images of national and local aspects are produced, reproduced and reshaped on an every day level (Valentine 1999:48). For the anthropologist Sidney Mintz, who has published texts on the production and importance of sugar during different times in history, the use of food products comes before the symbolic meaning of the product; meaning emanates from the use of the product in various social relations.

"'Meaning' […] is not simply to be 'read' or 'deciphered' but arises from the cultural applications to which sugar lent itself, the uses to which it was put. Meaning, in short, is the consequence

Is EU to regulate the contents all over Europe, and will Swedish lingonberry jam be known as European lingonberry jam in a few years? Photo: Maths Bogren.

of activity. This does not mean that culture is only (or is reducible to only) behaviour. But not to ask how meaning is put into behaviour, to read the product without the production, is to ignore history once again" (Mintz 1985: 14).

Here, Mintz refers to a phenomenological perspective where the view is held that the conception of something does not come before the practice of that conception. A story has to be told before it becomes a story, and in the same way a dish has to be cooked at some point before it can be representative of a food culture.[9] The conception of a place the way it's expressed in a restaurant must be preceded by the experience of that conception (Jackson 1996:39). But that experience may just as well be related to a Greek restaurant as to Greece itself. Both experiences lead to the same place, albeit on different levels, and even if the two experiences of Greece are different from each other.[10] The geographical conceptions play a major role, however, in how food cultures are expressed and experienced. They form a link between an everyday practice and a discourse. The empirical research from Kastav shows, for example, how restaurants can express the friction between global trends and conceptions of national food cultures and local practices.

A phenomenological view keeps the individual and every day aspects in perspective and at the same time making an analysis possible as to how the practice interacts with contextual factors. Using the theoretical concept of place as the starting point involves the direct physical experience as well as the experience within a cultural and social context (Casey 1996:19), in the relevant *space* as well as in *place*.

"This is not to say that human experience is without preconditions; rather, it is to suggest that the experience of these preconditions is not entirely preconditioned. A human life is seldom a blind recapitulation of givenness, but an active relationship with what has gone before and what is imagined to lie ahead" (Jackson 1996:11).

When restaurants express local affiliation they simultaneously relate to a geographical notion of how their own food culture relates to other food cultures. In Sweden we have a certain amount of sugar in jam, in southern Europe the sugar content is considerably higher. Food products can be used for a geographical positioning; they describe a belonging while at the same time defining other food cultures as different, as "other". This was the case, for example, with the Istrian *cevapçiçi*.

Since food is a down-to-earth, empirical area which may appear as an easy and obvious object for a phenomenological study from an every day, experience-based perspective, it is of vital importance to balance the analysis by focusing on the geographical conceptions that interact and affect the actual shaping of food cultures.

"The geographical imagination is a highly significant part of that "real world" which we socially construct, and has immense influence upon the ways in which people act within it" (Massey 1999:17).

Massey puts reality, "the real world" within quotation marks, in an attempt to distinguish between a level of consciousness where reality is what people claim to live in and a researcher's perspective where reality is a social construction. The point made in this quote, however, is that in order to understand and be able to analyse the interaction between "the real world" and the socially constructed world, it is important to take into consideration not only how things are produced, but also how things materialise and embody geographical conceptions (Massey 1999:18). A geographical conception is not about where that other place is located, but what it contains – the meanings *associated* with that place. Which moods and settings are associated with, for example, Europe, Istria, Greece, Italy? Thus, food can function as an interaction between local and global trends and geographical conceptions. All this interacts in that place which is the restaurant. Karen Olwig's definition of place, or site, seems useful in the case of restaurants:

"'Cultural sites', cultural institutions which have developed in the interrelationship between global and local sites. These cultural sites attain their significance because they are identified with particular places, at the same time as they accommodate the global conditions of life" (Olwig 1997: 17, see also Howes 1996).

Although Europe may be difficult to situate on the map – it could even be said to exist merely as an idea[11] – I would like to maintain that experiences like the one I had in Kastav *create* Europe. When we act with an existing Europe as our starting point, we also situate Europe on the map. This process may not always be a conscious one, but Europe is nevertheless part of reality, of "the real world", and as a territory it is present in our actions. Since Europe exists, it forms a territory which can be related to through existing, every day actions taking place within or outside that area – either consciously, as in the case of the jam debate, or subconsciously, as in Kastav. Europe does not appear out of a vacuum, it exists to the extent that the continent is used and experienced, and that is also when the geographical concept of the continent is created (Jackson 1996:10). These geographical conceptions are created in places, the "realities" which form the starting points for people's actions, but they also have an effect on our conceptions of, for example, Europe and food cultures.

The identity of the place is created in the identification process, i.e. when affiliation is expressed and/or experienced, identification and its relation to other identities of place take shape. In the same way the affiliation of a dish is found in the meeting point of its ingredients and the conception of that particular dish. In the friction between the place and the food, food culture happens – that is where we find Istria as a (regional) place, for example, and *Kukuriku* can be seen as the interpreter and presenter of this place.

The examples from Kastav point to the importance of close-range studies of what happens with geographical conceptions during the interaction between food culture and affiliation to place. Gunnar Törnqvist claims that today's increased globalisation leads to the rebirth of regionalism. From the point of view of food culture, this prediction does not appear to always hold true, since the emphasis on national cuisines remains. Still, the national cuisines we see today do have a regional character; local produce, local manufacturers and local traditions are held in high esteem. The preservation of traditional jam production, *Culinaria*'s emphasis on European diversity and *Kukuriku*'s Slow Food concept with its focus on local food culture and local produce, may all, in spite of the differences between them, be seen as phenomena expressing an alternative to the general notion of the standardising effects of globalisation. In the tension between local and global, food, with its focus on territory, manages to use opposites such as close – far away, fast – slow, traditional – modern, centre – periphery successfully. In light of my examples, European food cultures appear to remain resistant to the predicted effect of globalisation: culinary standardisation. Food-cultural characteristics emanating from a place-related origin are still strongly articulated within the field of food. Although food cultures are constantly shaped and reshaped, and new ingredients, presentations and methods of preparation are added all the time, these new food-cultural variations live on thanks to the emphasis on their place-related distinctive traits.

Notes

* This paper has earlier been published in *Fönster mot Europa*, Studentlitteratur, Lund 2001.
1. In using the term "place-bound affiliation", I refer to when something, food or people, define themselves or are defined according to where they come from. Synonymous with this term I will also use territorial affiliation and geographical origin.
2. In using the term "food media", I refer to articles about food in the daily press, food programs on TV, cookery books and food magazines.
3. In the article Scenes from a Troubled Marriage. Swedish Ethnology and Material Culture Studies, Orvar Löfgren (1997) has pointed to the recent reluctance within the field of ethnology to deal with material studies, and how this has led to a neglect of, for example, the materialisation of national states and the effects of mass consumerism on individuals. He propagates a revitalisation of empirical fields focusing on the material importance of every day life. Food, in this context, becomes a way for me to approach issues dealing with the importance of materiality in society.
4. It may seem that the map of Europe is permanent, but there are also colourful EU-maps that show which countries were among the founding members. The different colours on these maps indicate which year the respective countries entered the Union, which states are expected to join before 2005, etc. There are also other maps of the EU area that indicate participation in other trade and exchange treaties.
5. Many theorists bring up as a point of social criticism the importance of remembering the social, historical, cultural and economic processes behind food-cultural representations, like global food transports and complicated social conditions (cf. Cook and Crang 1996, Howes 1996, Hooks 1998).
6. The term "geographical imagination" is a development of Benedict Anderson's "imagined community" which refers to the imagined community of national states, and Edward Said's discussion of the Orient as an idea and as a socially and culturally constructed territory.
7. The geographer Doreen Massey would assume a different starting point, emphasising the need to see space as something socially constructed, where place is defined as a part, a level of the space: "If, however, the spatial is thought of in the context of space-time and as formed out of social interrelations on all scales, the one view of a place is as a particular articulation of those relations, a particular moment in those networks of social relations and understandings" (Massey 1994:5, see also Saltzman & Svensson 1997:13).
8. A helpful discussion on how a "direct perception of environment, formed out of a practical activity, generally speaking comes before all constructions" can be found in Hornborg 1997:213.
9. Cookery books are a special case here, since they contain instructions as to how dishes should be prepared. However, these instructions are preceded by an actual preparation, a practice. A recipe is a synthesis of an experience, a transformation from experience into notion.
10. This line of reasoning highlights the issue of how "genuine" a food-cultural presentation is. Many restaurants market themselves as more genuine than others in order to show how well they have succeeded in recreating their geographical origin, and even in the context of tourist tours, some experiences are pictured as more genuine than others (Burstedt 1999). The act of defining something as genuine may involve a subconscious exclusion of something else as false. I mean that all food-cultural experiences should be interpreted as genuine, since they actually happen (cf. Persson 1999). Every place becomes genuine when it is experienced, no matter if the experience takes place in Greece or in a Greek restaurant in Sweden.
11. Although I argue in this article for a phenomenological experience-related perspective as opposed to a more constructivistic view, I would like to underline that I am not saying that the idea and notion of Europe is less real or that it exists less. An analysis of empirical findings, based on either experience of text must refer to both as equally "genuine".

References

Abnersson, Veronika & Burstedt, Anna 2000: Matkultur eller kulturmat? *Kulturella Perspektiv*, no. 3.
Beardsworth, Alan & Kiel, Teresa 1997: *Sociology on the Menu. An Invitation to the study of Food and Society*. London: Routledge.
Bell, David and Valentine, Gill 1997: *Consuming geographies: we are where we eat*. London: Routledge.
Bringéus, Nils-Arvid 1994: Den skånska matprofilen In: *Hyllning till Madariget. Hävd-Humor-Hälsa-*

Husmanskost. Skåneländska Gastronomiska Akademien.
Burstedt, Anna 1997: Always go for the local! *Lundalinjer*, vol. 115.
Burstedt, Anna 1999: Besök i främmande kök. In: O'Dell, Tom (ed.) 1999: *Non Stop. Turist i upplevelseindustrin*. Lund: Historiska Media.
Casey, Edward S. 1996: How to get from place to space in a fairly short stretch of time: Phenomenological Prolegomena. In: Feld, Steven & Basso, Kieth H. (eds.): *Senses of place*. Santa Fe: School of American Research Press.
Cook, Ian & Crang, P. 1996: The world on a plate: culinary culture, displacement and geographical knowledge. *Journal of Material Culture* no. 1.
Culinaria, Europeiska Specialiteter 2000. Könemann. Cologne.
Delanty, Gerard 1996: *Europa. Idé, identitet, verklighet*. Göteborg: Daidalos.
Eriksson, Catharina, Eriksson Baaz, Maria & Thörn, Håkan (eds.) 1999: *Globaliseringens kulturer. Den postkoloniala paradoxen, rasismen och det mångkulturella samhället*. Nora: Nya Doxa.
Frykman, Jonas 1999: Hem till Europa. Platser för identitet och handling. *RIG*. No. 2.
Frykman, Jonas 2000: Europeiska mellanrum. Om långsamhetens ting och platser. Ansökan till Riksbanken 2000.
Goody, Jack 1982: *Cooking, cuisine and class: a study in comparative sociology*. Cambridge: Cambridge University Press.
Harvey, David 1996: *Justice, Nature & the Geography of Difference*. London: Blackwell.
Hannerz, Ulf 1990: Cosmopolitans and Locals in World Culture. *Theory, Culture & Society. Explorations in Critical Social Science*, Vol. 7, No. 2–3.
Herzfeld, Michael 1997: *Cultural Intimacy. Social Poetics in the Nation-State*. New York & London: Routledge.
Howes, David 1996: Introduction: Commodities and Cultural Borders. In: Howes, David (ed.): *Cross-Cultural Consumption. Global Markets. Local Realities*. London: Routledge.
Hooks, Bell 1998: Eating the Other. Desire and Resistance. In: Scapp, Ron & Seitz Brian (eds.): *Eating culture*. New York: State University of New York Press.
Hornborg, Alf 1997: Landskapet som "text". Några funderingar kring ett stycke svensk skärgård. In: Saltzman, Katarina & Svensson, Birgitta (eds.): *Moderna landskap*. Stockholm: Natur och Kultur.
James, Allison 1996: Cooking the books: Global or local identity in contemporary British Food Cultures? In: Howes, David (ed.): *Cross-Cultural Consumption. Global Markets. Local Realities*. London: Routledge.
James Allison 1997: How British is British food? In: Caplan, Pat (ed.): *Food, Health and Identity*. London & New York: Routledge.

Jackson, Michael 1996: Introduction. Phenomenology, Radical Empirism and Anthropological Critique. In: Jackson, Michael (ed.): *Things as they are. New Directions in Phenomenological Anthropology*. Bloomington: Indiana University Press.
Löfgren, Orvar 1997: Scenes from a Troubled Marriage. Swedish Ethnology and Material Culture Studies. *Journal of Material Culture*. No. 1.
Massey, Doreen 1994: *Space, Place and Gender*. Cambridge: Polity Press.
Massey, Doreen et al. 1999: Issues and debates. In: Massey, Doreen, Allen, John & Sarre, Philip (eds.): *Human Geography Today*. Cambridge: Polity Press.
Miller, Daniel 1998: *Material Culture. Why some things matter*. London: UCL Press.
Mintz, Sidney 1985: *Sweetness and power: The place of sugar in modern history*. New York: Viking.
Murcotte, Anne 1996: Food as an expression of National Identity. In: Gustavsson, Sverker & Lewin, Leif (eds.): *The future of the Nation-State. Essays on cultural pluralism and political integration*. London: Routledge.
Nielsen, Niels Kayser 1997: Madens kulturella verderner – mellem opbrud og permanens. *Dansk Sociologi*. No. 4/8.
Nielsen, Niels Kayser 1998: Madkultur mellem det lokale, det nationale og det globale. Arbejdspapir 3. Kultur og formidling. Centre for Kulturstudier. Odense Universitet.
Olwig, Karen Fog 1997: Cultural sites. Sustaining a home in a deterritorialized world. In: Olwig, Karen Fog & Hastrup Kirsten (eds.): *Siting Culture. The shifting Anthropological object*. London: Routledge.
Persson, A. Eva 1999: Queenstown – Cobh, tur och retur. In: O'Dell Tom (ed.) 1999: *Non Stop. Turist i upplevelseindustrialismen*. Lund: Historiska Media.
Persson, Hans-Åke & Lindström, Fredrik (eds.) 1999: *Europa – en svårfångad historia*. Lund: Studentlitteratur.
Ritzer, George 1993: *The McDonaldization of Society*. Newbury Park: Pine Forge Press.
Salomonsson, Karin 1999: Utmärkt mat. Kulturella förtöjningar i europeiska flöden. (u.u.).
Saltzman, Katarina & Svensson, Birgitta (eds.) 1997: *Moderna landskap*. Stockholm: Natur och Kultur.
Shore, Cris 1999: Inventing Homo Europaeus. The Cultural Politics of European Integration. *Ethnologia Europea*. Vol. 29:2.
Sydsvenska Dagbladet 24 February 2000.
Törnqvist, Gunnar 1999: Europas nya karta: In: Persson, Hans-Åke & Lindström, Fredrik (eds.): *Europa – en svårfångad historia*. Lund: Studentlitteratur.
Valentine, Gill 1999: Imagined Geographies: Geographical Knowledges of Self and Other in Everyday Life. In: Massey, Doreen, Allen, John & Sarre, Philip (eds.): *Human Geography Today*. Cambridge: Polity Press.

Contents

Articulating Europe – Local Perspectives. Introduction 3

Reinhard Johler: Local Europe. The Production of Cultural Heritage
and the Europeanisation of Places 7

Kjell Hansen: Festivals, Spatiality and the New Europe 19

Eva Reme: Exhibition and Experience of Cultural Identity.
The Case of Bergen – European City of Culture 37

Jonas Frykman: Place for Something Else. Analysing a Cultural
Imaginary 47

Maja Povrzanović Frykman: Violence and the Re-discovery of Place   69

Michi Knecht & Peter Niedermüller: The Politics of Cultural
Heritage. An Urban Approach 89

Kirsti Mathiesen Hjemdahl: History as a Cultural Playground 105

Karin Salomonsson: The E-economy and the Culinary Heritage . . 125

Anna Burstedt: The Place on the Plate! 145